DEFORESTATION

Armando A. Ang
Copyright 2006

Printed in the Philippines by:
SCR

ISBN No. 149-746-01-0-7

An Ode to a Tree

Nothing con earth can compare to a tree,
God's special gift for you and for me;
One of His first and greatest creations,
Priceless and matchless, a blessing to all nations.

This is one natural resource we should all be thankful,
God's creation of the trees was very thoughtful;
A gentler living thing there is none to compare,
Without wonderful trees we will all suffer.

Have you ever seen a tree standing high,
With her slender arms outstretched to the sky?
Even the lowly plants that caress Mother Earth,
They strive to hold back the sands of the deserts.

From roots to crown, in old grandiose and tall
Spindly or thick, young and old, God made them all.
From the mountains to the valleys and the plains
In unison the trees sway while waiting for the rain.

Created in a variety of species, sizes and forms
They stood steadfast to the ground, weathering the storms;
From green in summer to other colors during the cold,
A tree is a thing of beauty – a great sight to behold.

Whether narra, mahogany, ipil-ipil – teak or pine,
Almaciga or mangrove, they're all God's special design;
What could be more majestic than a stately old tree,
A boon to mankind, so unique all will agree.

The trees have served mankind for millennia
From the America to Africa, Europe and Asia;
Until we learn to take good care for them,
Our worse fear for an inhospitable planet may just happen.

It's God's intent that we cherish with joy
To protect this heritage, cuddle it like a toy;
Should we let this land, full of life go to waste,
Or let ruthless men cut our trees in great haste?

All trees were created for mankind to use,
Instead they have been decimated, subjected to abuse;
Each grown up tree could fill many of our needs,
Yet man chops it down to satisfy his own greed.

Everytime a tree has been chopped down,
You know it has been done by foolish clowns;
These cowards only know how to hide behind,
The trees that should be praised to divine.

If only man were treated like a tree
Will he be happy if he is cut down for a fee?
Or would he rather rise up with his head bowed low
To thank the great Creator, shouldn't it be so?

The forests once filled with resonating sound
Have become silent without wildlife to be found;
The once teeming native animals and plants
They are all gone except for the bees and the ants.

Where are the ferns, the orchids, and the bamboos
That once interspersed with the woods?
Have they too gone out of existence,
Caused by human greed for more opulence?

Timber for houses, ties for the rails,
Toys for our children, poles for the sails;
Paper from pulp, pallets for industry,
Fruits and food are there to feed the hungry.

Houses and furniture, bridges to cross
Without trees all these would be lost.
With trees left to die – Mother Earth ponders her fate
What can man do when it's almost too late?

What then is our world without a tree?
Desolate and barren, so naked she'll be;
Where can man go to seek shelter and food,
In forest lands wasted, are they any good?

Dark summer clouds bursts, monsoon winds blow,
Floods, drought, famine and death they soon follow;
Misery and woe, will set in to enfold,
Man becomes so bitter, where is his green gold?

There must be something good that can be done
For mankind to atone before all the trees are gone;
Give them a chance to grow and to abound
And fill a world with beautiful trees all around.

No creation can match a tree that is sturdy and tall,
Yet mankind has no time to appreciate them all;
Let us ponder what would life be,
In a treeless planet what is there to see.

Now, can you tell me, what's there to compare
To a tree that He made for us all to share;
There is nothing, no nothing, do you agree?
I thank my Lord for giving us a tree.

Armando A. Ang
Sesenio C. Rivera

Books by the same author

Saving the Trees

Saving the Animals

The Dark Side of Catholicism

Trips and Traps When Buying or Building a Home

The Plain Truth About the Unorthodox Protestants

Sonnets from the Bible

Greed & Scams, Inc.

The Brutal Holocaust
(Japanese WWII Atrocities)

Child Abuse: A Growing Menace

**SPECIAL DISCOUNT FOR BULK PURCHASE
CONTACT NO. 0915-6964-732 or
0916-5423-523**

Words of Wisdom

To forgive is always the right thing to do except for those who claim and preach that they hold the key to the absolute truth when in fact they have perverted the gospel of Christ. They have absolutely no right to take others with them to hell with their distorted interpretation of the Bible; let them be accursed (see Galatians 1:8)

One true friend is all you need and your life on earth will not have been in vain. Beware, your best friend today may be your worst enemy someday.

There is a fine line between love and hate, friendship and enmity, loyalty and betrayal. All it takes is one mistake or misinterpretation of facts to turn things upside down.

Cheating and lying have become a Christian way of life;
What better way of crucifying Christ in the eyes of others.

Half-truth and half-lies are less discernible and therefore more dangerous than total lies. Many souls have been lost because they have trusted their pastors instead of reading the gospels for themselves. There is no room for complacency when dealing with the eternal destiny of our immortal soul.

A true church should never be afraid that her doctrines
Are being challenged; only then can the truth be realized.

Procrastination is the secret weapon of the Devil. He makes full use of man's greed and weakness for worldly lust. People are blinded by the love of money and refrained from seeking righteousness while they seek and enrich their coffers.

A true and wise Christian is conscious of anything
Wrong and refrains from doing it. A foolish hypocrite continues doing the wrong and tries to justify it.

Greed is the main reason for poverty and slavery of the masses.
Money has become the modern form of slavery. It has blinded many greedy Christian that they willingly became slave to it.

The existence of cults is not because they are interested in one's salvation, but because they find religion a convenient way to control the minds of people and gain wealth and power.

God's greatest commandment is thou shall have no other gods before me
Man's greatest commandment is thou shall have only gold before me.

A bad church is one that refuses to acknowledge its wrong teachings in the
face of overwhelming evidences from the Bible. A worst church is one
that searches unbiblical documents to justify its wrong teachings.

God may not want any to perish but He will not hesitate to send anyone to
hell. Jesus Christ is the only redeemer and mediator. Believing otherwise
shall put the soul in jeopardy. You never know what God will do to
those who pray to other entities for solace and mediation.

The truth can be very unpleasant to hear, difficult to accept,
and even dangerous for those who speak them out! Anything
that deals with the eternal destiny of the soul must be told.

There is an adage. "You can give without loving or caring, but you
cannot love or care without giving. It is just as important to give
without malice and for the recipient to receive without question."

Money and friendship often do not mix well. When lending to a friend,
be prepared to lose the loan or lose a friend. Never go into business
with a friend for greed is bound to reel its ugly head. It could be
the start of the end of a friendship.

In life there is death, in death there is eternal life. What happens after
death
is determined while we are still alive. We are destined to die once and
life is so short and death unpredictable so let us be prepared.

Most Christians are no better than non-Christians.
Anyone who wants to be called a Christian,
for Christ's sake must live like one. Shame on those who take
the name of the Lord in vain for evil gain.

To be filthy rich and to refuse to share is obscene
for we are only stewards of the wealth bestowed on us
by God. The gift must be used for His glory but
shame on those who are greedy and miserly.

Beware of pastors who claim that salvation can
only be found in joining their church. Salvation is
an act of personal faith and not an act of membership.

Some filthy rich people are so deceitful they think they are
smarter than others. The measure of a man is not in his wealth,
but how he uses it for the benefit of mankind.

Miracles should never be the basis of one's faith
All major religions of the world have their fair share of them.
Some miracles, especially those glorifying other entities
may be the work of the devil to lead people astray.

Corruption is so endemic that even innocent officials
are eyed with doubts and suspicions.

Some church leaders think they are inspired by the Holy Spirit that
they are infallible in interpreting the Bible and men must conform to
what they think are the correct teachings. How then do you explain
why there are so many sects in Christianity?

People who deal with vices are vicious and heartless. They
would rather take your money or your life before letting you off.
Their only interest is how you can enrich them and satisfy their greed.

Some lies are more dangerous than others especially those
concerning salvation. Millions have been led astray because some
holy men think they have the solution to your eternal destiny.
The worst of them are those who brandished the Bible and claimed
they alone arc inspired by the Holy Spirit to interpret and preach the
gospel. Not only do they distort the spirit of the Bible, they have
completely changed the way of salvation and worship.

Beware of the churches that forbid their laity to read writings
concerning their teachings. They may have something to
hide that would explain this irrational fear or behavior.

Know your friends by the places where
they bring or entertain you. Only a true friend will not
bring you to unsavory places like gambling and vice dens.

Money is not everything. Some people waste then life making money
only to be cursed after death for the fortune left behind when
then children killed one another for then fair share.

Those who think they have been saved when they were baptized
as babies may be in for a big surprise. Discernment is a
necessary part of faith in the saving grace of God.

TABLE OF CONTENTS

REFERENCES

Allaby, Michael, *Green Facts*, Hamlyn, 1986

Allen, Robert, *How to Save the World*, Littlefield, Adams and Company, 1980

Ang, Armando. *Saving the Animals*, Bookman Printing House. 1998
   Saving the Trees, Bookman Printing House, 1996

Banks, Martin, *Conserving Rainforest*, Weyland, 1989

Bernarde, Melvin A., *Global Warming*, Wiley, 1992

Brown, R. Lester, Flavin, Christopher, Postel, Sandra, *Saving the Planet*,
   Norton, 1991

Brown, R. Lester, (ed). *World Watch Reader*, W. W. Norton & Company, 1991

Brown, R Lester and Kane. Hal, *Full House*, W. W. Norton & Company, 1994

Button, John, *How to be Green*, Century, 1989

Cairncross, Frances. *Costing the Earth*, Harvard Business School. 1992

Candy, Thomas Y., *Our Changing Earth*, National Geographic Society, 1994

Caplan, Ruth, *Our Earth, Ourselves*, Ballantine, 1990

Carson, Patrick & Moulden, Julia, *Green Gold*, HarperBusiness, 1991

Clarke, Robin, *Water: The International Crisis*, MIT Press, 1993

Collins, Mark (ed). *The Last Rain Forests*, Oxford, 1990

Conca, Ken & Dabelko, Geoffrey (ed). *Green Planet Blues*, Westview Press,
   1998

Cowell, Adrian, *The Decade of Destruction*, Channel Four Book, 1990

ODay, David, *The Environmental Wars*, Ballantine Books, 1989

Diamond. Jared, *Collapse*, Viking, 2005

Dubley, Nigel, Jeanrenaud, Jean-Paul & Sullivan, Francis, *Bad Harvest?*
   Earthscan, 1995

Ehrlich, Paul and Anne, *Extinction*, Ballantine Books, 1981
   Healing the Planet, Addison Wesley, 1991

Ellis, Richard, *No Turning Back*, HarperCollins, 2004

Farrelly, David, *The Book of Bamboo*, Sierra Club book, 1984

Field, Barry, *Environmental Economics*, McGraw-Hill, Inc., 1994

Friends of the Earth, *How Green is Britain?* Hutchinson Radius, 1990

Gale, Robert. Barg, Stephan, and Gillies, Alexander, *Green Budget Reform*.
   Earthscan Publications, Ltd 1995

Gelbspan, Ross, *Boiling Point*. Basic Books, 2004

Ghai, Dharam (ed), *Development and Environment*. Blackwell Publishers. 1994

Goldstein, Jerome. *Recycling*, Schocken books, 1979

Gore, Al, *Earth in the Balance*, Houghton Mifflin Company. 1992

Gradwohl, Judith & Greenberg. Russell, *Saving the Tropical Forests*, Island
   Press, 1988

Head, Suzanne and Heinzman. Robert (ed). *Lessons of the Rainforest,* Sierra
   Club Books, 1990

Hecht, Susanna & Cockburn, Alexander, *The Fate of the Forest*, Harper Perennial, 1990

Hurst, Philip, *Rainforest Politics*, S Abdul Majeed & Co., 1990

Huxley, Anthony, *Green Inheritance*, Gaia Books Limited, 1984

Javna, John, *50 Simple Things Kids Can Do to Save the Earth*. Andrew & McMeel, 1990

Kemf, Elizabeth, *Indigenous Peoples and Protected Areas*. Earthscan, 1993

Kinder, Peter, Lydenberg, Steven D., Domini, Amy L, *Investing for Good*, HarperBusiness, 1994

Lamb, Marjorie, *Two Minutes a Day for a Greener Planet*, HarperPaperbacks, 1990

Langone, John.*Our Endangered Earth*, Little Brown, 1992

Lilienfeld, Robert & Rathje, William. *Use Less Stuff*, Fawcett Books. 1998

Lim Teck Ghee and Valencia, Mark (ed), *Conflict Over Natural Resources in South-East Asia and the Pacific*, United Nations University, 1990

Mather, Alexander. *Global Forest Resources*, Timber Press, Inc. 1990

McCully, Patrick, *Silenced Rivers*. Zed Books, 1996

Mitchell, George, *World on Fire*, Macmillan Publishing, 1991

Myers, Norman, *The Primary Source*, W. W. Norton & Company, 1992

Norse, Elliott A., *Ancient Forests of the Pacific Northwest*, Island Press, 1990

Null, Gary, *Clearer, Cleaner, Safer, Greener*, Villard Books. 1990

Philippine Center for Investigative Journalism, *Saving the Earth* (4ft Ed.), PCIJ, 1997

Ponting, Clive, *A Green History of the World*, Penguin, 1991

Rampton, Sheldon & Stauber, John, *Trust Us, We're Experts!* Tarcher, 2001

Rifkin, Jeremy, *Beyond Beef*, A Plume Book, 1992

Repetto. Robert & Gillis, Malcolm (ed). *Public Policies and the Misuse of Forest Resources*, Cambridge University Press, 1988

Rosenblum, Mort & Williamson, Doug. *Squandering Eden*, Paladin, 1987

Saign, Geoffrey C., *Green Essentials*, Mercury House, 1994

Seymour, John & Girardet, Herbert, *Blueprint for a Green Planet*, Dorling Kindesley, London, 1987

Taintor, Jerry & Taintor. Mary Jane, The Oral Report, Ballantine, 1989

Utting, Peter (ed). *Forest Policy and Politics in the Philippines*, Ateneo de Manila University Press, 2000

Vallely, Bernadette, *1001 Ways to Save the Planet*, Ballantine, 1990

Vitug, Marites Danguilan, *The Politics of Logging: Power From the Forest*, PCU, 1993

INTRODUCTION

Mother Earth is undergoing an environmental upheaval as never seen before. The unprecedented number of people bearing down on earth has greatly affected the environment of our planet. Whether we are rich or poor, developed or underdeveloped nations, we are all together for better or for worse for the well-being of this planet.

Of all the problems besieging the planet, rampant deforestation is probably the single most important problem we face today. The ecological problems directly and indirectly connected with deforestation are numerous and require immediate remedies. Global warming and loss of biodiversity are two problems of universal ramification for mankind that need to be resolved if mankind is to continue to exist for the next thousand years.

After air, water, and food, trees are the most important natural resources that mankind need. Otherwise, God would not have created trees in the third day of the creation story in preparation for man's beginnings and existence. It is also one of the most important renewable resources that will serve mankind for eons if we only learn to respect the role they play in our lives. Since men first walked on the planet, he was surrounded by trees with all their fruits and wildlife for his benefit. For centuries, it has provided mankind with all the resources necessary for him to survive the harsh climate. With so much of our forests lost to human needs and greed, it is necessary for us to change the way we appreciate the immense value of trees.

All the wealth of the nations around the world is found in their natural resources. They could be the under the sea, under the sand, under the forests and over the top of the land surfaces. Without these resources, civilizations would not have advanced to this point in time. Except for the food from the sea and the forests on the land, all the other natural resources are considered non-renewable. Yet, at the rate we are exploiting some of these resources they too would become non-renewable and even extinct.

According to a World Bank report in 2001, "Forest resources directly contribute to the livelihoods of 90% of the 1.2 billion people living in extreme poverty and indirectly support the natural environment that nourishes agriculture and supplies food to nearly half the population of the developing world. Forests are also central to growth in many developing countries through trade and industrial development. However, mismanagement of this resource has cost governments revenues that exceeded World Bank loans to these countries. Illegal logging results in additional losses of at least US$10 to 15 billion per year of forest resources from public lands. If retrieved by governments, these losses could support expenditures in education and health that would exceed current development assistance to these sectors."

The International Tropical Timber Organization (ITTO) report of 2001 essentially gives the same assessment. "In spite of the noble intentions expressed repeatedly and variously, actual achievements have been disappointing, evidenced by the current situation in the forestry sector: illegal logging and encroachments; continuing and increasing deforestation and land degradation; loss of bio-diversity; increasing occurrence of forest fires; denudation of watersheds; truncated parks and protected areas; failure of forest plantations; unprofitable investments; indifference of concessionaires to sustain forest management."

The Food and Agriculture Organization (FAO) reported in 2001 that "In many countries, illegal operations proliferate and governments are unable to control their own bureaucracies or to enforce adherence to the 'rules of the game' by commercial corporations and civil society entities. In extreme circumstances, private corporations or powerful groups are able to sway government policies and 'purchase' decrees, legislation and regulations for their own benefit."

Greed and poverty are behind the destruction of the world's remaining forests. The world has already lost 80% of its original ancient forest cover and the twin factors continue to play out its ugly roles. The insatiable demand of humanity, especially those powered by the economic growth of many countries and the greed of many companies and concessionaires are expected to continue the road to destruction. Calls on them to stop the destruction are met with promises that are never carried out. If actions are ever undertaken, it is only half-heartedly done to show a semblance of compliance.

Poverty has driven many to seek their fortunes in the forests. Some practice slash-and-burn while others try to eke out their livelihood by small-scale mining in the hope of striking it rich. But more often than not, they end up with nothing to show but sufferings and ill-health for all their efforts. The same is true for all the workers in the forestry sector. They toil long hours under difficult hardship only to enrich the concessionaires who stay in their air-conditioned offices in the cities.

The poor indigenous people have lost most of their livelihood and are forced to turn to swidden cultivation to survive. As their ancestral lands are taken over by greedy government bureaucrats and given away to domestic and multinational companies, their only recourse was to fight a losing battle.

There have been some effective actions undertaken mostly by the NGOs. It is doubtful if it will put a dent against the destructive forces now in place and deeply entrenched. The only way to stop the greedy scums is to legislate stiffer laws against illegal poaching and even wanton destruction of forestlands by licensed loggers and impose on them the ultimate death penalty and carry it out without delay. It is often the fear of death that can force a greedy person to act rationally.

In this book I have tried to set down the many causes of deforestation, the consequences of what will happen if we fail to act to protect the trees and enact measures to minimize the problems.

Chapter 1

EFFECTS OF DEFORESTATION

According to the Food and Agriculture Organization (FAO) of the United Nations, the world is covered by 9,557,553,850 acres (4 billion hectares) of forests in year 2000. At the same time, 22,200,000 acres (9.2M hectares) of the forests were converted to non-forest land such as crops, roads, settlement, etc. The breakdowns of the distribution of the world's forests today are: [1]

- Europe contains 27% of the world's forests
- South America contains 23%
- Africa contains 17%
- Asia contains 14%
- Canada and USA contains 12%
- Oceania contains 5%
- Mexico and Central American contain 2%

Between the years 1990 to 2000, only Europe, Canada and the USA were able to gain additional forested lands of 1% while the rest of the world's fasts experienced a decline. Mexico and Central America experienced the most decline by 12%, followed by Africa (8%), South America (4%), Oceania (2%) while Asia's loss stands at -1%.

During the same period, on a country-by-country basis, China gained 12% forested lands, New Zealand (5%), USA (2%), Canada (0%), while the following countries. Ecuador. Indonesia and Indonesia each lost 12% of their forested lands. Brazil with the largest tropical forest lands experienced a decline of 4%.

Forests are not just a source of timber, food, fuel wood, and medicine, but also perform a wide range of social and ecological functions not available from other natural resources. It was estimated in 1997 by Robert Costanza that the annual value of forest ecosystem services is worth £4.7 trillion.[2]

Rates of Deforestation

There is no hard and fixed figures that could account for the exact rates of deforestation. Most of these figures are only educated estimates According to the 1989 figures of biologist Norman Myers in his book *Deforestation Rates in Tropical Forests and Their climatic Implications,* the global rates of deforestation is placed at 31 million hectares annually. In Brazil alone, the country with the biggest tropical forests, 50,000 km² or 5,000,000 hectares are lost annually. It has lost more than one million I km² of its original forest cover of 2,860,000 km² to the present 1.8 million km². Along with the loss of forest cover, of the 6 to 9 million indigenous people that once inhabited the Brazilian rainforest in 1500, less than 200,000 remain by 1992.[3]

In its State of the World's Forest 2001, the Food and Agricultural Organization (FAO) figures put the deforestation during the 1990s at 16.1 million hectares per year of which 15.2 million occurred in the tropics. Deforestation is also highest in the Africa and South American regions. The sad fact is that 14.2 million hectares were converted to other land uses and 1.0 million hectares were converted to forest plantations.[4]

On a worldwide basis, about half of the mature tropical forests, between 750 to 800 million hectares of the original 1.5 to 1.6 billion hectares that once graced the planet have already been brought down. The devastation is already acute in Southeast Asia, the second of the world's great biodiversity hot spots. Most of what remains is in the Amazon Basin, which ranges across nine countries, and its forest covered more than 600 million hectares, an area nearly two thirds of the size of the US.[5]

The forests are being destroyed at an ever-quickening pace. Unless significant measures are taken on a world-wide basis to preserve them, by 2030 there will only be 10% remaining with another 10% will be left in a degraded condition. Eighty percent will have been lost and with them the natural diversity they contain lost forever [6]

The Philippines, once covered with forest to an area of 250,000 km² out of a land mass of 300,000 km² is now down to 8,000 km² (800,000 hectares) of virgin forests or 3% of the original cover. The annual rate of deforestation in 1989 was 2,700 km² and has been greatly reduced due to the diminishing forest cover today.[7] We have lost 97% of our original forest, the worst in any country.

Lungs of the World

Imagine a world where people keep on inhaling oxygen and spewing out carbon dioxide (CO_2) with each breath. In due time, there will be no oxygen left without the trees absorbing and converting the carbon dioxide into oxygen. We would all end up gasping for oxygen. This is the reason why forests are considered die "lungs of the world" for its crucial role in the recycling of carbon and oxygen. Trees, contain roughly 50% carbon, are our natural defense in the battle against global warming. They absorb carbon dioxide in the process of growing and release oxygen. When trees are cleared by burning, the carbon they contain, as well as some elements in the underlying soil is released back into the air causing global warming. Deforestation is responsible directly for about 20% of the carbon released to the atmosphere. There are other greenhouse gases such as methane and nitrous oxide that indirectly caused by deforestation.

Oxygen is essential to life and is expensive to produce in the laboratory. A large amount of energy is required, but the trees with the aid of radiant energy from the sun are producing it for us free through a natural chemical process called photosynthesis. In this process the carbon dioxide, a waste produced from our body is absorbed by the tree which in mm releases oxygen that is needed by our body. In spite of that we have not appreciated the important function of nature with our wanton destruction of the trees. Although farfetched, any reduction of oxygen contents in the atmosphere to below 15% maybe a disaster to the planet. There would not be sufficient oxygen to allow fire to bum. Life would be very different without die process of combustion.

The present state of our atmosphere is made possible by the growth of forests throughout the world eons ago. It made it possible for other higher forms of life to exist in this beautiful green planet. Too much carbon dioxide vis-á-vis oxygen would be disastrous to human life. Carbon dioxide in die atmosphere is not only poisonous to humans and to the animal kingdom it is also a major cause of global warming. Without the forests to keep the planet's atmosphere in balance, people and many life forms could become extinct.

* * * * *

Today, the destruction of the forests is like a malignant cancer growing out of hand. Most of the cancer growth is spreading throughout the tropical countries and many cures being advocated do not seem to work. The cancer is slowly taking over the entire lungs of the world and unless put under control and eventually regenerated, it could eventually destroy civilization if not mankind itself. Another part of the lungs is being invaded in the form of the Russian forests. Forestlands make up 70% of Russia's territory and span 12 time zones out of the 36 time zones. It is known as Europe's lungs and second only to the Amazon in the amount of carbon dioxide it holds within the trees and that it absorbs. There are also many rare species within its territory found nowhere else.[8]

At present, there is a plan to sell some of the forestlands to private enterprises amounting to $164 billion. This has raised fears among environmentalists that the forests will be wantonly destroyed. There are not enough funding to ensure that the extraction of the forest can be done sustainably Part of the fear is that the price of the logged wood will only sell for $1 per cubic meters whereas it sells for $30 in Finland and $15 in Estonia.[9] This legal price is not conducive to protect the forest for the future.

There is already an illegal trade in forest products with China and Japan with Russia losing about $30 billion in hard currency a year, according to the World Wild Fund for Nature (WWF). This is compared to the legal exports of $4.1 billion in 2001.[10] The $30 billion is probably an exaggeration as another more recent report by the same NGO reported the annual loss at $1 billion in revenue due to illegal logging and the associated trade.[11]

Aside from the damage as a result of logging, there is the potential harm to some of the endangered species. The far eastern leopard, of which there are only 30 left, the Siberian tiger, of which 400 remain, would suffer from widespread destruction of their habitat. Rare trees such as the Siberian cedar pine and the Korean cedar pine are also threatened in Russia's far east, and the wild chestnut, already being logged in the Caucasus is also at risk.[12]

---

* In the US and Canada, it is known as the World Wildlife Fund

Biodiversity

Trees are important to our daily lives and to the ecology of the planet that it is hard to conceive of a world without them. Without trees, civilization would not have advanced so fast and our living standard improved so much Life would be harsh, difficult, and very different from what we enjoy today. Billions of trees are cut down annually worldwide for various purposes. It has more than 10,000 diverse uses and important ecological functions that through the ages it has been the single most important natural resource of this planet. A treeless planet is a lifeless planet.

Tropical forests occupy roughly 6% of the Earth's land surface, down from twice its size before mankind started utilizing and wasting the forest. Tropical rainforests are the world's oldest living ecosystems. Fossil records show that the forests of Southeast Asia have existed in more or less the present form for 70 to 100 million years.[13]

It also contains an estimated 10 to 30 million species of plants, animals and organisms on the planet. As of 1989 only 1.4 million different life forms have been catalogued. At the present rate of destruction, hundreds of thousands of species may become extinct before scientists have time to catalogue them. Some of them may contain genetic materials that could combat some of the dreaded diseases faced by mankind.

Tropical forests are the richest reservoir of living things. According to the National Academy of Science, a typical four square mile patch of rainforest contains as many as 1,500 species of flowering plants, 750 species of trees, 125 mammal species, 400 species of birds, 100 reptiles, 60 amphibians, and 150 different species of butterflies. In another study of one square meter of leaf litter, when analyzed, turned up 50 species of ants alone.[14]

The rainforests harbor many species of animals that can only survive within an intact forest. It is the best place to preserve biodiversity as long as it is not disturb in their natural ecosystems. Men have not learned to manage biodiversity, instead have destroyed them at an unprecedented scale. Spurred by greed, poverty, and the runaway population, men are destroying many plants and animals that make up the planet and make life comfortable for humanity. According to the National Academy of Science, at least 50 million acres a year are lost for various reasons.

Even degraded forests that have been reforested by monoculture plantations of genetically cloned trees could no longer harbor biodiversity. Logging companies, as well as their buyers and lenders should fund the planting of genetically diverse forest that will preserve the heritage of genetic diversity. This is a tall order and it requires vigilance.

* * * * *

Even plant species found in the temperate zones such as the US has important biological roles. Brien Meilleur and Oliver Philipps, two biologists estimate that rare plants in the US could be worth billions of dollars a year. They compiled a comprehensive database of plants used for food, animal fodder, timber, medicine and other products and compared them to similar US rarities belonging to the same genus. Close relatives of medical plants are likely to produce similar, perhaps more potent, versions of the active ingredient. Wild relatives of crop plants are a repository of genes that could be used to improve today's varieties. The survey they made revealed that 80% of American threatened plants belong to a genus that includes one useful species. Some of the wild species in the US have already shown some potential. American grape vines saved Europe's wine industry from die ravages of the root-sucking phyiloxera louse late 19th century. The hybrid sunflower grown throughout the US is a product of breeding with wild Helianthus-species, which have given the crop its improved yields and resistance to fungi.[15]

* * * * *

To address the problem confronting die loss of biodiversity, the Rio Earth Summit of 1992 was convened. During the summit, the Convention on Biological Diversity (CBD) was adopted It was signed by 182 countries, including Japan. The aims of the CBD were to conserve biological diversity, the sustainable use of its components and the fair and equitable sharing of the benefits arising out of the utilization of genetic resources. The only way this can be achieved is to stop deforestation and land degradation. Like all other conventions and conferences, adopted, nothing has been done to put the spirit of the agreements into concrete and concerted actions.

Extinction

Extinction of species is an admitted fact of life but the present rate is occurring at 1000 times faster than the natural rate. By carefully examining fossil records and ecosystem destruction, some scientists estimate that as many as 137 species disappear from the earth each day, or as astounding 50,000 species every year. [16]

Extinction of species is mostly due to habitat (forest) destruction. So much destruction has been done to the old-growth forests that many animals and even plants are now near extinction. Many forest plantains have become monoculture species to the exclusion of other crops and a threat to wildlife that depends on a variety plant species in order to survive. Animals have been forced to migrate to other dwindling areas as forested lands are decimated.

Saving tropical forests is vital to preserving biodiversity. This is because tropical forests contain more than half of all known species of plants and land animals in the world. Just one hectare of Peruvian rainforest contains nearly 300 tree species compared with just 50 tree species m the whole of northern Europe. Costa Rica, with just 52,000 kms of land, contains 8,000 species of plants while Britain, with nearly five times the land area, has fewer than 1,500 species. Peninsular Malaysia has 8,500 species of plants.[17]

Forest Products

Tropical forests are rich potential sources of valuable food, timber, medicines, and industrial products. When we inadvertently destroy entire ecosystems, resources of enormous potential value are lost forever. Deforestation is contributing to a decline in biodiversity and extinction of the world's flora and fauna. It is estimated that one-fourth of the plant species could die by the year 2020.[18] This is serious because continued advances in food production depend on the availability of a broad genetic base of wild strains of plants related to the world's major food mid industrial crops. The economic contributions of most tropical species have barely been exploited. Somewhere in the forests may also be found the answer to our growing food problem to feed the exploding population.

Forest products are essential to the world economy, worth about $400 billion annually in timber, pulp, paper, and fuelwood. Forest products other than wood, such as medicines, vegetables, and fruits, provide another $20 billion and are growing in importance.[19]

Genetic diversity found within the rainforests provides invaluable additions to the gene pool which help maintain and improve domestic crops. Wild strains often contain genes which can be crossed with their domesticated counterparts to better protect crops against pests and diseases. This diversity accounted for half of the two to five times gains in agricultural yield in the US from 1930 to 1980. However, those gains that made possible genetic diversity have actually resulted in a sharp decrease in diversity as a few exceptional successful crop strains I squeezed out native varieties.[20]

Healthy forest boosts food production. Trees soak up and store water from season to season, slowly releasing moisture during dry periods. Without tree cover, water runs off faster during the tropical rainy season, canying away valuable topsoil. A World Bank study found that the rate of soil loss was 10 times higher on forest lands where slash-and-burn shifting cultivation was practiced than in undisturbed forests. One reason that agricultural yields have fallen in sub-Saharan Africa is that vast amounts of forest cover have disappeared, hastening soil erosion and loss of soil nutrients.[21]

* * * * *

Numerous studies have shown that harvesting of sustainable forest products can be more profitable in the long run than harvesting the logs for timber export In one study in the Peruvian Amazon, $1,000 can be generated whereas the annual yield by harvesting forest products is $6,330 per hectare. This does not include the medicinal drugs that are still underdeveloped.[22]

Some products can only be collected from a fully functioning forest and cannot be raised in plantations. The Brazil nut tree is a canopy species that grows in forest with a full canopy. The cashew and Brazil nuts account for $300 million in sales in the US alone. Those who engage in sustainable harvesting of rubber, Brazil nuts, palm hearts and others earn four times more than the city workers.[23]

Rattan, a common rainforest liana is a valuable non-timber forest product used m the manufacture of furniture fetches $3 billion annually in the global market. Like timber, these products must be harvested on a sustainable basis.[24] It takes about ten years for a fast-growing rattan to teach an optimal 3 cm. in the Philippines, but due to dwindling supply and the competition for harvesting, they are being harvested at half the diameter.

Medicine from the Forests

The tropical forest contains 155,000 of the 250,000 known plant species. Less than 1.5 million have been screened for their medical value. Forty percent of the world's drugs come from the wild worth $40 billion annually worldwide.[25] This is not surprising as thousands of years ago ancient civilizations have learned the importance of some plants for their medical values such as ephedra and the opium poppy. From these plants came the drugs ephedrine, morphine and codeine that are still in use today. In fact, ephedrine from ephedra has multiple uses as a drug to prevent low blood pressure after spinal anesthesia in surgery, stimulant for coma victims and treatment for hay fever and asthma (Huxley, 113, 121)

Some plants, animals, bacteria, and fungi are essential for modem medicine They are used directly in the production of medicines or indirectly as starting materials for drug synthesis and other chemical compounds that they help synthesize or otherwise help in the general advancement of biological and medical understanding As much as 25/0 of western medicine came from plant species found in the tropics, accounting for about 7,000 medical compounds prescribed by Western doctors.[26]

The potential for medicine from the forests is almost unlimited. Each plant is like a chemical factory. They can produce specialized substances called secondary compounds that are of great value to mankind. Even closely related species of plants can produce different chemicals with slight changes in genetics. Seventy percent of the 3,000 plants identified by the National Cancer Institute as useful in cancer treatment are found only in the rainforest. Drugs have been developed to treat leukemia, Hodgkin's disease and other cancers.[27] The rosy periwinkle flower, found in Madagascar, contains alkaloids called vinblastine and vincristine. (Huxley, 122) Together they have been successfully used to treat several forms of cancer, including Hodgkin's disease with a 58% chance of success from 19% chance of success in 1960 with a different drug and 99% chance of remission for childhood (lymphocytic) leukemia. The newly discovered *Ancistrocladus korupensis* vine in African may hold the key to a new AIDS treatment.[28]

Medicine for the treatment of malaria, quinine can only be found in the bark of the cinchona tree harvested from the forest of Latin America and Africa. Even the poisonous bark of various curare lianas has been used to treat diseases such as multiple sclerosis, Parkinson's disease and other muscular disorders. It also permits tonsillectomies, eye, abdominal and other kinds of surgery due to its anesthetic qualities. The wild yams of Mexico and Guatemala were used as active ingredients for the birth control pills diosgenin and cortisone. There are actually about 4,000 plant species offering contraceptive possibilities.[29] The wild yams from China and India are still processed to make oral contraceptives.[30]

* * * * *

Even animals have provided some important drugs. Compared to plants, they may be a minor source, but nevertheless an important one. They supply us with about 3% of the drugs currently in use today (AnSL Animals, 28)

Some of the medicines gathered from wild animals include ancrod from the Malayan pit viper and used as an anticoagulant in the treatment of heart attacks. Capybara from South American jungles has blood containing compounds that combat leukemia. Venoms from poisonous snakes have been synthesized to help snake bite victims.

Climate Change

For millions of years, the forests have helped regulate the earth's climate making it habitable for all life forms. In the last 100 years, almost half of the forests have been destroyed, altering the environment of many countries. Barring some dramatic changes, most of the rest will be gone in the next few decades It may take hundreds of years to restore the rainforest ecosystem at great cost to the economies of the world.

The crucial ecological roles of forests are less approbated than their social and economic values. Forests influence the wind, temperature, humidity, mitigate the force of typhoons and soil erosions, a source of water supply and benefits in ways often discovered only after the trees an cut. Forests assist in the recycling of water, oxygen, carbon, nitrogen, md mitigate the effect of air pollution. Climate changes on a small scale happen in places where forests are denuded. About half the moisture in clouds hovering over the tropical forests is taken into the trees by inspiration. Without trees, annual precipitation drops making the climate hotter and drier. Rainfall runs off the bare soil quickly instead of being trapped by the trees or vegetation. Low moisture will result in futility decline resulting in further denudation.

The air around the forest, in contrast to farm and pasture remains relatively cool and humid on hot days, so that showers are more frequent. Rainforests can generate up to 50% of the region's rainfall as in the Amazonia But deforestation can greatly reduce the amount of rainfall and adversely affects the climate of the region. James Lovelock, the creator of the Gaia Theory estimates that the cooling effect generated by the Amazon forest alone is worth $150 trillion annually. (Ang, Saving the Trees, 13)

Reduced Rainfall

A phenomenon known as the "albedo effect" caused by the increase in shininess or reflectivity of the earth's surface due to loss of tree cover could influence convection currents, wind patterns, and rainfall in the countries affected. Changes in rainfall in once forested regions are increasingly acknowledged by local people. The Panama Canal watershed has been losing its forest cover throughout the last century and has shown a marked decline in rainfall. About 12,000 ships use the canal annually But in the late 1970s, a drastic drop in water level has forced the government to turn away the largest ships, losing around S350 million a year. The reason is that settlers have been cutting down the forest around the watershed that supplies the needed water all year round. (Collins, 105) Similar processes exist in southwestern Ivory Coast, montane areas of Tanzania, several parts of India, northwestern peninsular Malaysia, and some localities in the Philippines. Although the mechanism is not yet established there is no doubt there is a strong link between rainfall and tree cover. (Ibid)

Large scale clearing of forest can alter the climate of an area by reducing rainfall and allowing too much sunlight to fall on the soil creating a dry and dusty surface that is easily eroded. This is very apparent m areas such as West Africa where rainfall has dropped to below average for 21 consecutive years and crop cultivation has become more difficult, soil quality deteriorated and deserts have increased in size.

The world's cloud forests are under threat of destruction, and their disappearance could have a devastating effect on millions, according to a report entitled Cloud Forest Agenda. This report gives us maps of forest distribution, the threats they face and an agenda for action. Cloud forest areas have been over-estimated and amounts to less than 2% of the world's tropical rainforest or 400,000 kms^2 and are found mostly in Asia rather than in Latin America It is estimated that 40% of water used in the capital city of Honduras comes from cloud forests of La Tigra National Park. The forests are under threat from agriculture, logging and construction, and their ecology and location on mountain slopes makes them sensitive to climate change. Changes in temperature and rainfall will drive some into extinction and force others to higher altitudes. The amount of clouds at lower altitudes will cause drying of the cloud forests.

Deforestation can cause major changes in hydrologic cycle - reducing evapo-transpiration and hence reducing moisture transfer inland. It is the deforestation in southern and eastern China that is cited as the main reason for rainfall decline in northwestern China where the dust bowl is forming. The deforestation is reducing the moisture transported inland from the South China Sea, the East China Sea, and the Yellow Sea. Where land is forested, the water is held and evaporates to be carried further inland. When tree cover is removed, the initial rainfall from the inland-moving, moisture-laden air simply runs off and returns to the sea. As this recycling of rainfall inland is weakened by deforestation, rainfall m the interior declines. Reversing this degradation requires a stabilized population, planting trees everywhere possible to help reduce rainfall inland, converting highly erosion-prone areas back to grassland or woodland, reducing livestock populations, and planting tree shelterbelts across windswept areas of cropland, as US farmers did to end dust storms in the 1930s.[31]

Evidence from across West Africa indicates that deforestation has lowered rainfall, increased ground temperatures, dried up rivers and spread deserts. In the past five decades in the area, 650,000 km² have been overrun by the deserts.[32]

Global Warming

The plant kingdom plays an important role in determining how much solar energy heats the land and regulate the temperature of the planet. This is done through the transpiration, respiration and photosynthesis of plants For the past thousand years, forests have maintained a balance between the biomass and the carbon dioxide in the atmosphere. This continuing cycle controls the amount of carbon (dioxide) and the temperature of the air surrounding the planet. Few living things can absorb carbon dioxide gas from the atmosphere and store them in the form of living plants that we can use in the form of energy.

Since 1850, with the advent of the industrial revolution and the population explosion, the demand for fossil fuels to run engines, the burning of fuelwood and the logging of timbers have resulted in the increase in carbon dioxide. The burning of fossil fuels discharges about 6 billion tons of carbon while deforestation and forest fires account for 2 billion tons.[33] The result is an upset in the balance of gases with more Concentration of greenhouse gases in the atmosphere.

Global warming has become a big problem for the planet as the mean temperature is expected to increase about 1.8°F by 2030 and 5.4°F before the end of the century. This amounts to a warming rate 10 to 1000 times more rapid than the fastest warming period in the last 10,000 years. This is the consensus of 300 leading scientists formed by the united Nationals and the World Meteorological Organization (WMO)' Panel on Climate Change (IPCC) formed in 1988 to assess the risk of global warming.[34] It is caused mainly by the burning of fossil fuels that came from die trees that once existed on earth millions of years ago. Once the fossil fuels or trees are burned, one of the products released to the atmosphere is carbon dioxide. This gas, once released to the atmosphere acts like a glass in a greenhouse that traps the heat on earth instead of releasing it to the outer space. The problem is being aggravated by deforestation. The nations of the world pump over 7 billion tons of caibon dioxide into the air annually from all sources. Three billion tons come from the burning of tropical forests.

In 1850 the concentration of carbon dioxide in the atmosphere was about 265 parts per million (ppm). By 1995 it has jumped to 359 ppm, or an increase of 170 billion tons since the beginning of the industrial revolution. At present the Co_2 concentration in the atmosphere stands at 370 ppm.[J5] Other greenhouse gases such as methane concentrations have more than doubled from 650 ppm to 1,700 ppm in the last 300 years. Six of the warmest recorded periods occurred in 1980, 1981, 1983, 1987, 1988, and 1991. The trend was only interrupted by the eruption of Mount Pinatubo in 1991 which cooled temperatures around the world for several years due to amount of dust emitted into the atmosphere. In 1995 the warming trend was reestablished, with 1995 being the warmest years yet, coming in at 59.7°F. This has been verified by the Goddard Institute of Space Studies NASA. It may sound like small incremental increases, but during the height of the ice age, the average temperature was only 6°C cooler.[36]

Global warming has a tendency to bring havoc to the climate. Cases of simmering hot days on one part of the earth and flooding on others are common occurrences. 1998 was one of the hottest years on record Australia experienced devastating droughts and bushfires. On the other hand, Indonesia saw weeks of incessant rain and the worst flooding in decades. In India, 1,000 people died in a heat wave. Rivers burst their banks and crashed through Germany, Russia and the Czech Republic. As temperatures rose in Antarctica, 3,250 square kilometers of the Larsen B ice shelf collapsed. Scientists found that the global icemelt rate had doubled since 1988 and predicted the sea could rise by 27 centimeters by 2100. Many are already making plans to move to higher ground. The native Alaskans were leaving their shrinking island village of Shishmaref. On the opposite side of the world, the 10,000 citizens of the low lying Pacific island of Tuvalu were making plans to emigrate.[37]

* * * * *

In this millennium, some of the warmest days happened early in this century. The cycle of bad and stormy weather and heat wave is a common occurrence around the world. In the spring of 2003, 1,400 people died after heat wave struck India and Pakistan. On the other hand, in only the month of May of the same year, the US experienced a record 562 tornadoes A brutal heat wave in Europe set new temperature records in Britain, triggered Portugal's worst forest fires in fifty years, and killed as many as 11,000 people in France in a four-week period. (Gelspan, 79)

* * * * *

At present, the tropical forests contain more than two trillion tons of carbon while the atmosphere contains about 800 billion tons and Increasing at the rate of 1% annually.[38] The long term effect of global warming can cause more forest fires due to higher temperature of the atmosphere Historical data on the forests of northwestern Minnesota bear out this fact. Over the last few centuries, when the climate was warm and dry, forest fires burned more often than when the climate was cool and wet. With increased warming, more forest fires are inevitable. (Ang, Trees, 93)

The trees play an important role in the future of the world's problems of global warming. It could be the only significant way of taking carbon from the air and storing them in trees. Trees contain about 50% carbon taken from the air naturally without human intervention. The cost of sequestration of carbon could be an expensive undertaking, but nature is doing it at minimal cost. By planting, replanting, growing, and then regular harvesting the timber without burning, the carbon in the trees will forever be stored in the wood.

The main culprits in the emissions of carbon dioxide come from the industrialized countries, mostly from the burning of fossil fuels. It accounts for 80% of human-made carbon dioxide emissions. On a per capita basis, each US citizen emits 19.1 tons of carbon per year followed by Australia at 16.9, Canada at 13.67, Britain at 9.53 and Japan at 9.28.[39]

Deforestation also contributes a substantial emission of carbon dioxide into the atmosphere. The conversion of each hectare of forests into pastures could contribute more than 500 metric tons of carbon dioxide. The reason for this is each hectare of forest could hold as much as 600 tons while the cropland can only hold about 5 tons Besides this there are the methane and nitrous oxide emitted from deforestation.[40]

Planting enough trees could be the only way to stem and eventually contain the greenhouse effect. Of course, trees can be planted anywhere, but mere is no environment so good for growing trees in a hurry than in the humid tropics with its year-round warmth and moisture that is conducive to growth. Tropical forests can sequester up to ten tons of carbon per hectare compared to 2.7 tons from the temperate forest annually. It will require 700 million hectares of growing trees to remove the 7 billion tons of carbon released to the atmosphere annually. This is a tall order considering that at present, deforestation is growing much faster than reforestation. Furthermore, many of the reforestation projects have failed miserably to provide adequate trees to put a den on the loss of carbon to the atmosphere.

To stabilize the global climate, the UN-endorsed IPCC has stated that emission reductions of 60% by 2050 initially suggested is not enough. Many experts now think that 70 to 90% is needed. This is due to the climate rapid change that is happening to our world which is heating up 50% faster than originally believed, according to the British Meteorological Office's Hadley Centre report in 2002. They predict that most of the world's forest will begin to die then.[41]

* * * * *

There are many evidences of the rising sea levels as a result of the large bodies of ice melting in the poles. In 2001 NASA scientists published a major study on observations by satellite and aircraft that ice-sheet from the margins were dropping in height at a rate of roughly one meter a year. In 2004, a team of scientists recorded falls as dramatic as 10 meters a year in some places. New cracks are opening up in the icy surface, sign of ice melting. The glacier has dropped an astounding 150 meters in the last 15 years.

Global warming is responsible for die rise of sea water level in many parts of the world affecting the low lying and coastal areas. Nothing can compare with the effects on the plants and trees because they cannot migrate fast enough. Historically, forests migrate at a very slow pace roughly 10 to 50 kilometers per century'. To survive the coming global warming many trees have to move ten times faster Long before they are able to do so, they would have been inundated by the rising sea water. In places where human beings reside, plant migration is impossible.

Kyoto Protocol

The Kyoto Protocol is an international agreement set up under the auspices of the UN in 1997. The agreement adopted a mechanism for reducing greenhouse gas emissions such as CO_2, methane, hydrofluorocarbons, perflurocarbons, and sulphur hexafluoride. Under the agreement, the 38 industrialized countries must reduce their greenhouse gases by 5.2% to their 1990 levels by 2012. It has been ratified by 178 countries except the two biggest polluters, the US and Australia and took effect on February 16, 2005.[43]

The US who is responsible for a whopping 25% of the Co_2 emissions refused to sign the Protocol on the ground that it would harm the American economy. Oil lobby and right-wingers see it as economic interference and that there are no proven scientific evidences to back up the claim. Many environmentalists accepted the agreement despite reservations that it is too weak and full of loopholes in getting the job done with the small cuts.[44]

Under the Kyoto agreement, one of its features is the adoption of the carbon credits where those who continue to pollute over and above their allowable limits can make use of carbon credits. Those who emit less carbon can sell the credit to those who pollute more. The polluters can also invest in forest and green development projects which can be used to offset their continued pollution or if they fail to reach their allowable target.

At present most of the billions of dollars changing hands are concentrated in the industrialized countries. More tropical countries need to be included in the program to help them alleviate the poverty problem plaguing them. Two independent boards are needed to verify if they have managed to keep the "carbon sinks" intact.

* * * * *

An alternative agreement is being proposed by Michael, the prime minister of Papua New Guinea He is supported by a block of developing countries who proposed it during the UN Conference in Montreal on climate change, in November 2005. Under the plan, the industrialized nations are requested to pay the tropical countries for preserving the

forests and its environmental services. However, there are doubts if it is possible to determine a fair-market value for nature as well as whether governments can protect the forest against illegal logging.[45]

* * * * *

The latest conference on climate change in Montreal in December 2005, ended with a high beat. The 159 members of the Kyoto Protocol approved several crucial decisions on strengthening the treaty's mechanisms. They also agreed to launch negotiations starting next May 2006 on cutting gas pollution beyond 2012 when the present agreement expires. Included in the decision are two messages to the US president George W. Bush and US politicians and business interests. The message to the president was that his format for tackling global warming through voluntary emissions cuts, smart energy techniques and "partnership" with Asia Pacific nations will not work. The second message for the politicians and businesses warn that US corporations will lose out on the profits that can be reaped from the global carbon cleanup as long as the country stays out of the Kyoto club.[46]

The US delegates were invited to the meeting but on the last day the chief American negotiator, Harlan L. Watson walked out of the meeting because of disagreement on the final statements to be released. He later dropped the US opposition to the nonbinding talks after a few words were adjusted in the text of the statements.[47]

Carbon Credits

The burning of the tropical forests and fuelwood is responsible for roughly 30% of the 4 billion tons of carbon emitted to the atmosphere every year. The rest come from the burning of fossil fuels. Fortunately, the same trees harvested for industrial use and fuelwood can be replenished by planting trees. Each hectare planted in the rainforest can hold up to 10 tons of carbon for decades upon maturity. It will require 4 million kms^2 or 400 million hectares to offset a billion tons of carbon. This can be accomplished by increasing the areas under forest stand by 15% worldwide at a cost of about $80 billion for a period of 10 years or $8 billion a year. This is a small amount in comparison to the damage possibly produced by severe weather changes to crops estimated at $200 billion a year beside other damages such as flooding of coastal areas and low lying areas, intrusion of salt water into our water system, destruction of fresh water trees and lakes, and the redesign of irrigation systems.

There is no question that the buildup of carbon dioxide and other greenhouse gases will raise the average temperature on earth. The size of the effect remains unclear and there are many uncertainties about the consequences of further buildup. There could be a synergetic effect every time there is an incremental increase. To counter further increases, a system of carbon trade-off has been set up in the US. Companies that emit more than their allowable limit of carbon are required to pay for their excess by the planting of trees to absorb what they emitted.

Before the Kyoto Protocol came into existence, Sweden and Finland have passed laws levying taxes on the amount of carbon dioxide emitted by burning fossil fuels as an attempt to reduce die output of greenhouse gases. In 1992, the tax generated $1.1 billion for Sweden. About half of it is issued for environmental projects in the areas of energy efficiency measures, renewable energy sources and support action for the Baltic region. The same law can be extended and adopted by other countries to tax the use of timber products such as log, plywood and lumber and the money collected must be specifically used to support reforestation in tropical countries where it is most needed. Similar laws can be passed to protect the other environment against degradation caused by pollution.

* * * * *

The carbon trading has been formalized in the Kyoto Protocol's Clean Development Mechanisms (CDM). There are however, problems that need to be resolved for the program to be effective. There are fears that the carbon-trading will spawn vast tree plantations with monocultures of non-native tree species on land already claimed by local people. There is also the question of risks undertaken by the local communities. National governments need to protect and formalize land tenure rights of communities or the deal will be riddled with conflict, increasing the financial risk of investors. Assessing the social impact of carbon-trading also has to be appraised. There are questions on how the portfolio will be shared by investors and tree planters.[48]

It is hoped that carbon-trading deals would sharply reduce poverty among the rural poor while providing businesses with an inexpensive way of offsetting their carbon emissions. There is also the potential of recovering millions of hectares of heavily populated forest and farmlands for the indigenous people.

The expected global market price of each ton of sequestered carbon is between $15 and $25. The latter is the going price in Europe and is in high demand.[49] A project study to restore 10,000 hectares of degraded community forests in the Handia Forest range of Madhya Pradesh, India, shows a potential to earn at least $300,000 every year for some 95 very poor rural villages.[50]

Applied Energy Service Thames, a Connecticut electric utility company, contributed $2 million to plant 52 million trees in about 100,000 hectares in Guatemala to offset an equal amount of carbon that will be emitted during its 30 years of burning fossil fuels. Another $14.5 million was contributed toward the effort later.

A large portion of the fossil fuels is turned into gasoline to operate the automobiles. Before each automobile is sold, the buyer or the seller will be imposed a carbon tax to pay for planting trees to offset an equal amount of carbon that will be emitted during the life of the automobile.

* * * * *

There is a single-cell algae called euglena that is a voracious eater of carbon dioxide. This algae is used to feed cultured fish and could also be used to feed domestic livestock and even humans. Growing them is not difficult because and they reproduce rapidly in air containing 15 to 20% carbon dioxide. A one-hectare tank of cultivated algae would absorb about 410 tons of carbon dioxide.[51]

Floods and Droughts

Deforestation is responsible for flooding and droughts in many tropical forest countries. The forest soaks or absorbs up the rainwater with its tree root systems before releasing it gradually later. The water is soaked into the ground instead of running off and eroding the topsoil, thus reducing erosion and flooding. Slowly moving water is likely to seep into the underground pools and springs from where we get our groundwater for irrigation. In areas where there are no trees such a paved roads or anything that is not permeable, more rain water rolls down the streams and drainages, carrying with it sand, silt, nutrients, fertilizers, and pesticides that cause flooding and destroy the local ecology.

A denuded forest with less tree cover increases the intensity of flooding and soil erosion. The flash flood of November 5, 1991 in Ormoc City, Leyte killed more than 7,000 people and is blamed on rampant deforestation and conversion to sugar cane plantations. Despite this knowledge, illegal loggings are still going on. Although on a smaller scale, uncontrolled flooding and higher rates of siltation reduce the useful lives of reservoirs, hydroelectric dams, and irrigation systems. Flood damages in India below the deforested areas of the Himalayan range have ruined emergency infrastructure averaging $210 million annually. In the Ganges Valley of India, along the foothills of the Himalayas, each monsoon season is often visited by massive flooding in the wake of deforestation that have caused huge losses to crops and property, estimated at an average of SI billion a year. Thousands of lives are also lost. (Ang, Trees, 8)

The Yellow River is so named because of the yellow colored soil that flow with it from erosion coming from upstream. The main cause is the unabated clearing of the forests for fuel, coffins, and construction materials in northern China that has resulted in disastrous floods. It regularly results in major changes of the detouring rivers in the lowlands causing huge loss of lives. The same situation exists in many countries in Asia and Africa.

Deforestation that resulted in huge damages is particularly hard on Bangladesh, one of the poorest countries in the world. Population growth has caused the people to strip the trees along the Himalayan mountain ranges to build homes that protect them from downpours coming from the mountains. A flood in 1988 killed tens of thousands of people and destroyed homes for at least 50 million people out of a population of 115 million then. The extensive destruction will stop only if the forests are restored.

In many rural areas and even urban areas, flooding has caused the contamination of drinking water from the wells and water pipelines. People who live in low-lying areas where their homes are flooded are likely to be at risk from waterborne diseases. It is common knowledge I that whenever disasters strike, contagious diseases naturally follow.

Severe flooding in Kachin State in Burma (Myanmar) in 2004 was reported to be the most serious catastrophe in 30 years. Other surrounding areas have water levels that reached their highest point since records were kept. The cause of the flooding was deforestation but the military authority refused to admit it and instead blamed it as a normal occurrence. They even denied all reports of casualties and damages and even had three local residents who filmed footage of the flooding detained for three days before being released after the intervention of a prominent local church leader.[52]

Hundreds of millions of dollars are spent worldwide each year on dam and embankment projects to control floods, but the solutions are not addressing the basic cause of these problems. Flooding has become a way of life for many. Deforestation has caused so much soil erosion that reduced the capacity of reservoirs. Overflowing water is inevitably released to relieve pressure on the dams. This results in destruction downstream of crops, buildings, lives, and equipment along its path while exacerbating further erosion. Soil erosion is the main cause of siltation, sedimentation and desertification.

It is no wonder that the editors of the UN magazine Ceres wrote in 1975, "It is no coincidence that in all the countries with major crop failures in recent years due to drought or floods such as Bangladesh, Ethiopia, India, Pakistan, and the Sahel countries, the forests had been razed to the ground. In the 1990s, hurricanes, floods, and fires affected more than two billion people and caused in excess of $608 billion in economic losses worldwide, more than the preceding four decades combined. The root causes of these catastrophes were destructive practices and overpopulation.[53]

Deforestations in Bangladesh and India have caused the increasing frequency and force of floods. In the past, major floods occurred only every 50 years. By the 1980s they have began occurring every four years. Between the late 1960s and late 1980s, India's flood-prone areas grew from 243,000 kms^2 to 575,000 kms$^{2.}$ [54]

In another report on India, the area subject to annual flooding there expanded from 190,000 kms² in 1960 to 502,000 km² in 1984 due largely to deforestation in the Himalayan Mountains. The 1988 flooding in Bangladesh covered two-thirds of the country and caused extensive crop damage. The one that hit in 1998 made 30 million people temporarily homeless.[55]

* * * * *

Droughts are the exact opposite of floods. They often occur in the same Areas where the other calamity occurred but only at different seasons. they have greatly increased in number and severity in many parts of the world. They are obviously the result of rapid deforestation caused by disastrous farming methods, cattle ranching and logging. All these can be witnessed in the mighty Amazon that is even experiencing droughts during the dry and even wet seasons.

Rainfall is essential to the growth of the trees. Together with the nutrients from the soil, these elements are transported into the growing crown through the leaves and branches. Tall dipterocarp trees usually have very few leaves and branches to maintain their growth. They get the water they need from the crown. Knowing that half of the rainfalls in the Amazon and other thickly forested areas come from the transpiration of The trees themselves point to another consequence of deforestation. Replacing the forests with grassland with a much reduced leaf area, will lead to greatly reduced rainfall. With such a reduction, the amount of savanna and other arid vegetation types will increase at the expense of the forest trees.

Drought and deforestation together form a vicious cycle. The deforestation going on in the Indian subcontinent is reducing the amount of water that is refilling the aquifiers and spring. Roughly four-fifth of India's land area is now subject to repeated droughts, often on a two-to-five year cycle. With such lengthy dry season, trees are dying for lack of water.

In recent years, the world's attention has been drawn to the nations of Africa by the plight of millions of people affected by drought. They are unable to provide themselves with food, water and other necessities of life. The cause of all these problems is drought leading to famine. Few plants can withstand the long drought which is followed by famine. And unlike humans and animals, trees cannot migrate to drought-free areas. Without any vegetation to hold on to the soil, erosion becomes a problem that leads to desertification.

Prolonged droughts even in arable lands can be devastating. Once the crops and vegetation are harvested, the topsoil will be subjected to scorching heat. Trees are not as effective in retaining the topsoil although it takes a long time before the tree will wither and die. Soil erosion caused by wind inevitably follows and there is almost no way to stop it. Even some of the most-resistant desert plants will find it difficult to survive. When the rainfall finally comes, the remaining topsoil will only percolate into the groundwater where it is beyond the reach of most plants.

Droughts in the Philippines occur frequently in Luzon and Vi say as due to the early denudation of forests in these areas. It won't be long before Mindanao will feel its effects too. With the presence of lush forest, the rainwater could easily be absorbed by the leaves and roots or seep into the soil instead of being runoff rapidly to the sea. Transpiration locally would mean more showers in the vicinity.

Prolonged drought in pastoral areas is equally damaging. It reduces the forage supply and the land is prone to overgrazing if the animal population is not kept low. The large herds overgraze vegetation to such extent that even the plant roots are uprooted. In their desperation for food, shrubs and trees are not spared by animals that effectively remove vegetation which has helped to protect the exposed and loose soil particle from being carried away and taking away the ability of the land to support plant and animal life.

Another problem worth mentioning is that prolonged droughts often trigger bush fires that quickly spread by the hot air and wind. The 1990s were marked by periods of severe drought, setting the stage for devastating wildfires to occur in practically every comer of the world. Hundreds of thousands to millions of hectares were burned annually in dry Weal Africa, large areas of Africa south of the Equator, central Asia, southern South America and Australia. An estimated 200 million hectare south of the equator in Africa went up in smoke.[56] As the erratic climate change continue, the possibility of more pronounced and deadlier bush fires can be expected.

Erosion, Siltation and Sedimentation

Boil erosion is a natural phenomenon whenever soil is disturbed. What is not natural is the way humans have intensified the problem by their greed. The effect of siltation of rivers, watersheds, and streams under normal condition is minimal. However, human alteration of the forests has made a significant difference. Studies have shown that a hilly region, once deforested of its cover is prone to erosion. Studies have also shown that the annual soil runoff from forest areas is only a few hundredths of a ton per hectare. Grassy pasturelands average four tons per hectare. Land cultivated for com production produces an average annual sediment yield of fifty-four tons per hectare; for abandoned farmlands, an astonishing 450 tons per hectare; and for forest cleared for agriculture, grain^ logging, or firewood gathering, the silt load rises dramatically over 1,000 tons per hectare.

The lives of approximately 500 million people in 30 countries are adversely affected by soil erosion. Sedimentation as a result of deforestation of watershed forests can dramatically reduce the economic life of reservoirs, hydroelectric facilities and irrigation systems.

A survey of twenty-two irrigation reservoirs in India shows that in many instances the annual flow of sediment is at least four times the estimate when the dams were built. Preliminary calculations for Taiwan s Shihmen Reservoir suggested a useful life of seventy-one years, but in one five-year period, from 1963 to 1968. 45% of its capacity was lost to sediments, rousing the government to take quick action to stop authorized forest clearing and farming on steep slopes upstream.

The economic life of earth dams usually lasts for fifty years. The Philippines' Ambuklao Dam, located in the Benguet region is the biggest earth-and-rockfill dam in the Far East. It was built in 1956 with three turbines generating three megawatts of power each and expected to last sixty two years, is down to thirty-two years, due to excess logging that caused some 3.6 million m³ from an anticipated 2.6 million m³ of silt to accumulate each year in the Upper Agno River watershed. By 1990, an estimated 110 million m³ of silt has piled up in the water reservoir. Experts blamed the massive erosion to deforestation caused by burning, logging, mining, and grazing.[57] True to prediction, the dam was shut down sometime in the 1990s. A move to rehabilitate the hydroelectric plant proved to be unsuccessful.

The Panama Canal is an important source of foreign exchange. The continued operation of the Panama Canal is jeopardized by deforestation upstream, which suffers from heavy sedimentation during the wet season and a lack of sufficient water during the dry season. This deforestation is also affecting the quality of drinking water in Panama City.

Ecuador is one of the most biodiversified countries in the world. It occupies only 0.2% of the Earth's land surface yet contains 10% of known plant species. It has the greatest number per unit area of any country in the world. Unfortunately, it has one of the highest rates of deforestation estimated at over 300,000 hectares per year. The life span of its largest hydroelectric dams in Paute has been reduced by half due to sedimentation caused by deforestation in its watershed. During dry years electricity shortages are experienced by the major cities being supplied by this dam.[58]

The life of the Tarbela Dam in Pakistan, which was originally planned for 50 years, has been reduced to less than 20 years as a result of excessive sedimentation brought about by upstream deforestation, overgrazing, and cultivation of steep slopes. Colombia, Ethiopia, Haiti, India, Indonesia, Madagascar, and Nepal are experiencing similar problems. Soil erosion on deforested slopes affects half of Ethiopia's land area. The country is faced with problems of famine and starvation for years to come. Other African nations where deforestation started a long time ago will soon suffer the same fate.

Deforestation has also led to electricity rationing in areas served by hydroelectric plants operating at less than normal capacity due to lack of water. It also reduces the productivity of irrigated agriculture, due to sedimentation of irrigation works and a lack of water during the dry season. This especially affects rice farming programs such as the "Green Revolution" in Indonesia Malaysia and the Philippines.

Damages to fisheries and coral reefs caused by sedimentation have been documented around the world. The harvesting of timber worth only $14 million from the drainage of South Fork of the Salmon River in central Idaho in the mid-1960s caused an estimated $100 million in damage to the river's Chinook salmon fishery. That industry has still not recovered. Fisheries in Bacuit Bay near Palawan in the Philippines were depleted after getting sediments from logging operation started in 1985 on surrounding hillsides. Uncontrolled flow of sediments into the bay killed up to half of the living corals that supported the fishery and thus deprived local villages of their source of protein.

* * * * *

When whole mass of soil and rocks on a steep slope slips from a higher plane, it is considered a landslide. It is a common occurrence in deforested mountains. Sometimes the landslide is accompanied by logged timber, making it much more dangerous to people below. This is what happened during the landslides of November 2004 in Aurora and Quezon Province that left more than 1000 people dead. During the 1985-1988 periods in Thailand, deforestation costs the destruction of the homes of40,000 people.[59]

The death toll of 202 people in a landslide in Ziyang country in Shaanxi province was caused by four days of heavy rains. This brought to at least 647 the number of people reported killed in floods during the summer rainy season Flooding often is worsened by excessive farming and tree-cutting that leaves stripped hillsides that are unable to trap rainfall.

Hurricane Mitch killed 15,000 people in Central America, mostly in Honduras From a treeless hill above the capital city, Tegucigalpa, tons of topsoil turned to mud and flowed down from hills and into a river that jumped banks to destroy markets, factories, and homes. Mitch left 2 million people jobless, homeless, or otherwise damaged. In the past the country was almost entirely forested Now, Honduras loses about 250,000 acres a year to logging, burning, and clearing of rainforest to create pasture, and to erosion from poor farming practices. About 80% of the land is sloped, so that when rainfall is heavy, without trees to break the flow of water or hold the soil in place, the land turns to sliding mud and the rivers chock, causing floods.

* * * *

Forests contain huge amount of nutrients and nitrogen in the soil. When the trees are uprooted, these nutrients are brought down the stream along with the eroded soil into the lake and the river. It would have a devastating effect on the body of water. This is what happened to Lake Victoria, the world's second largest freshwater lake. Satellite sensing detected a plume of nitrogen-and-phosphorous-rich sediments feeding the water hyacinths. As a result the fish starved to death while the planktons were deprived of oxygen and sunlight. The stagnant lake became a breeding ground for mosquitoes and snails that host bilharzia, a parasite that attacks the liver, lungs, and eyes. Vegetation that used to filter this water of sediments flowing to the lake has been removed.[62]

1998 is one of worst years in China. During the August 1998 floods, the Yangtze River's flow peaked at less than 2 million cubic feet/second, a rate it had surpassed 23 times since 1949. So by any measure, the flow should not have been a problem, but the combination of land reclamation and population growth created an environmental time bomb. The lakebeds, which used to soak up excess water became giant traps. Throughout the region, over 5.6 million houses were washed away Storm runoff from deforested hillsides drowned 750 people and left 1.5 million people homeless along the Yangtze. Yangtze, once comparably clean is now about as muddy as the Yellow River. At one flood in 1980, the Yangtze in Sichuan Province was carrying 2.35 million yards of sediment per hour.

Desertification

Tropical rainforests are sometimes called "green deserts" because they are planted on predominantly clay soils that are lean in nutrients. The profusion of vegetations has evolved ingenious life-support systems. Trees and plants send out shallow roots in all directions, soaking up available nutrients from forest's waste products - fallen leaves, dead trees, and rotting organic matter Unlike temperate regions, virtually all the nutrients are recycled back into the forest canopy, leaving little in the soils.[63]

Stripping away the trees causes the exposed soils to deteriorate rapidly, eroded by the torrential rains that can deluge tropical forests with sometimes over 2.5 centimeters of rain in 30 minutes. A single storm can remove up to 185 metric tons of topsoil from one treeless hectare. After the rains cease, the sun bakes the earth into a hard ochre-colored mass. Such "laterization" often renders the exposed soil incapable of supporting any kind of vegetation and can be irreversible. Burning is particularly damaging as most of the nutrients are released into the atmosphere.[64]

Large-scale clearing of forests not only reduces rainfall, but also allows too much sunlight to fall on the soil that creates a dry and dusty face that easily erodes. This is apparent in areas such as western Africa where rainfall has dropped to below average for 21 consecutive years. This has made crop cultivation more difficult because soil quality deteriorated and deserts have increased in size. (Ibid, 11)

The most extreme form of soil loss resulting in desertification is caused by people practicing shifting cultivation, cattle raising, firewood gathering, and logging. The 20th century has seen the steady advances of deserts into once productive land areas resulting in widespread degradation. Desertification commonly follows deforestation because water runs off the bare hills too quickly, carrying much of the topsoil with it and making it difficult to reforest and cultivate crops. This is one reason why slash-and-bum cultivators would raze trees to get to nutrients or wait for years of fallow to fertilize the land.

An estimated one-third of the earth's land surface is arid or semi-arid. Some 850 million people inhabit this land area of approximately 40 to 50 million square kilometers. The incidence and threat of desertification within this area is widespread. So is die threat of hunger, disease and poor sanitation. Desertification now affects the south western parts of the US, northern Mexico, north Africa, the Sahel, large parts of South Africa, and parts of Australian and Asia. In Mauritania, the advance was so rapid during the 1980s that homes and businesses were buried by sand dunes caused by sandstorms rolling south at the rate of several kilometers a year in recent years. (Ibid)

The Sahara Desert is advancing into Spain and Italy so much so that in 1990 the EC allocated 8.8 billion to combat its spread. The desert once confined to Africa can be seen in eastern Europe and the Caucasus region of the Soviet Union, due in part to unprecedented overgrazing by huge herds of sheep. Between 1925 and 1975, the Sahara Desert grew by about 640,000 square kilometers along its southern edge. In Sudan die desert edge moved about 190 kilometers south between 1958 and 1975 and is expanding north at the rate of about 100,000 hectares a year.

The estimated loss of 79 million hectares of forests over the past 40 years in China has accelerated the destruction of farmland through wind and water erosion, leading to desertification. Serious erosion and silting now affect 15% of the land. The most extreme example is the vast Loess Plateau, a barren area of bald mountains that stretches half a million square kilometers north of Xian along the Yellow River.

The US has lost approximately two-thirds of its topsoil, 85% of this loss is attributed to livestock overgrazing. Cattle and sheep consume 90% of the forage on 70% of all public lands in western US. The damage caused by overgrazing has brought approximately one-thirds of US drylands into various stages of irreversible desertification.

Findings by the UNEP Global Assessment of Soil Degradation survey revealed that more than one billion hectares of land, or 11% of the earth's vegetation surface land has been severely degraded since 1945. Two-thirds of all these eroded lands are in Asia and Africa, whereas both Central America and the US lost 25% of the productive cropland. The most prevalent cause is overgrazing by livestock, accounting for 35% of all degraded land. Loss of vegetation to livestock encourages wind and water erosion. Trampling by animals compact the soil and prevents water absorption. Deforestation, which affects 30% of the earth's damage land is most prevalent in Asia and South America and consumes an average of 42 million acres a year in the 1980s. Destructive agricultural practices account for 28% and two-thirds of the damage has occurred in North America. Because restoration of these damage lands is often expensive, the land is simply abandoned.

Desertification in northeastern Brazil has caused refugees not only to flood to the cities, but many have moved into the Amazon basin where they are helping the other migrants cut down the forests for farming.

* * * * *

Although droughts are often transitory, a prolonged drought that lasts for years can lead to unexpected desertification. This adverse climate condition is mostly a responsibility of human activities that often start with cutting down the trees surrounding an area followed by overgrazing by livestock. Estimates put as much as 6 million hectares of the Earth's surfaced under this precarious condition every year.

Once desertification gets hold of a fragile area, there is the tendency for it to increase in size unless drastic actions to arrest its spread is undertaken. In many places where drought-resistant plants were cultivated, it is still a losing proposition against the expanding desert.

Modern agricultural systems of monoculture that allow the soil to lie exposed and unprotected after each harvesting season is also partly to be blamed. When wind and rain erode the topsoil, it is only a matter of time before the land deteriorates to a point that even grass find it hard to survive. Desertification reduces the land available for agriculture.

Experiences in the US had shown that good land-use management and planning can prevent soil degradation. To be effective in an area such as Africa the region should enact restrictions on grazing and monoculture in many regions. The carrying capacity of the land should be estimated so that land management can be undertaken without putting too much stress on the soil Good land-use planning would recognize areas sustainable for forest, fuel woodland, grazing and agriculture. Any plan involving soil conservation must consider all factors related to soil fertility now and in the future.

Many techniques which could be employed to prevent desertification are also capable of reversing the process. Land-use planning and soil conservation techniques such as contour ploughing which conserves water and prevents erosion, strip cropping, and windbreak can be employed. Irrigation has become common practice and rain making has been attempted. Dry farming techniques have been introduced and probably the most effective way is reforestation.

* * * * *

Livestock are known to cause widespread soil erosion when the undergrowth are consumed by them, leaving the soil without any protective cover from the wind and the rain. It is estimated that cattle in Africa totaled more than 500 million today. If not due to famine and disease, the herd can double every ten years, much faster than the land can afford to feed them.

There is no controversy that cattle eat too much and drink too often and overgrazing has created desert patches on 90% of Sahel-Sudan rangelands. In southern Africa, the figure was near 80% and rising fast. Huge tracts of Central Africa were eroded severely by overgrazing. In one report, it was calculated that herds were overstocked by 50 to 100%. This can only be the result of unsustainable grazing and eventually leads to desertification. Selling the overpopulated livestock will reduce overgrazing and allow the soil to regenerate before the land is permanently turned into desert.

* * * * *

There is no question that the only solution to halt the marauding desert is by planting trees. One such gigantic project is the Great Green Wall of China. It is located in northern China where for decades since 1949, the Chinese have been planting trees roughly parallel to the Great Wall in an effort to hold off the advancing desert and reclaim the degraded land More than 30 million hectares have been reforested stretching more than 7,000 kilometers.

* * * * *

Millions of hectares of once rich farmlands have turned into desert because of overgrazing or poor farming practices that left them barren The rehabilitation of the desert is one of the most difficult undertakings to achieve. It takes a lot of manpower, patience, resourcefulness, and money to do the almost impossible. A well-known conversion of desert into a blooming area was accomplished in the Negev Desert, Israel. The desert was one of the worst pieces of lands in Israel. Through contributions from Jews worldwide, the Israelites have planted trees and orchards in this desert and turned them into a land of milk and honey. They made use of greenhouses, trickle irrigation and plastic mulch in reclaiming thousands of hectares of desert lands.

The land under plastic mulch is used to slow down evaporation The trickle irrigation or more commonly known as drip irrigation uses a system of thin plastic pipes with perforated holes laid along the surface or buried in the soil and delivering water to each plant root system where it is most needed and in exact amount that is needed. Great savings in water ranged from 50% to 80% compared to flood or sprinkle irrigation is accomplished and evaporation is greatly minimized. It increases plant

health and raise productivity by as much as 80%. The greenhouse also saves water by 90% to 95% compared to open field farming.

Drip irrigation is favorable for use in areas where water is scarce or expensive, although the initial cost can be expensive. A well-designed drip irrigation system or subsurface drip irrigation system will lose practically no water to runoff, percolation or evaporation. Scheduling the of drip irrigation can also increase crop yields and quality.[65]

Chapter 2

POPULATION PRESSURE

The greatest threat to our planet and our forest in particular is the unstoppable increase of the human race. The increases are mostly due to the high fertility rate especially in the Third World countries, the low mortality rate and the longevity of the people. During the early Christian era, the population stood at 250 million people. It reached its first billion in 1824. The second billion was reached in 1925 or 100 years later. The third billion took only thirty five years from 1925 to 1960. The fourth billion took fifteen years by 1975 and the fifth billion in 1987 or twelve years later. The sixth billion occurred before the end of the 20th century. Today, the population stands at 6.3 billion people and increasing by the minute.

Every year roughly 77 million people are addod to the world's population or roughly a little over a decade to add another billion. This is expected to continue for at least several decades before people finally put drastic measures to control population growth or nature will take over through means such as pestilence, disease, famine, etc. as predicted by Thomas Malthus. The current worldwide growth rate is 1.2% but the 50 least developed countries average 2.4%. The population growth is governed by the concept of population momentum. The population momentum is like a moving vehicle, it will take some time after applying the brake for a moving vehicle to come to a stop. The only way to stop the momentum is for each couple today to have two children to replace them. Even then, it will take two generations to stabilize the population.

People need living space for human activities such as housing for shelter, school rooms for education, offices and stores to work, malls and shopping centers to shop, amusement enters for leisure, factories to produce consumer goods, roads to go places, and a variety of other activities requiring products coming from the forest. The demand for trees and forest products is outstripping the natural growth by as much as 25% annually.

Population and Forest

The economic well being of the planet depends on the natural resources around the world and the forests supply a disproportionate amount of it. The demand of the exploding population on the forest is numerous and in many cases it is unable to support the huge population in many developing countries. Most of the needs of the people can only be found in the soil, and the economy of the world is based on the natural resources of the planet. Forests play a vital role and within the forests can be found many of the needs to keep up our living standard. Many of our needs can only be in the forests with its myriad functions.

The present demand on forest products and the need for living space for the continuing population growth is reducing the forest cover by about 50 million hectares annually. If the trend does not stop, there will be no virgin forest to speak of except patches of trees throughout the world. The time to develop the forest on a sustainable basis is now and it can only be done if we stabilize the population.

* * * * *

More than 80% of the populations today were bom in the last century. The trend is expected to continue and most of the growth is occurring in poor families and in the developing countries. African countries, with some of the lowest per capita income are expanding faster than anyw here else. Kenya, with an annual growth rate of 4% will double its population every 17.5 years. Brazil, China, India and Indonesia have slowed considerably, but the sheer size of their existing populations translates into a huge increase in people.

Deforestation and degradation of woodlands are primarily the consequences of the human population growth which have accelerated settlement and enlarged the land under cultivation for crops and grain. Harvesting of woods for export, local use, and for fuel, contributes significantly to the process. The industries located in the rural areas have abetted the overcutting of wood.

European conquest of new lands in the Americas, Africa, and Asia triggered ofT vast destruction of forests. In 1770 when settlements in the US were confined to the eastern seaboard, forests covered about 2.3

million square kilometers. By 1850, as the settlements expanded westward, about 40% of these ancient forests had been destroyed. Another 35% were cleared in thirty years. By 1930 only 13% of the US original forests were still in existence. Today less than 10% old-growth forests are available and loggers are aiming to harvest the remains as demands continue to increase.

Since the first settlement in Australia at die end of the 18* century about half of the original forests have been destroyed. Most of the destructions were due to the construction of road networks and buildings, and firewood usages.

Logging often paves the way for uncontrolled settlement,. Government should ensure that the practical plan for assisting settlers to develop the land sustainably without destroying the forest ecosystem is put in place.

The 19th century marked the expansion of the population settlements from the more fertile plains and reliable water supplies of the lowlands to the forests. By the early ZO* century, most lands suitable for homesteading were marginal or upland places unsuitable for cultivation under existing farming methods. The continuing population growth has made many rural areas reach its maximum carrying capacity. The excess population has no recourse but to move upland for their livelihood and survival.

In the densely populated regions of the world, there are great difficulties for die poor to own a fertile plot. Many are forced by necessity to look to the forests for their food and shelter. This has only led to clearing of the forests. In most instances, their actions are tolerated because governments were allocating more resources to the urban dwellers and are unable to provide for their needs.

* * * * *

The rapid depletion of forestlands due to demand is too great compared to the financial resources working to reverse it. The drive to sustain economic development in many parts of the tropics may be too late for some unless the population is stabilized so that economic gains can uplift the masses In almost all these countries, their carrying capacity has been exceeded making it almost impossible to reverse the environmental degradation unless the population is first stabilized and gradually reduced.

Man is the greatest polluter and destroyer of the planet's ecosystems Human pressure can be seen everywhere in connection with the destruction of forests. The continuing rise in population will continue to increase the demand for wood products with no end in sight. Some environmentalists attribute population as the primary cause of deforestation. Population growth in the first half of the last century has contributed to increased settlement expansion of cultivated land, and the penetration of agriculture into upland and forest areas. The acceleration of this process is reflected in the rising density and mobility.

The areas set aside for crops and grain in developing countries increased by nearly 100 million hectares or 11.5% from 1954 to 1983. Much of these increases came from clearing forested lands. During the last four decades, the areas occupied by the forest and woodlands have declined by more than half in many places in Central America and Africa. All these clearing are done to feed the teeming populations and supply the needs of the western world.

China's population has been particularly marked for centuries. It is estimated that the natural forest once covered about 75% of the land. The slow extension of farming, together with firewood gathering steadily reduced this area to about 5% by the early 20th century. These areas are covered mostly by inaccessible and mountainous areas. Only in the late 20th century' has most of the forest been reclaimed. In India, the Thar Desert in Rajasthan and Punjab, an area of about 160,000 kms² was once an impenetrable jungle 2,000 years ago.

* * * * *

Because of the high population growth for the past decades, the economic and industrialization growth cannot keep pace with it in order to absorb the excess labor force. Due to the unequal distribution of lands and poverty surrounding the lowland, those who are poor and unemployed are forced to use common property or private resources such as forest for food and fuel. Population growth has increased the pressures on natural resources, and in some cases to the point of destruction. Low wages in the private sector are also partly blamed for workers taking to the forests for a livelihood.

Malaysia has one of the highest deforestation rates in the world. In its drive to industrialize and reduce poverty and unemployment, it is destroying the forests at four times the sustainable rate. The federal government planned to convert one-thirds of its original forests into cash crop plantations.

Population and Food Supply

The world's population is expected to reach more than 10 billion by 2050. This huge number needs to be fed three meals a day with nutritious food if they want to enjoy a healthy life. There are those who think that the planet can produce more than enough to feed the growing population and even deliver a higher standard of living. On the other hand the pessimists argue that only an intensified agriculture can meet the demand for a time but at the expense of grave environmental damages.

There is actually a problem with feeding the world's population. Those who advocate that there is no problem are often the rich and well educated who have not experienced the suffering of the hungry and the ill-nourished. Every day millions of people go to bed hungry or without consum ing three square meals.

According to one report, the people from the richest developed nations eat between 30 and 40% more calories than they need while the poorest nations on average get 10% less than this basic minimum. Over one billion people, one in every five on earth do not get enough food to lead fully productive lives. At least 400 million of them get less than 80% of their basic needs, and are condemned to stunted growth and constant danger of serious illnesses. Two-thirds live in Asia, another fifth in Africa. Two thirds are probably under 15 years old and their numbers are growing. Every year about 11 million children under the age of five die from hunger or hunger-related diseases. Those who survive may never reach their full potential. One third of Peru's children are so underfed that their growth is stunted.[66]

Even if there is enough food to go around feeding everyone, there is still the problem of unequal distribution of wealth. Not every one has enough

money to buy the needed food and other basic needs All it takes it just a disastrous year of harvest to compound the problem. Per capita grain production, which grew from 246 kilos to 345 kilos between 1950 and 1984, fell back to 296 kilos by 1988. For the first time that year, the US produced less grain that it needed for its own people. In 1989, for the third successive years the world as a whole produced too little to satisfy demand. World gram stocks fell from a record high in 1986 to approaching their lowest levels ever. Prices rose by 48% between 1986 and 1989. In some of the hottest years, drought hit India in 1987 and the US, Canada, and China in 1988 as a result of the greenhouse effect [67]

* * * * *

There is currently a lack of arable land in many tropical countries In many countries the actual number of arable lands needed had peaked and even though there is a decline as urban centers has engulfed some of the fertile land. Farmers have also fled from irrigated land that has become unproductive because of salt accumulation.[68] Whenever famine strikes there is the serious problem of getting the food to those who are in need. The cost of transporting these goods may be too prohibitive for some countries to shoulder the cost.

The falling harvest is due to overuse of the arable lands, soil erosions and desertification. Every year, the world's farmers lose about 24 billion metric tons of topsoil. At one stage, in the 1970s, American farmers lost six tons of soil for every ton of gram grown. The world has some spare capacity; 20 nulhon hectares of US farmland were held in reserve in 1988, and brining them back into production would increase the world's cropland by 2%. But according to the FAO estimates, soil degradation could take 65% of all the Third World's rainfed (non-irrigated) land out of production by the year 2000. Every year the world also loses 1.5 million hectares of irrigated fields to salinization.[69]

* * * * *

The runaway population growth in the Third World, comprising about 90%.ofthe world s birth rate needs to be fed and sheltered. Because of the finite habitable areas, most of the lands converted to housing and roadworks often come from the very best farmlands that are needed to produce food for the growing population. Every year more than 300,000

hectares of farmlands are lost to urbanization. These losses can only be compensated by encroaching on the forest whose fragile soil is good for a few years of farming. Already there is lack of adequate shelter for the teeming population and growing population will guarantee that more farmlands will be lost to urbanization.

The Philippines has never been self-sufficient in food production except for a brief period in the past. Yet we are continually converting prime agricultural land into other uses that will only aggravate the food situation. The diminishing yields coupled with the disappearing croplands are manifested in the increased number of malnourished children.

Transmigration

Transmigration is a state policy to move people into government owned forests to help alleviate poverty, reduce tension by granting land to the landless as a form of land reform and alleviate unemployment by turning them into farmers. In many cases, the dwellers are induced by government with subsidy for a few days or months before they have to fend for themselves. But once let loose, the migrants often turn the forests into victims of neglect and unsustainable development.

Even before transmigration has become a modem trend in some countries, the European colonizers have used their military power to expropriate land for the settlement of their countrymen. In Algeria, after the French conquest, some of the good prune lane's were expropriated for European settlements. The local inhabitants had to move into new areas and dear the forest to provide enough land for food production.An area of about 500,000 hectares was destroyed.

Population pressure has forced government to open way to forest lands and build highways to move people from one place to another. Many of the road systems today were once covered with forest lands. The trend is continuing as urban congestion and lack of employment forces people to move to other regions.

In the 1950s and thereafter, many Third World governments were unable to provide livelihood for their teeming populations, so they opted to open up the forest lands to migration and shift people from densely populated

cities and towns to thinly populated forests to relieve population pressures and open up agricultural areas to cash crops. Large-scale transmigration had occurred in the Amazon forests and the Indonesian forests and to some extent in the Philippines and Malaysia. Rural people from the lowland have been encouraged to seek their livelihood in the highland through shifting cultivation and other means for survival. As a result many forests that should have been protected have instead become degraded as more people are forced to open up the forest for livelihood. People who migrated to these areas are required to make a clearing for agriculture which is done by burning down the forest. Forest fires often go unhampered for days destroying more areas than are necessary for subsistence.

The noble aim of resettling the unemployed members of society is to alleviate poverty and decongests the cities. However, it does not always work as planned. The Pahang Tenggara project in Malaysia allocated one million hectares of forests for resettlement. After decades of trying to improve the living standard of the migrants and aborigines, they are still living well below the urban standard. This is repeated throughout the world. There is no way of uplifting the living standard as these people as they have no access to capital intensive ventures that could really put a dent to improve their living standard.

In Ecuador, the Agrarian Reform Laws of 1964 and 1972 encourages people to colonize the forest as a solution to relieve social pressures caused by inequitable land distribution. The colonizers are forced to expand agricultural frontiers to avoid expropriation of their land. The colonists are required to clear 50 to 80% of the forests as proof of utilization. By the time the law was changed in the 1990s most of the forest is gone and the practice is still going on.

* * * * *

Transmigrations have been facilitated by die opening up of road networks used for log harvesting and mining for oil and mineral resources. Readily available loans from the international financial institutions have made it possible for government to clear forests for settlements and private corporations with their logging and mining operations. These two factors have been linked to the vast resettlement programs going on in some of the moderately congested tropical

countries. Coupled with population pressure and unemployment problems, hordes of people have migrated upland, a move never experienced before the 20th century.

Not all road networks are constructed by corporations for the purpose of exploiting the natural resources lying inside the forest lands. Some are constructed by the governments to entice settlers to move into the forests for resettlement and as a conduit for connecting towns and cities, Transmigration in the Amazon in the past was done through massive ad campaigns undertaken by the government that promised migrants thirty dollar subsidies to each family for the first six to eight months, and guaranteed crop financing for lowland workers to occupy the thick jungle. Sometimes the farmers are encouraged to settle in sparsely populated areas as a means of claiming land ownership by countries on border territories.

Military considerations are often behind the decisions to develop forests many tropical countries. In the Amazon, road buildings are promoted to encourage local inhabitants to populate the jungles to gain a foothold the land surrounding the border states.

They have been responsible for allocating funds to build huge and lengthy highways in the hope of improving the economic well-being of their poor citizens. One of these projects funded by the World Bank is the 6,000-km Trans-Amazon Highway with its 6,000-km feeder roads. The seemingly beneficial project that was to connect the Pacific Ocean to the Atlantic Ocean turned out to be one of the most destructive undertakings against the Amazon Transmigration, cattle ranching, illegal trade in wildlife, and the introduction of modem diseases to the indigenous people were made possible by this highway.

Another highway also sponsored by the World Bank is located in Polonoroeste, Rondonia has resulted in massive forest destruction. Government subsidies for transmigration cost the government about $12,000 per family, and the destruction brought about by their farming method is immeasurable. Many farmers have found out too late that swidden (shifting) cultivation does not work for long and have abandoned them after a few years. The land is then sold to cattle ranchers for land speculation. As in Indonesia, the conversions would not have

taken place at an alarming rate without the heavy public expenditures that supported them.

Experiences from the past have not put a dent on road construction inside tropical forests. There is plan to open a new 2,100 miles of additional roads through the wilderness. This could lead to clearing up to 70,000 square miles of forest over 30 years. The tendency of each route is to increase deforestation along the highway to a depth of 50 kilometers on each side, according to the Feamside's Amazon Environmental Research Institute.[70]

* * * * *

Indonesia is one of the most densely populated nations with the second largest tropical forests in the world. Its Transmigrasi Program started in 1973. To make transmigration attractive, the government gave settlers in Irian Jaya two hectares of land, tools, clothing, and a year's supply of food. Thousands of hectares were colonized from freshly cut rain forests and cabins lined in rows were constructed. Each plot was set aside and ready for every migrant to toil. The government envisioned 65 million people to be settled in the outer islands of Sumatra Timor, and Sulawesi from the highly congested islands of Java Bali, and Madera By the 1990s more than 3.5 million people have been settled, degrading more ' than 50 million of forested lands. The WB estimates that for every colonist resettled under the official transmigration project, two or more unofficially move into the forest due to the drawing effect of the program.[71]

The Leuser ecosystem zone in North Sumatra and Nanggroe Aceh Darussalam covers an area of 2.6 million hectares and is one of the world's richest tropical rainforests. It is a sanctuary for biodiversity with more than 3,500 floral species. 89 rare wildlife species, 130 mammalian species, 325 bird species, reptiles and amphibians, and others, all under the protection of the law. The ecosystem is also made up of magnificent lowland forests, an alpine park, fresh water marshes, valleys and a volcano. It serves as a buffer zone for the life of surrounding communities by providing clean water, controlling erosion and flooding, and other climatic services.[72]

Before the 1980s, the Leuser ecosystem is the last remaining pristine forest of Sumatra As a result of granting some concessions to timber barons and illegal logging it is expected to be ravaged further with new highways linking the east-west and north-south region running through the ecosystem The noble idea is to end the isolation of the local people and to aid their economic advancement.

In Sumatra Indonesia, a new highway network being proposed, the Ladia Galaska highway project plan is to build roads connecting the Malacca Strait to the Indian Ocean. This 504.69-kilometer tnmk road will pass through protected forests and the Leuser National Park. It is expected to rip the ecosystem apart. There is also the 713-km road running from the north to the south and a 369-km support road on the border with North Sumatra Already there are skirmishes between groups of soldiers and policemcn as they try to protect their respective illegal loggers. Legislation to conserve this zone seems to be ineffective as loggers ignored the presidential decree to stop illegal logging.[73]

Even before the Rpl.5 trillion project started, squatters have already moved with their own trails to carry out the felled logs. They were ticked by security personnel and financed by timber barons to plunder the forests.[74]

* * * * *

The rate of conversion of forest lands is directly proportional to the population growth. At the time of the colonization of the Spaniards in the 16th century, there were about 750,000 Filipinos throughout the archipelago and our forest covered 92% of the lands. By 1800, the population has risen to about 1.8 million and along with it 1.4 million hectares of forestlands have been converted for human habitation. Most of the trees were cut down for building ships and for human habitation. (Vitug. 11-12)

When the American took over the country, commercial logging accelerated such that by 1934, only 17 million hectares of forestlands remained Despite the loss of valuable forest, the government of Pres. Manuel L. Quezon during the Commonwealth period began to purchase big landed estates for distribution to tenants. Most of these estates were forestlands and had to be cleared for settlement. The resettlement

program accelerated after the Republic was set up to accommodate the growing population. The Philippine government sponsored resettlement schemes brought about 200,000 families into upland areas in the 1950s and 1960s. To survive, the migrants were encouraged to become farmers or hired by big estate owners to plant sugar and coconut and thus more forests have been cut down or burned to make room for fanning. The sites are selected without environmental impact assessment and even if there are, there is no guarantee that it will be followed. Wide tract of forest lands in northern Luzon and Mindanao were cleared for settlements. Once they were settled there, the forests becamc a source of livelihood and firewood gathering. Road building and other suppori programs attracted new migrants and eventually 1.3 million more people occupied the forest lands.

The upland migration has exacted a heavy tool on the forest. Cultivated upland areas increased from 582,000 hectares in 1960 to more than 3.9 million hectares in 1987. Soil erosion was estimated at about 122 to 210 toni/hectare a year for converted pastures compared to 2 tons/hectare for land under forest cover. Many upland areas reached population density of 300 persons/km^2 leading to high rates of deforestations and erosion. Timber concessionaires often hire rural people for cheap labor. The family often followed and cleared land for cultivation. By 1985, more than 62% of the total upland population resided in timber concession areas.

* * * * *

Throughout the 1990s many developing countries with rapid population growth had turned forests into agriculture land while cutting down the trees for housing and wood for fiiel. The tropical countries continue to export forest products to meet the rising demand and for incoming dollars from developed countries.[75]

Put it in another way, the forest area per capita fell by half between 1960 and 1995 as a result of both population growth and the disappearance of forest cover. In 1995 close to 1.7 billion people lived in countries with less than one-tenth of a hectare of forest cover per capita. This is expected to be reduced further to a third by 2025 when the population is expected to reach 4.6 billion people in the same finite forest area.[76]

Today, even without a transmigration program, the rapid population growth is expected to increase the movement of people unilaterally to the highland. High rates of deforestation are expected as forest areas are converted in agricultural land while the latter are converted into housing projects.

Viable resettlement areas need to be identified through better and improved surveys. Titles to land need to be awarded to settlers who have demonstrated a capacity for sound management. Land-use zoning usually fail to achieve its objectives because of lack of services and facilities in these areas It must be supplemented with modem provisions of essential services, land title, and penalties for noncompliance. Innovative approaches to integrated land management that allocate land to settlers, loggers, and extractive reserves while ensuring the rights of indigenous people are under way in the Amazon, West Africa and Malaysia. Adequate funding is essential to be successful.

* * * * *

Many of the programs implemented before have not worked. In some densely populated countries, it has been the policy of the government to disperse the people to the countryside or forested areas to engage in agriculture. Even after decades of fanning at the expense of forest denudation, the living standards of the farmers have not been uplifted. Experience have shown that this practice have not worked and will never work.

In the early 1900s, Brazil built a railroad into a portion of its vast forest in an effort to encourage settlement there. More than 2.7 million hectares of the Amazon were stripped of forests in an effort to grow crops. The experiment did not work, and today the area remains a desolate scrubland. However, Brazil did not learn from its mistake. Today it is still continuing the resettlement program. It is a disaster for Brazil and the rest of the world. The wealth of the Amazon forests is in the abundance of trees and not in the soil. Land cleared by slash-and-bum techniques support a farmer for a few years before the soil is totally degraded and the farmer is forced to repeat the destructive process elsewhere.

Transmigration can foster animosity among the original forest dwellers and the new settlers. The former are often displaced when government opened up their territory for the latter use with their new form of agricultural practices and even tree plantations. This is what happened in Ethiopia when the government in 1986 started a program called Producer's Cooperative (PC) by mobilizing "voluntary" families to resettlement sites in the hope of improving agricultural production or in curbing natural resource degradation. Most of the large tact of lands were allocated to the newcomers. Those who were left out resisted the government's program of environmental rehabilitation by stealing the fruits of the reforestation works.[77]

The ongoing civil war only exacerbated the problem. The disgruntled forest dwellers were helped by the insurgents in cutting down the trees of the government and community plantations. Even after the conflict is over, lands were transferred to communities that in turn converted the forestlands to farmland, leading to more deforestation.[78]

Indigenous People

Indigenous people are marginalized people who prefer their ancestral way of life in the forest. But their peaceful existence has often been disrupted by greedy businessmen wherever forests are situated. Whatever and whenever businessmen undertook activities on their ancestral lands it is inevitable that their lives will be disrupted.

More than 300 million people around the world belong to indigenous tribes. They are the original inhabitants of their land and have greater rights to these ancestral lands. But millions are being forced off the land, dispossessed, or pushed toward the more remote areas of the forests Many have died or perished from diseases where they have no immunity Of the six to twelve million Indians originally frcm the Amazonia, only 200,000 have survived by the 1990s while a third of the tribes have become extinct. (Hecht, 3)

In 1957, Darcy Ribeiro published a report about the conditions of the Indians of the Amazon. From a high of one million indigenous inhabitants in 1900, their population has dropped to two hundred thousand while some eighty Indian tribes had become extinct and others are on the verge of extinction. One 140 tribes occupying the Amazon

basin would one day be extinct if they are not insulated from modem society by the Indian Protection Service (SP1) sets up to protect them. Unfortunately, this government agency was run by corrupt officials during the 1950s. In 1967 the Ministry of Interior and private investigators found that among other crimes committed against the indigenous tribes were massacres of entire tribes by dynamite, machines and poisoned sugar. One French medical attaché, Patrick Braun, found that between 1957 and 1963, tribes in the Mato Grosso had been deliberately infected with smallpox, influenza, tuberculosis and measles and that tuberculosis had been introduced into the tribes of the northern Amazon in 1964 and 1965. Braun spoke also of evidence of landowners and speculators utilizing a mestizo previously infected to infect other tribesmen resulting in countless deaths. (Hecht, 154)

In February 1969, Norman Lewis reported in the London Sunday Times that officials of the SPI joined forces with ranchers and land speculators in murdering Indians and stealing their lands. He quoted Attomey-General Albuquerque Figueiredo as saying, "It is not only through the embezzlement of funds but by the admission of sexual perversions, murders, and all other crimes listed in the penal code against Indians and their property, that one can see that the IPS was for years a den of corruption and indiscriminate killings. The agency was abolished by Interior Minister Lima and a new agency FUNAI was set up and promised restitution to the Indians. The following year, Minister Limsa was gone from politics and the Trans-amazon highway was announced to pass through the Indian lands. FUNAI was an initial improvement but it could scarcely have been worse than its predecessor. The good old ways were back again. In 1970, the new head of FUNAI, Bandeira de Mello, issued several certificates to large-scale livestock operators claiming that no Indians lived in the ranchers' area of interest when in fact it is the homeland of the Nambiquara. (Ibid, 154-155)

* * * * *

Indigenous people have learned to protect the forests even though some practiced swiddcn farming. With very low birth rates and population density, they were able to use the same plot for years before opening a new plot for their farming. After the soil had lost its fertility, they were allowed to fallow for 20 years before they return for a secondary

farming. Beside these, they can harvest many other products coming out of the rainforests.

Products from the rainforests are ubiquitous. Varieties of coffee, chocolate, nuts, fruits, rubber, and medicine are collected from the wild |

forests. For centuries, these people have existed in balance and harmony with nature. But today, native people in the tropical regions have been decimated by greedy developers, loggers, and miners of natural resources. Stopping the destruction will give them and their children a chance for survival. We are greatly indebted to them for protecting the forests today as they have done in the past. Support organizations work to protect them from the new "invaders." Buying indigenous products will help their survival immeasurably. More government funds should be allocated to improve their livelihood.

The most severe problem faced by indigenous people in Asia and other countries with tropical forests is the lack of recognition of their ancestral rights to their land. Governments have forcibly taken over the land for exploitation by vested interests in partnership with the multinational companies (MNCs). The only recognized rights are those areas under permanent cultivation or occupied under ambiguous terms. In Indonesia, agrarian laws and policy discriminate in favor of urban and industrial users. In Malaysia, areas can be allocated at the stroke of a pen. In the Philippines, the new Constitution and laws grant them some ancestral rights to lands, but it is often not respected.

The lack of security of land tenure has resulted in massive take over of indigenous lands by expanding lowland populations, logging, and mining interest. The infringement of their rights by confining them to smaller plots has reduced or eliminated the long fallow period that often leads to accelerated soil erosion and loss of soil fertility and ultimately poverty of the people.

When President Ferdinand Marcos signed Presidential Decree 704 categorizing all land steeper than 18 degrees in slope as forest reserves, he in effect alienated all indigenous and upland dwellers from land ownership. Fifty-five percent of the country is now inalienable and some 15 to 20 million people are practically squatters in the land they have occupied for centuries. Government policies often ignored their welfare and rights to improve their living standard.

Just as forests are best left to nature, so are the indigenous people. They have sustained themselves for centuries without outside help and interference and will continue to do so in the future. Government intervention often leads to breakdown in relationships between government and indigenous people. PANAMIN was created in 1968 for the purpose of protecting the indigenous peoples' rights and interests, but instead it collaborated with the armed forces in depriving the people of their ancestral lands by awarding them to the mining and logging companies. The indigenous people were forced to join the militant oppositions, many joining the National People Army (NPA), a communist insurgent group.

Not only are their unique ecosystems being devastated, their lives, culture and the survival of their tribes are also at risk. This is assisted by a corrupt regime and its public officials as they allow private companies colonize the land. The expansion of cattle ranching and soya cultivation has forced indigenous peoples to be evicted out of their ancestral lands.

The human rights abuses resulting form the expansion of cattle ranching in the Amazonian states of Mato Grosso, Rondonia and Par6 are severe, especially with regards to indigenous peoples and landless peasants. There has been an enduring conflict between indigenous peoples and invading cattle ranchers over land, and in most areas, the cattle ranchers win the struggles, largely thanks to corrupt political protection and the use of violence. There have been repeated cases such as that of the Guarani-Kiaowá in Mato Grosso, whose struggle for their lands in the face of invasion by cattle ranches in the past 20 years has led to displacement, violence, murder, loss of livelihoods, famine and suicide.[79]

Stabilized Population

Food for human beings is the driving force behind the conversions of the forests into farmlands. This is mostly brought about by the runaway population growth in the tropical countries. People need to be fed and sheltered and the upland dwellers are mostly too poor to afford both necessities of life.

Unlike the temperate regions where populations have stabilized or if there were any increases, the density of the population is still low, the

tropical countries have a much higher density, poverty is rampant and the upland dwellers are mostly uneducated. This makes it necessary to control or reduce the population growth if we are to reduce the pressure on the forests. The supply for more food can only come from additional farmlands taken from the forests. Most countries have reached their food growing capacity and are forced to take over forestlands.

The carrying capacity of the land is a complex issue especially for the rural communities. The need for food, shelter, schoolrooms, health facilities, recreational areas, and firewood are some of the necessities of life that can only come from the land, especially in forested lands. The need to stabilize the population is urgent. Just as the population growth in the urban areas is putting the essential services in jeopardy, so does the exploding population of forest dwellers that put too much pressure on the forest.

Studies have shown that there is a close correlation between population growth, agriculture and deforestation. Population growth is directly proportional to the expanding agricultural and contracting forest areas. A stagnant or slow growing population on the other hand can maintain the forest integrity. The expanding population needs additional food that can only be cheaply supplied by agricultural crops planted on newly cleared forest lands. Population growth also increases the gathering of firewood for fuel that ultimately leads to a decrease in forested areas. The obvious and practical solution to a lasting forest cover is to stabilize the population at a sustainable level. Once the critical point of sustainable development is breached, that is, the level of harvesting is greater than the sustainable growth it is difficult to replenish the resource.

In the French Alps, extensive reforestation has been making large headway because of declining population that led to abandonment of agricultural land, and a reduction in the number of grazing animals. The agricultural lands are reverted back to forests. Afforestation is also extending to other European countries as most European countries have stabilized their population.

Chapter 3

TIMBER HARVESTING

The business of timber harvesting is a difficult undertaking requiring huge investments and government connections. It is more so today because of the economic and political crisis faced by many countries in the tropics. Under this scenario, timber investors have a tendency to go in and get as much as they can without regard to the welfare of the forest. The virgin forests are being raped and left to fend for themselves. More often than not, they are not able to recover from their past glory.

Timber harvesting per se is not a devious way of operating a business venture. People need wood and its derivatives as a way of maintaining our standard of living. It is an important part of the economy of countries with huge forest reserves. It could have reduced poverty if the money had been managed efficiently In the Solomon Islands, half of the revenue comes from the export of timber In Indonesia, it accounts for 13% of the economy.

Trees are renewable living things that we cannot do without But the problem is that we are destroying them in an unprecedented scale unknown in history In the tropics, it is being harvested 25% more than it is being regenerated. In short, the harvesting of tropical timber is not sustainable in the long run. For every tree harvested from the forests, ten to twenty trees young and growing are destroyed as the logs are hauled out of the jungle. The reforestation efforts cannot seem to keep pace with the rate of deforestation.

Illegal loggings have always been blamed for the deforestation around the tropical countries. I believe this is not always the case. Licensed loggers are also to be blamed as they try to extract as much as possible for fear of a change in government policy or political regimes. A timber license is a license to steal illegitimately in many cases. Loggers have been known to cut outside the concession and even bribed. They would even threaten the government watchdogs with harm and death for reporting any violations.

Politics and Patronage

Unlike mining, forest trees are there for any interested party to easily evaluate its potential worth. But it will take more than money to get to own a concession in this country and throughout the tropical countries Behind the destruction of the tropical forests are politicians and cronics of high government officials who tolerate the loggers in their unsustainable logging activities. These loggers, knowing that their ventures are a matter of patronage would not hesitate to destroy the natural resource and get what they wanted out of the forests. During the 21-year reign of President Marcos, many concessions were dominated by his cronies and powerful politicians or their own cronies.

Years ago, a friend told me that their logging concession and sawmill operation were cancelled prematurely by the forestry department. He had to seek the intervention of a senator to get the president to revoke the suspension. In order to convince the president, the senator got his name into the roster of owners of the company. This is probably one reason why powerful politicians and cronies got their names into the ownership of concessions. A very interesting book on nepotism, cronyism and the granting of logging concessions can be found in the book. *The Politics of Logging: Power from the Forest* by Marites D. Vitug.

Behind every concession is a politician, high ranking officials or their cronies. These people are not above aboard in helping destroy the forest when their pecuniary interest is involved. Once these powerful vested interests are involved, it is almost impossible for government to protect the forest should these loggers violate the forestry laws. Government s foresters assigned to oversee the logging operations depend on the loggers to supply all their needs. They are like underpaid underlings dealing with warlocks and even rely on the logging companies for their transportation water, electricity, health care and even shelter. Those who are honest are hounded out of the concession and even threatened with death. It is ironic that sometimes warlords are necessary to protect the environment against illegal loggers but only if they are allowed to operate it themselves.

* * * * *

It is not necessary to own large concessions to cut more than the fair share allowed under the agreement. With fewer logging permits being allocated for the once vast forests, the small concessionaires only need a cutting permit to extend their area of operation. Cutting outside the concession is a common practice employed by loggers to extend the life of the concession. In an investigative report, it was reported that one concessionaire got his permit to cut trees under an Integrated Forestry Management Agreement (IFMA) canceled in 2003 after it was found that it was cutting beyond his designated area. When a new DENR secretary was installed, an appeal for die lifting of the suspension was allegedly granted. This was sometime in September 2004 and supervening events forced the president to cancel all logging operation in the country.[80]

The IFMA is an agreement between the government and private enterprise allowing the latter to exclusively develop, manage, protect and utilize forestland of public domain for a period of 25 years, renewable for another 25 years. The name may sound rewarding as if we have found the solution to our denuded forest, but the opposite is true. The loggers are not interested in protecting the forest, our politics and padrinos system is at work and they know that anytime their concession may be axed.

According to some forestry officials, forestlands have been deliberately misclassified by poorly supervised DENR personnel under the IFMA system to evade new restrictions on logging. IFMA holders are supposed to cut in forests classified as "inadequately stocked or open and denuded," but with the connivance of forestry personnel, the dense forests are deliberately classified as "inadequately stocked" allowing the loggers to ravage the land. One high ranking DENR official claimed that about 15% of the IFMA sites are misclassifted. But this is disputed by one field inspector who claimed the figure could be much higher, more and half of them. (PCIJ, 36-37)

* * * * *

Government officials should never be in business dealing with our natural resources. However, many are known to be involved in logging or mining directly or indirectly through their friends. Their influences are known to be detrimental to the forestlands. They act selfishly if their own interests are involved. It has emboldened those loggers with connections with high government officials to violate logging rules when it affects their profits. Logging rules and regulations are violated if it is to their convenience Name-dropping is common when it comes to violating the laws.

In Thailand, illegal logging being done by people with political connections is still very widespread. More than half of the wood processed came from illegal sources. In Sarawak and Sabah, Malaysia, the state s environment minister and a former governor are the biggest concession holders in the region respectively.

Politicians throughout the world should be banned from the profitable business because their presence and power are inherently destructive to the environment. Politicians have been known to stop at nothing to enrich themselves to fund their political ambitions at the expense of the environment. They are a very powerful force to reckon with and they will go all out to preserve their interests or those of their cronies. It should be made a crime whenever they are involved in scams and the ban should extend to their immediate family as well.

In the US, politicians from the timber producing states have been in the forefront fighting for increases in allowable cut and passage of road building networks into the forests. Self-interest often take precedent over the environment.

During the discussion on the total log ban in the Philippines, powerful politicians in timber-rich provinces were vehemently against the total log ban because of the possible effect on their self-interest or that of their friends.

Throughout the country, many politicians have been involved in timber harvesting for decades. Many have been given concessions as reward for their political support and continued loyalty. In Mindanao, the Moro rebels and political leaders were given concessions to cut trees, but mostly for a short duration. The effect is that no reforestation is undertaken. Meanwhile the tendency is to cut as much as possible in as short a time as possible. Tumcoatism is rampant among politicians with logging and mining concessions to protect their interests.

When then Secretary Fulgencio Factoran of DENR undertook to revamp the department, he was met by stiff opposition from politicians and private individuals with vested interests. The threat of budget cut often work wonders for the politicians. He had to be cozy with the politicians for fear that he would be denounced publicly. When he cancelled several concessions for logging outside their concession area, he was maligned in Congress and was forced to resign in frustration. (Vitug, 49-50)

Factoran was aware of the problem that stands in die way when dealing with vested interest involving members of Congress. When he cancelled the one concession being lobbied by a congressman for violation of forestry laws by logging outside the concession area and cutting prohibited species, he was denounced as a "fraud" and the "phantom of the environment" in the halls of Congress. During one interview, he says, "Clearly, there should be no politics in natural resources. The political pressure I experienced was not from a higher-up asking me to do something against my will. President Cory never intervened. It was from the two houses of Congress." (Ibid, 50)

* * * * *

In a research made by Robert Deacon making use of historical records, he found that stable democratic governments play a key role in slowing the rate of deforestation. It is only the government that has the power to protect the environment by defining and enforcing secured property rights. The absence of secure ownership induces both trespassers and forest owners who cannot defend their own property to cut timber on short rotations and not to replant. A well-defined, secure private property rights discourage deforestation in two ways. Potential harvesters will allow trees to grow longer, to secure that the mature timber will be safe for them or their descendants to harvest and they will be more likely to replant. The absence of secure property rights also threatened forests by deterring agricultural investments in irrigation, terracing and soil enrichment.[81]

Dictatorship is always bad for the country. Even if the country is rich in natural resources, only the cronies and relatives are able to benefit from the bounty of the natural resources. The practice of nepotism is seen everywhere where the ordinary people suffer from poverty while only a few rich families benefit. Nowhere else is patronages more apparent than in Indonesia under President Suharto. Logging concessions covering more than half the country's total forest area were awarded by him to his relatives and political allies. In 2002, ten companies control 45% of the total logging concessions in the country. Cronyism in the forestry sector left timber companies free to operate with little regard for long-term sustainability so much so that legal timber supplies declined from 17 million m3 in 1995 to less than 8 million m3 in 2000.[82]

Asian Invasion

Asian logging companies are the worst in the world. They have destroyed their own forests and are now invading forests halfway around the world - in the Amazon. The Brazilian Amazon still contain about one third of the world's timber supply of about 60 billion m3 worth about $4 trillion. Most of these destructions have been driven and financed singly by Japan's insatiable appetite for foreign timber while keeping their own forest intact. They often use prize virgin hardwoods for disposable concrete moulding in the construction business.[83]

There is a major concern about the Asian logging companies invading the forests of South America. They have already moved into Guyana and Surinam and for the big prize, the Amazon rainforest. They shy away from the African continent because of the peace and order and political instability problems. In the Amazon, large parts of still intact forest in remote areas where government agencies are weak and unmotivated are for the taking. Without international vigilance, there is a real risk that the disaster that happened on die Southeast Asian forests will be repeated by the same companies in an unprecedented pace.

In Guyana, Malaysian companies have obtained government concessions to vast forest areas, and timber production multiplied fivefold between 1991 and 19%, forcing the government to decree a three-year moratorium on new concessions until environmental laws can be tightened. In Brazil, the Asians have begun buying up local timber companies, often keeping their own names. WTK of Malaysia paid $7 million for Amaplac in January 1997, and also bought 300,000 hectares of forest near the Jurua River, an Amazon tributary, for around $2.4 million. Total WTK investment in timber is reported to be $18 million Saraling, another Malaysian giant, is negotiating to buy Amacol

Compensa, a local timber firm, now belongs to China's Tianjin Fortune Timber Company. (*Guardian Weekly*, 19 Jan. 97)[84]

Logging Roads

Before any logging activities can commence, roads leading to the logging sites are necessary to harvest the timber that were cut down. This is the first destructive phase of the logging industry. Whole swathes of forest trees, big and small will have to be cut down to make room for the roads. The roads needed to get to all the matured trees will require not only the main thoroughfare, but even more feeder roads to reach other areas. The system of roads is like our circulatory system where veins and arteries serve as the main road and capillaries serve as secondary feeder roads. (Norse, 173)

In a report commissioned by the Washington Department of Natural Resources, it was found that for every square mile of commercial forest. five miles of logging road are needed. Each stretch of road needabout 10 to feet wide but the right-of-way generally cleared is about 40 to 80 feet. As a result, about 10 acres are deforested for every mile of road. This amounts to about 8% of the land. (Ibid)

In the logging of the nearly 30 million acres of commercial forest in northwest California, western Oregon, and western Washington, 233,000 miles of logging roads were constructed occupying 2,400,000 acres of land, an area twice the size of the state of Delaware. (Ibid)

During the construction and the maintenance of the logging roads the disturbance of the soil will continue as long as it is being used. The topsoil have to be compacted with gravel for trucks and other heavy vehicles to traverse and soil erosion and sedimentation will continue to be carried to the streams and finally deposited downstream and into the river or ocean. The problem is especially acute during rainy seasons. Mini avalanches have been known to destroy roads cut from steep areas. As a result, the damaged roads have to be replaced and the cycle of erosion continues. Loss of topsoil is a serious problem in the future when it comes to reforestation.

Many forest managers and scientists came to the same conclusion as one author wrote that road and skid trail layout construction, use and maintenance affect erosion from forest land more than all other forest activities combined. (Norse, 175)

It is the road networks that made it possible for logging trucks to penetrate deep into the once inaccessible old growth that has reduced the forest cover. Even before the loggers have halted their operation, forest inhabitants start to move in with their century old shifting cultivation. All these are made possible because of the existence of a system of road networks.

* * * * *

Selling logs abroad is more profitable than processing the logs back home. Most of the loggers in the Third World do not have the funds or refuse to risk investing in the business without a readily available foreign market. The hungry foreigners will always help out by funding the road projects to get the logs out. This is the way the Japanese get a foothold in the timber concessions in the tropical countries.

Malaysia was once the biggest exporter of hardwood logs. In 1985, it exported 11.4 m³ for which 5.8 million m³ went to Japan. Many operations were financed by Japanese companies under an intricate credit system with the right of first refusal. As a result, few buyers are willing to negotiate with the logging companies while the Japanese importers were very particular about the logs they will buy. The logging companies felled their logs and floated them down the river where Japanese fmancers/buyers were waiting. The prices of logs are dictated by the law of supply and demand. If the buyer and seller cannot agree on the price of the logs, they are left to rot. Millions of cubic meters were wasted. (Hurst, 108)

Logging roads are not confined to the movement of vehicles. The use of railroad systems can be more devastating to forests traversed by their mammoth locomotives. This is what happened in most parts of the US. Large-scale devastation logging began with the arrival of a swarm of railroads dunng the 1880-1920 era. Not only could timber and lumber be hauled out on trains, even heavy logging equipment were easily brought in by trains along with powerful skidders that dragged logs for long distances, creating deep gashes in the soil.[85]

* * * * *

Construction of roads through the forests has become a convenient excuse for logging. Roads have been constructed to connect towns or help upland farmers bring goods to the lowland. These are legitimate reasons but often there are ulterior motives behind these projects. There are other reasons which only corrupt minds can envision. One of these is the logging on the reserv ation of Fort Magsaysay.

The 73,000-hectares military reservation was created in 1955 as a training camp for soldiers fighting in jungle warfare. Today, less than 20% remain forested as insiders from the Army Headquarters have commissioned loggers to cut down the trees by way of building new roads to make the deeper parts of the jungle more accessible to the soldiers. This would defeat the main purpose of jungle training where paved roads should not have existed. The original pretext for the construction of the road was the right-of-way to get to another logging concession. Instead of a roughly straight line, the road became a zigzag road passing through many of the big trees. (Vitug, 104)

Once money has changed hands, the forest is under the mercy of unscrupulous loggers and their cahoots. Loggers would enough clout could get insiders to grant them permit to cut trees in the name of development. Other spur or switch roads could be found branching out from the main road. Valuable trees were cut down outside the right of way and left lying in the roadside for later retrieval. Even after the contract has expired, trees continue to be cut. Such is the lure of the commercial logging wherever they exist.

Fragmentation

Fragmentation can occur in many ways. Road that cut through the forestlands is the most common way. Large scale fragmentation can also occur through burning or logging at different sites. Deliberately fragmentation of logging is a common occurrence among different concessionaires. There are many ill effects of fragmentations.

Logging roads as well as logging itself contribute to die fragmentation of the forestlands. Roads increase the possibility of slow-moving animals getting killed while crossing the road. In many highways in the US that runs through forested areas, roadkill is a serious problem. The fragmented forest increases the outer rim areas making animal-to-human contacts increasingly likely. In Florida, one panther is killed every year crossing the Alligator Alley Highway. This has forced the state government to build 36 underpasses fimneling the panthers to these crosswalks. Near Orlando, Florida, the State Road 46 had claimed 15 of] the more than 300 bears killed from 1976 to 1993. An eight-foot tall tunnel and fences on both sides running for a mile in both directions has been constructed to funnel the bear into it. (Ang, Animals, 276)

In Australia, every year about 100,000 hectares of trees are being cleared for development. The shrinking and fragmented forest could lead to inbreeding. The koalas are also forced to cross streets that often resulted in their being killed by motor vehicles. Of some 4,000 koalas killed annually, 2,500 died as a result of road accidents. The only remedy is to connect these fragmented areas with corridors, allowing animals to travel from one area to another without being molested. NGOs are working to stop new road developments that traverse their habitats. (Ang, Animals, 94)

Anybody with an automobile who drives recklessly can be a hunter without using a firearm. In the US alone, six times more deer are killed by the automobiles than those killed by hunters. In UK, 200,000 rabbits and hedgehogs and over one million toads are run over by automobiles each year. In Germany, over 500,000 hedgehogs are ran over by vehicles annually. (Ibid, 284)

* * * * *

Another problem with fragmentation of forests is that those small forests, ranging from one to 100 hectares may be too small to remain as self-generating ecosystem. Julieta Benitez-Malvido of the National University of Mexico in Morelia studied 11 fragmented forest near Manaus, Brazil. She found that the density of shade-tolerant seedlings which represent the majority of trees - decreases dramatically towards the forest edge, and is up to 40% less in the comers of a fragment than in the center. She concludes that below a certain size, rainforest segments cannot contain enough seedlings to fully regenerate the plant species within them. One of the key factors was the change in climate within the forest. The hotter, drier environment near the edges prevents the germination of shade-tolerant species. They were hindered by having to compete with light-tolerant species that have higher growth rates. The reduced number of animal species in small forests sections also reduces the pollination by animals. Fewer primates, birds and other animals means there is less "seed rain" dispersed in feces.[86]

* * * * *

The effect of global wanning by the clearing of rainforest may have been isly underestimated. A team from Brazil has found that carbon emmisions from the felling of tropical forests are generally 7% higher than previously thought and as much as 42% higher in some places. Recent estimates suggest that deforestation worldwide release about two billion tons into the atmosphere every year through burning and decomposition, a large portion of which comes from the tropics. According to William l.aurance at the National Institute for Research in the Amazon in Manuas, Brazil, the figures do not take into account the extra carbon dioxide produced by the fragments of forests left after clearing. In an 18-year study of 66 forest fragments, Laurance and his team found that the fringes of forests - within 100 meters of the edge - lose significantly more vegetation than the inner areas because they are exposed to higher winds and other extremes of climate. The resulting decomposition emits considerable quantities of carbon dioxide and methane, two major greenhouse gases. The loss of trees also means that there is less biological matter capable of absorbing carbon dioxide from the atmosphere during growth.[87]

The team calculates that annual carbon emissions from fragmentation of forests are between 3 and 15.6 million tons in the Brazilian Amazon and between 22 and 149 million tons for all tropical forests at the present rates of clearance. This suggest that current estimates for carbon emmisions from the felling of tropical forests are up to 7% too low, and as much as 42% too low in some areas. This is equivalent to an additional 150,000 to one million hectares of rainforest each year being destroyed.[88]

Selective Logging

In selective logging, only the fully matured and over-matured trees are chosen to be felled and the less matured ones are left standing. The forest is then left to regenerate for 35 to 45 years in most countries, unlike the

Japanese forest where the waiting period is 60 years. This is however, rarely followed as loggers disregard the fallow period and return to log the secondary forest at a shorter time. One typical example is the operation of Western Mindanao Lumber Company that selectively logged their concession between 1953 and 1955, taking an average of 150 m of timber per hectare. Fifteen years later, it returned to the same area and harvested some 120 m³ more. It is doubtfiil if a third harvesting will be forthcoming in the near future.

Researches have shown that even selective harvesting can be very damaging. One survey reported that only 3% of the trees were harvested but the damage to the other trees can be as high as 49%.[89] This is initially and partly due to the heavy machinery used to penetrate the forest and the roads constructed to get to them. Once logging commenced, the mountainous and steep slopes in the Philippine logging areas required the log to be forcibly dragged out with high tension steel cables instead of the safer skidding techniques. The FAO estimates that on the average 31% of the land surface are stripped of vegetation by the way our logging system is done. (Hurst 188)

On the average, virgin dipterocarp forests can contain 100-145 valuable trees per hectare. For every tree harvested, ten or more are broken or damaged Felling one tree tears down with it the climbers, vines, epiphytes and lianas, leaving a hole in the canopy that dries up the forest floor and make it susceptible to forest fire with its accumulated combustible fuel. The compacted soil also makes it hard to grow the seedlings. Once a tree is damaged, its defenses against insects, fungi, and other pests are impaired. In one study, the use of heavy equipment like bulldozers can damage a third of the area of operation.

According to the 1978 UNESCO report on tropical forest ecosystems, true selective felling is impractical regardless of the structure, composition and dynamism of the original stands. Logging is now taking place mostly in the virgin forest which contains larger volumes of marketable timber. For the second growth logging 35 to 50 years later, the trees will not grow as big in size or quantity with a higher percentage than today. The ecology of the environment is permanently changed for the worse. After the third harvesting complete denuding can be expected.

Commercial logging in Brazil probably has the worst record. Out of the 6,000 species of trees, less than 10 species are commercially logged and the damage to the surrounding forest using modem equipment is 50% in any given area.

Clear Cutting

Clear cutting is often done in the temperate countries because of the likelihood that most of the trees are old growth and matured. Most of these forests are pristine and harbor only a few species. Even then they have many things in common with tropical forests. There are biodiversity although on a smaller scale than the tropics. Indigenous people also exist in abundance. In North America, indigenous Indians tribes have been displaced because of deforestation. They livelihood of fishing have been destroyed due to the destruction caused by deforestation to the streams and rivers. Animals that once grazed the land for hunting have disappeared along with the forests. What is happening to Canadian forests is happening to Brazil that some ecologists are branding Canada as the "Brazil of the North."

The livelihood of the indigenous people is not protected by the central government. In 1988, the inhabitants of the Lubicon Indian Nation, one of the poorest in Canada were told to move out because the Alberta Government have given away their land to Daishowa in the form of subsidies for timber extraction in excess of $74.7 million, it was able to get away with the "crime" because the Lubicon are a small, poor population whose voice has been dampened by the government and Daishowa. There have been wide protests through the help of the NGOs to block Daishowa from cutting amid land disputes. Another group under the gun is the Bigstonc Cree Indian whose lands are being threatened by Mitsubishi and Daishowa's clear cutting and the discharge of pollutants to the only river they depended on. Their only hope is a court action to stop the degradation on the ground that their livelihood depends on the Athabaska River where they get most of their food.[90]

In Canada where Aspen trees abound, paper and chop stick mills are setup to process the timber. This is necessary because Aspen trees are quick to rot and if rotting occurs, it will reduce the strength and brightness of the pulp resulting in substandard paper products.[91]

The massive pulp and paper mills are expected to dump thousands of tons of toxic waste into the rivers daily. The Great Mackenzie River has been turned into one giant chemical sewer of the pulp mill discharge. The mills are very dependent on the organo-chlorinc used to bleach the wood in making the paper whiter. So far, at least 150,000 tons or the chemicals have been discharged into the rivers and coastal waters.[92]

To hide the clear cutting expanse of landscape, a "beauty strip" 10 to 151 miles beyond is left behind the highway. Clear cutting have resulted in even worst soil erosion of the rivers and streams where most of the indigenous people depend on the salmon and trout for part of their diet.

Forest Product Certification

The unprecedented and wanton destruction of forests leading to deforestation have hit many tropical countries. Concern for the rainforests caused some environmentalists to offer loggers an opportunity to grant official recognition for their sustainable harvesting of timber products. The oldest program was launched by the Rainforest Alliance in 1991. It is called Smart Wood. So far the program has certified four logging operations in the US and six countries in the tropics including some firms in Indonesia, Mexico, Brazil and Papua New Guinea. Finished products such as lumber and furniture and the stores that carry them are also certified.[93]

Other environmental groups are joining the wood certification program. Basically, three important criteria must be complied with before a certification is issued. The first criterion is that timber must be harvested sustainably. The second is that the health of the ecosystem must be maintained at all times and the economic needs of the community must be respected. Another certifying organization is the Oakland-based Scientific Certification System (SCS).

Since the certification program came into force, some importers from the West are requiring tropical exporting countries to obtain forest product certification before they will purchase the products. Certifying products coming from the forests may be one way of forcing and ensuring that they come from forests that are managed sustainably. By 1998, about 10 million hectares of forested lands have been certified, mostly in Europe and North America. In tropical countries, where most of the forest destruction is taking place, only tiny areas have been certified as providing sustainable yield.[94]

To assure credibility, environmentalists and certifiers need someone to grant authority to the certifiers. They created the Forest Stewardship Council (FSC). It is an independent international nonprofit NGO that provides standard setting, trademark assurance and accreditation services for companies and organizations interested in responsible forestry. FSC was set up in 1993 and headquartered in Germany and well-funded by businesses, governments, foundations and NGOs. (Diamond, 473)

It sets international standards for responsible forest management through consultative processes. Not only is the forest certified with its logo, the products are traced from their sources through a chain of complex network of suppliers all the way to the consumers. So far, it has certified some 10 million cubic meters of tropical wood worth $5 billion in 90 countries. Over the past ten years, 50 million hectares in more than 60 countries have been certified according to its standards while thousand of products are produced using FSC certified wood and cany the FSC trademark. The FSC operates through its network of National Initiatives in more than 34 countries.[95]

TracElite is another NGO set up to keep track of the timber from the stump, through the supply chain up to the retailer. It claimed to be the number system of timber traceability. Everyone connected with the supply of timbers from the buyers, suppliers, auditors, trainers, and verifiers are organized into a single system where monitoring is made much easier.[96]

The successes of the certification programs and its strict criteria have forced some business organizations to come up with their own certification programs with weaker standards to confiise the public. They include the Sustainable Forestry Initiative in the US that was set up by the American Forest and Paper Association, the Canadian Standards Association: and the Pan-European Forest Council. None of them require third-party certification and some can even certify themselves. (Ibid, 479)

The central government of United Kingdom, which accounts for 15% of the purchase of timber products, has finally decided on a buying policy based on the certification schemes. Only products that are certified will be purchased. The two certification institutes chosen are the Forest Stewardship Council and the Canadian Standards Association.[97]

* * * * *

One way of going around this process is to export finished products. Most importing countries, companies and individuals appear to care little about the source of their timber, or as one Chinese exporter puts it, "Our clients are concerned about the type and quality of wood that is used. But nobody has ever asked us if the source of the wood is legal or illegal Despite many recent international, regional and bilateral initiatives to combat illegal logging, many importing countries still legally allow the importation of timber coming from illegal sources. The timbers are produced in breach of the laws of the country of origin and exported into consuming countries including the G8 nations and China. Once the timber has been 'substantially transformed' into finished products such as wooden furniture from logs or processed timber, its designated country of origin becomes the country where the timber was processed, not whore it was logged. Timber illegally logged in one country and subsequently made into furniture in another, could theoretically be legally exported to the US.[98]

The internationally recognized definition of what amounts to 'Country of Origin' effectively legitimizes the laundering of illegal timber in trade. Interestingly, wood sourced in Burma is often labeled as having a 'southwest' origin and appears to be treated by the Chinese in the same way as domestically-sourced timber.[99]

* * * * *

The WWF has a different approach to the same problem. Instead of certifying the suppliers, it is certifying the companies that are doing the buying. Companies certified are given the logo of Forest & Trade Network (FTN) as long as they increase their purchase from sustainable forest harvesters. In the UK, there are 55 members and they accounts for 20% of the purchase.[100]

All the measures so far adopted by EU countries are voluntary and no punitive actions against violators are imposed. But Germany has gone

one step ahead of the other EU members by proposing legislation outlawiing import or marketing of wood sourced illegally in non-EU countries. Under a draft law, German timber companies will be obliged to certify that timber they import or use was procured legally. The proposal affects all companies with annual sales of more than 100,000 euros.[101]

According to the German environment minister Jurgen Trittin, illegal ing has been responsible for 80% of Brazilian timber exports, 73% fenesian and 30% of the Russian exports.[102]

Sustainable Forest Management

Sustainable forest management is good in name only. Loggers are out to take as much out of the forests without regard for the future of the forests. Actual experiences from the field have found that even long concession tenure will not encourage sustainable management unless it will benefit the loggers. This is not financially profitable in the long run as the loggers are out to harvest as much as they can the first time out. Loggers abhor regulations of whatever kind.

Sustainable forest management is a very difficult undertaking and can be quite expensive. Methods of harvesting with little impact on the forest and the ecology may be available but not adopted because of the cost. Lack of resources is usually the reason. The only way to get them to comply with their sustainable forest management is strict enforcement and monitoring of their activities. High penalties and cancellation of license are the best ways to get their compliance.

Political consideration in the awarding of forest concessions only invites problems of unsustainable harvesting. The loggers are always fearful that they would lose the license once their patrons are out of office. There is no incentive to protect their forests for the benefit of others in the future. The best solution so far is to award the concessions to the communities. Let them benefit using the least form of impact harvesting like carabao logging. The use of mechanical and electric equipment should be outlawed. When it will take generations to log the concession, the regeneration power of the forest would be left to nature. It would be to the interest of the community to guard against illegal logging.

* * * * *

A forest is considered sustainable if the volume of trees extracted is equal to those replanted trees and on a more or less equal species. Instead, other kinds of species are replanted that will not restore the same biodiversity in the long run. Even if reforestations have been undertaken, it is a half-hearted effort that could not compensate for the lost forest. One good example is the deforestation in West Malaysia. During the 1970s, lodging affected 300,000 hectares each year while enrichment planting of chosen species for the whole decade was only 47,000 hectares. (Hurst, 50) This is being replayed all over the tropical countries.

Loggers who want to go into business of timber harvesting should only be allowed after they show their capability to reforest. What better way to prove their worthiness is to have them replant some of the denuded forests in their vicinity before they are granted the privilege of logging in our forests. How they manage to care and the reforestation and the survival rates of the trees is the key element to prove their sincerity and | worthiness for sustainable harvesting of our natural resources. In short, plant first before cutting.

Historical surveys have shown that the world's tropical forestlands continue to dwindle with each passing year. There is no way of bringing back many of these forests that have been converted to settlement sites or crop plantations.

Millions of people especially those living within the confines of the forest rely on forest products for their livelihood. Sustainable forest management will require not just strict enforcement of laws that protect forests, stamping out corruption that allows damage to the forest but also provide alternative sources of livelihood for many rural people. This is not expected to put a dent at present because of lack of resources and money to take care of the rural communities.

Mahogany, a dark-red tropical wood has become a rare species that is highly prized around the world. It has been placed under the protection of the Convention on International Trade in Endangered Species (CITES). CITES requires producing countries to define sustainable levels of mahogany production and limit their export permits accordingly. There are other problems surrounding the production of this species. In Brazil, it has become a problem as reports of slavery threats to indigenous South American tribes and unchecked illegal logging abounds.[103]

Indigenous workers have been hired like slave laborers in the mahogany business. In 2003, more than 1,400 of them were freed by the Brazilian government Because some of the prized mahogany could only be found deep in the jungle, loggers have penetrated these sites bringing with them diseases that the local people have no immunity or little resistance.[104] The timber harvesting in Amazon typically extracts one tree per hectare or about 3% of the forest but the damage to the environment with the construction of road networks and the use of skidders, kill or damage more than 52% of the other areas. The loggings are done on Indian lands. (Hecht. 158)

News of the illegal nature of harvesting mahogany coming from Peru and Brazil have forced the US and European countries to reject Brazilian mahogany exported under fraudulent permits. As a result, the Brazilian government suspended mahogany logging. However, in other pails of South and Central America, many communities were able to harvest Eahogany in an environmentally sustainable way.

* * * * *

Sustainable tropical logging is a difficult undertaking to achieve and often incurs costs that eat into the profit. The only possible way to achieve sustainable logging is not wholesale timber harvesting as practiced by most loggers to make a profit. The Yanesha forestry cooperative, an Indian forestry cooperative in the Peruvian Amazon, has been operating since 1985. By clear cutting down timber in narrow strips of 20 to 50 meters wide and a variable length, much like small-scale natural disturbances, it hopes to create areas of sunlight that will allow new seedlings on the ground to grow faster. This thinning also allows the seedlings from the uncut areas to colonize the stnpes. Reforesting will hasten the process.

Each harvested strip must be at least 200 meters from those cleared in previous years and an additional section is set aside to act as a reserve lor old growth. During the harvesting the small branches and foliage are left behind to provide nutrients. Draft animals are used to remove the logs] out of the forest to minimize soil damage.

* * * * *

There is no doubt that during logging operations there are too many wastages spent. This has to do with the log ends of the cut trees. These small diameter wood are often left in the wood to rot and can put the forest at risk of wildfires. This is because it is difficult to process the small log into lumber or board as they can crack easily. However, they can be used as they are as poles. They can actually be used as post for log homes in the rural areas or as railings for balcony and stairways or even as firewood.[106]

* * * * *

Sustainable forest management could be the solution to fight illegal logging. But the problem is that those who engaged in them are often not conscientious enough to undertake the task. Instead, they take advantage of the government efforts with their own hidden agenda. Many of the forest management agreements are nothing but fronts for illegal logging Just before Secretary Michael Defensor of DENR filed his leave of absence, he cancelled 8,000 of these agreements or logging permits. All these agreements covered areas in Luzon and Visayas while sparing three integrated forest management agreements in Mindanao.[107]

The reason for the cancellation is that there are too many of them and monitoring is difficult if not impossible. Other reasons given are violations of the agreement such as failure to submit comprehensive development and management plans and payment of rentals and fees.[108] His act has been long in coming considering that despite spending billions in reforestation, the rate of deforestation is going on faster than we can reforest The country cannot afford to continue in this state if we are going to leave some forests intact for the future.

Social Forestry

Forest lands are owned by the government in most of the tropical countries. And they have the discretion to allocate to individuals or community for specific purpose such as tree planting. It is an ideal setup that protects the forest against intruders harvesting timber or otherwise destroying the forest. At the same time landless farmers are required to plant trees and crops for their immediate subsistence. The tenants are given the right to dispose the products at their discretion as long as they keep the land under tree production. In the Philippines, livestock programs were used initially as an incentive to get farmers to participate in tree growing. This is essentially social forestry at work.

Social forestry is the involvement of the local rural people in growing trees for their own use. It involves planting a few trees wherever spaces are available. It is a local community development project to provide products for their own use and to generate income. Everybody is involved in growing different species of trees for different uses such as wood for housing, fuel wood for energy, fruits, mushrooms, herbs, etc. Only conscientious people who are willing to sacrifice and see the projects through will succeed.

The Philippine National Communal Tree-Farm Program (CTF) was established in 1979 to promote social forestry in denuded upland areas for rehabilitation. Under the program, the farmers leased small plots of forested lands from the government for 25 years at no cost. The lease is renewable for additional 25 years if the work was satisfactory. The farmers were given seedlings and technical assistance. Each participant is required to cultivate in at least 80% of the area leased.

Although the program was not as successful as anticipated, it did reduce firewood gathering and greatly minimized slash-and-bum agriculture on forested lands. Each region has its own outlook toward social forestry. It is necessary to evaluate each project on a case to case basis. It also requires hard work and community cooperation in order to succeed.

Another program called the Integrated Social Forestry Program was undertaken in 1982. Like die CTF, qualified individuals and upland communities are given stewardships or tenure agreements using different agroforestry methods to protect the forests. Since most individuals prefer individual agreements, large tracts of critical watershed forests cannot be allocated. Only 21 leases of community-based programs were issued. Even then they have little knowledge and practical experiences to run the programs.[109]

During the term of President Corazon Aquino, a Master Plan for Forestry Development was initiated in 1990. Restricted loggings were undertaken and timber licenses were converted to Timber Production Sharing Agreements (TPSAs), program such as Industrial Tree Plantation (ITP) with loans from Asian Development Bank (ADB) while other forest areas were leased to local communities. Still the same problems of the past hound the new approaches.[110]

During the tenure of Secretary Factoran, he estimated that 15 percent of the funds spent on reforestation amounting to about P390 million was pocketed by corrupt DENR officials, politicians and parties granted the reforestation projects. There were reports of ghost contractors, abandoned reforestation because workers were not paid and some have resorted to burning down their reforested sites. Even funds allocated to congressional districts in the hope of getting the congressmen to cooperate in reforestation works are no better. Investigation by the DENR and confirmed by the Commission on Audit found that some contractors abandoned their projects after collecting the 15% "mobilization fee" in preparation for the reforestation sites. Some never did any reforestation while continuing to receive money through falsification of accomplishments reports. (Vitug, 61)

This is the same experience that visited Laos. Instead of reforestation, the ADB $11.2 million "Industrial Tree Plantation" project is seeing further deforestation and the replacement of forests with farms that only grow one (cash) crop. Private companies are reaping the commercial benefits while government subsidies further increase deforestation. Villagers must now walk farther to collect foodstuffs and forest products necessary for their survival. Wildlife increasingly migrated out of the plantations. leaving many Laotians impoverished and the forests in grave danger of being lost to the world forever.[111]

* * * * *

After decades of plundering the forests, there are more than enough denuded lands that can be used for tree planting without the need to destroy new forests for farming. One successful example is a group farm forestry scheme developed in West Bengal, India. A group of landless farmers were given a block of marginal public land for tree planting under this system, group control over the areas allotted and the number of trees to be planted guarantee enough wood to meet all domestic needs.

All work is done in a group for effective performance and assurance compared to individual work.

Forestry cooperatives supported by farmers is another innovation that may prove to be effective. A pilot project in Guzara, Pakistan envisages the establishment of some 15 forestry cooperatives, each with a minimum of 200 hectares of forest lands. Each cooperative is responsible for manning the forests in accordance with a plan approved by forest department. The cooperatives receive assistance and the services of field foresters, both paid by the government. Other expenses are borne by the cooperatives. The cooperatives are authorized to retain as much as 40% of the revenue from the sale of trees.

In Malawi, the residents of Katunga village were granted the management rights to a nearby forest plantation in year 2000. One of the conditions of the handover was that all the revenues derived from the plantation shall be used for community development initiatives, including re-investment in forest management. More than one hundred local communities were involved. The project was funded by the Norwegian Agency for Development Cooperation (NORAD) through the Malawi's Forestry Department. Much of the success was the result of villages' ability to democratically reach consensus among themselves and to successfiilly negotiate with outside organizations methods on how to develop their community.

Buying the Forests

In some countries, forest lands are not considered public domain and can be purchased by private individuals or corporations. This is the case in the U.S. Most of the old growth forests have been logged over by' timber harrvesters around the world. Presently, there are few old-growth forests in existence and they are being eyed by the greedy loggers. In California in 1850 when it gained statehood, there were two million acres of original Redwood forests, today less than three percent of them remain. Some of these Redwood trees stand more than 300 feet high in the sky with diameters of 15 feet and above. The owner of the concession, Pacific Lumber is planning to log the area and a group of concerned local citizens and environmental groups seeking funds to buy the grove called Nanning Creek Grove. It is the largest unprotected stand of primeval red forest in the world.[112]

This is nothing new in the US. Many foundations and individuals in the US have furnished the money for NGOs to buy up forests before they are logged by the timber barons. At one time, the MacArthur Foundation gave more than $7.5 million to ten environmental groups to acquire and preserve tropical areas in Hawaii, Puerto Rico, the Virgin Islands, and the Florida Keys. (Null, 10)

A Costa Rican door manufacturer, Portico, S. A. went as far as buying the forestlands where their only source of mahogany, caobilla was I endangered by deforestation. To protect their interest, they hired the I same people they bought the land from as part-time guardians against illegal loggers.

There is a least expensive way of protecting the environment adopted in I Boliva. This is paying people to sustainably manage their natural resources called Payments for Environmental Services (PES). The j scheme is to pay or reimburse the environmental service providers for not using the land and the forest in ways that jeopardize the environmental service. One example is for a city council living downstream of a river that is a major source of drinking water to pay people living upstream not to cut down the trees near the river so that water quality is maintained or improved.[113]

* * * * *

In many cases, developing countries are practically selling off their patrimony for pittance. Despite the huge debts many of them are harboring, they continue to grant concessions to foreigners at very little I cost and even to avoid excise taxes on the logs they removed. Part of the problem lies with the tax loopholes in legislation. One example is the 1994 agreement in Suriname that granted 7.5 million acres at less than $35 an acre There are no provisions in the agreement requiring reforestation, environmental protection or monitoring by the government In Belize, a Malaysian logging firm paid about $1 per hectare for timber rights. Other taxes were not included in both agreements.[114]

In Cambodia, the government was losing so much revenue from its failure to collect taxes on timber that the IMF cancelled a $120 million loan. The World Bank also suspended the aid to government until the corruption in the forestry sector was resolved in Papua New Guinea. The government failed to enforce an excise tax that would raise the price of timber to $8 per nr when the logger exported the log to Japan at $160 per m³, In Nigeria, a Hong Kong logging firm reportedly paid $28 to the government for each mahogany tree while selling the wood at $800 per m³ or roughly $2,900 per tree.[115]

Private Forest

The private tree farming is a concept designed to stimulate landowner interest in making their private forest more productive through better management. It is based on the premise that farms and forests have certain elements in common and special care and attention should be taken that has been given to the farmlands. Special public recognition should be accorded for owners who practice good forestry.

It was first realized in 1941 when the Weyerhaeuser Company of Tacoma, Washington, designated 50,000 hectares as the Clemons Tree Farm. This marked the beginning of a system of organized free-farm programs though the US, sponsored by American Forest Products Industries, a nonprofit education organization. To become a tree farmer under the system, the owner must not only protect his woods from natural elements but he must improve his immature stands of timber by weeding, thinning, and harvesting his trees to assure a continuing crop. A prospective tree-farm is inspected by a forester before he is accorded membership and a familiar green and white sign is posted on his land.

Another special feature of the program is that tree-farm owners are provided free management services by wood companies and are given first option to purchase their products. This scheme need not be confined to individuals or family. The community as a whole can also benefit.

* * * * *

We have plenty of denuded land that can be awarded to prospective formers who are willing to spend time to nurture forest trees for their descendants Some enterprising landowners have taken the time to plant high value trees such as mahogany, narra, and lauan trees early in life in the hope that someday, they or their children can harvest Investment in tree farms need not be very expensive. Trees are sturdy and can survive without too much attention.

Most governments are reluctant to give property rights to communities that would enable them to plant timber trees for the future and conserve the present resources. The open-access resources presently in force in many countries have only encouraged the gathering and use of fuelwood more than needed for fear that others may remove what is left. By giving title to lands for development, the community will defend their land and keep out encroachers or poachers. This is easier to accomplish than assigning individual private titles.

Rural community treatment of forestlands is very different from that owned by private companies or the government. The community or villagers owning the forestlands usually manage them better when they have their future at stake. In Nepal, the hill people managed to conserve the trees and soil by deliberately restricting, felling and grazing in the forests, which belong to them. When the Nepalese government took over, the people felt no responsibility for the trees and wanton destruction began. After a few years, seeing the damage done, the government gave back die forests to the people and the cycle of regeneration started again.

Land title is a good incentive for people to work hard and protect the lands. One incentive given to farmers in China is the title to the land they reclaim from the desert. Experts from China used this scheme to preserve the gains they have made against the marauding dunes since 1978 Peasants in dune-covered Yulin Prefecture were given deeds to farmland they have reclaimed in exchange for a commitment to plant trees as a barricade against the intruding desert. Millions have joined this undertaking planting trees that extend from Manchuria westward along the frontiers of Inner Mongolia and Xinjiang. The successful program depended on the participation of farmers, the incentives given, and the knowledge that they have a stake far more than just their livelihood.

* * * * *

Giving land titles do not always work. It usually depends on the recipients and how they cherish the land. The governments of a number of countries have sold their forest resources to private citizens or companies This privatization could spell the wanton destruction of the forests in countries where political stability is poor or where greedy owners or companies opt to harvest the newfound resources as soon as possible. In the once communist states of the Baltic, many forestlands are being handed back to the previous owners or their families. This has led to a 727% increase in volumes of timber produced there between 1993 and 1994. (Dudley, 21)

When Romania distributed 400,000 hectares to a million peasant families, the forest was rapidly cut down even though the country is already suffering a decline in forest areas. In New Zealand, the government has decided to sell off a massive part of its forestlands. It attracted so many foreigners that it is doubtful if the trees can survive very long. (Ibid, 21-22)

Chainsaws

Chainsaw is the single most important power tool responsible for the deforestation. It takes only five minutes to cut down a 300-year-old tree using this tool. The chainsaw is 30 to 50 times faster than human hands using the ordinary manual saw. Using the old crude way of cutting would create jobs and reduce the felling of trees.

In some villages surrounding the forest areas of Nuimi Berending, Gambia, the local women groups branded the chainsaw logging as the "HIV/Aids of the forest." Everytime the sound of the chainsaw could be heard, the villagers around the community would go out in search of the forest intruders to stop the logging. It has led to the removal of members of the village development committee (VDC) and the forest committee that has allegedly approved a permit for the chainsaw operation. In one case, the chamsaw owner paid D500 to the VDC for a mahogany tree that could be sold for D 150,000 in the open market. The trunk measures about 12 meters long and has a diameter of two meters.

Rights of the Indigenous People

There are more than 300 million indigenous people scattered through the world. They are found mostly in the forests and the hinterlands, protecting the natural resources. With the escalating growth in world population, forests are becoming victims of human needs and greed. Right after the colonial period and the post-World War 11, many elites and dominant groups with money and resources started to look for fortunes found in areas occupied by the indigenous people. They came in droves with the help of the military to wrest control or steal the natural resources from the indigenous nations that ignited open conflict They are often assisted by the international financial institutions such as the World Bank that has financed many megaprojects that further denied the indigenous people of their livelihood and natural resources.

The rights of the indigenous people are often ignored by companies granted the privilege to harvest the forests for trees, that turn them into pastures for raising cattle, or mine the areas for oil or mineral This is the story of the Hoktek T'oi community of the indigenous Wichi people in the Province of Salta in the northern part of Argentina. Their suffering has been replicated in many other indigenous communities in other parts of the tropical countries.

For 12,000 years the Wichi people have been living in the same territory surviving on the forests through sustainable hunting, food gathering and cultivation and other sustainable practices. When the land was colonized by the whites, loggers started to exploit the land for their selfish ends. With the stroke of a pen, their ancestral forestlands of 75,000 hectares were reduced to 27 hectares. Since 1910, the land has changed ownership, but it was in 1966 that the deeds to land surrounding their community was registered in the name of an agricultural company called Los Cordobeses SA.[117]

I

At first the company tried to move them to another place, but they resisted. Then they "donated" 27 hectares of the indigenous territory as their legal ownership and started to fence the area. Seeking advice and support, the Wichi community turned to the Permanent Assembly for Human Rights (PAHR) to defend their rights and territory. The agricultural company did not delay in taking reprisals. With the cutting permit, the company started to devastate the native forest. The numerous attempts to stop the destruction were in vain. Complaints filed with the provincial authorities responsible for the defense of indigenous communities and those responsible for the environment were also ignored.[118]

While the judicial hearings were undergoing court proceedings the company was destroying the forests with heavy machinery and chamsaws and burning the tree trunks, branches and roots in preparation for the plantations. By the time the indigenous community was granted legal rights to 44 hectares of the green island among brown fields, the company continue to fight to claim the land. In 1999, the indigenous community submitted an expropriation bill to the Argentine Congress in an attempt to recover an area of 3,000 hectares of forest about 4% of its own territory. Even while the bill is pending, the 3,000 hectares are being deforested. Even while the Argentine government solemnly signed environmental or social agreement prepared at international levels, the Wichi have been obliged to follow intricate administrative and legal channels to defend the forest and their rights. The slow justice system made the government and its functionary just as guilty as the exploiting companies.[119]

* * * * *

Forests are often denuded and degraded before government acts to grant tenure to the indigenous people or the small farmers. This is the new trend affecting Asia as the rapid process of forest tenure reform and transfer of forest management to small farmers is taking place. In China, 30 million hectares of wasteland and degraded forests have been distributed to 57 million households to plant trees under community forestry programs. They have also been introduced into Nepal and the Philippines.[120]

There are hundreds if not thousands of indigenous tribes in the Philippines. Several laws have been passed by Congress, through the efforts of NGOs and indigenous people organizations, to grant them titles or domains to their ancestral lands. The first law is the Comprehensive Agrarian Reform Law of 1988 that suspended logging activities in the areas considered their ancestral land. However, this was followed by the National Integrated Protected Areas Act of 1992 that prohibited them from resettlement or relocation within protected area. But it was only in 1997 that the Indigenous Peoples Rights Act (RA 8371) recognized ownership held by indigenous people in the form of ancestral lands and domains. It even authorized the issuance of evidences of titles called Certificates of Ancestral Land Title or Certificates of Ancestral Domain Titles. A National Commission of Indigenous People (NCIP) with seven indigenous commissioners was created to oversee the program. The NCIP is attached to the Office of the President .[121]

Only about 2,000,000 hectares out of 30,000,000 hectares were being claimed by the indigenous people. Even this small area cannot be accommodated by the greedy businessmen who are assisted by corrupt government officials. Since it took effect, not much has come out of the law to protect their rights. Obstacles have been put forth by vested interest in the logging and mining industries to railroad the spirit of the law. With so much money waiting to be earned, it is easy to use some of the funds to silence or corrupt people who stand in the way of their interest. Murder is not beyond their means as some activists have been assassinated as a result.

* * * * *

Indigenous people are found almost in every country where forests exist in abundance In the Americas, they are the aboriginal Indians found in North and South America. We are often under the impression that North American Indians have most of their rights protected by law. This is far from the truth. The Indian tribes of British Columbia and Alberta where forests are being clear cut by two Japanese conglomerates are suffering because their livelihood are being destroyed.[122] What made matter worse is that their livelihood is one of traditional subsistence without other recourse that are available in a more civilized environment.

Many ecologists feel that the provincial governments have violated the rights of the native Indians when they sold out the forests to the Japanese companies by allowing clear cutting that destroyed their only livelihood and pollute the land with chemicals from the pulp and paper mills. Their plights have been ignored by the governments. Their only hopes lies with the NGOs with their voice that could be heard around the world. In the meantime, every minute of delay means more deforestation, more pollution and less chances of survival.

* * * * *

Success can sometimes be dangerous. This is what happened to the Higaonon indigenous tribes of northern Mindanao. Through the help of the Cultural Survival from the US, they were able to set their own agroforestry project called Tribal Agro-Forestry Technology (TAFT) project. TAFT built a biodiversified buffer zone on logged areas around existing forest, expanding and protecting it, and maintaining ecological balance without compromising the Higaonon ancestral customary laws, The success of the project led to the expansion of other sites and attracted other neighboring tribes.[123]

This did not escape the watchful eyes of the illegal loggers and their cahoots. With the help of the locally stationed military, the paramilitary and the police, the members of the communities were harassed to stop them from continuing with their projects. One foreman was shot while others were forced out of their reforestation sites. This is despite the Memorandum of Understanding signed between the tribe and the Department of Defense to work together to promote environmental protection. The head of the project was threatened and went into hiding.[124]

* * * * *

Some indigenous people have become so desperate for the raping of their forests that they have taken the protection of the trees into their own hands and bodies. The have used roadblocks to stop delivery of truckloads of timber. Others have taken to the trees before they are cut. They would hug and even chain themselves to the trees.

It was related that this hugging movement started in India in 1733 when a girl embraced a tree to protect it from being axed by men of the maharajah. This was followed by other village tree-huggers that in die end resulted in die death of the girl and 363 other villagers. Finally the maharajah relented and allowed them to maintain their own forest resources. In 1973 this hugging movement was resurrected and called Chipko (meaning "hug") Movement when loggers attempted to open up their forests for exploitation. The villagers, mostly women threw themselves on the trees in the face of the chainsaws. This movement has spread to other ecological sites in the Himalaya where death and destruction often follow disaster. (Day, 256-257)

The originators of the Chipko Movement were Chandi Prasad and other Gandhian workers who started off by fighting job discrimination in Uttarakhand near the Chinese-Indian border. After the 1962 border war between China and India, the Indian government decided to develop the land surrounding the borders. Roads were constructed and trees were felled to develop the land. Forests are granted to outside companies who cut indiscriminately. Locals were discriminated from harvesting.

Firewood gathering became difficult. After years of plundering the forests, disasters such as flooding and landslides began to occur frequently. The local people were not blameless as they have also plundered the land for their own survival Since the government policies restricted their use of the forest products they decided that commercial logging has to stop to end their suffering.[125]

At first they' demanded from the government the abolition of the contractor system and instead to award contracts to the local cooperatives and generates jobs for the locals instead of awarding to outsiders who indiscriminately cleared the forests. All their moves went unheeded. When representatives of the Simon Company came to the forest with their permit to cut, they were met by local workers who marched in procession toward the Mandat forest where the marked trees were ready for cutting. Accompanied by the beat of drums, they sang traditional songs voicing their concern for their natural home. When the Simon Company with their lumbermen reached the forest, they were met with a crowd of 100 people and they abandoned their plans and withdrew without the trees.[126]

As a result of this victory, the Chipko Movement soon spread to other communities. Whenever the Forest Department sets up auction for tree felling, they were met by tree huggers out to disrupt the proceeding with rallies, demonstrations and posters. Even when the auctions were awarded, the loggers were never allowed to cut the trees because the local people were waiting to hug the trees to prevent them from being felled. Pleading with the government officials are ignored.[127]

* * * * *

In the village of Reni, the axemen tried to gain entry into the forest by avoiding the village during the bus trip. They were seen by a little girl who spotted them going to the forest. She ran and told Gaura Devi, an elderly leader of the village who rushed around the village calling the other women from their cooking chore. Within minutes about 30 women and children were mustered and they hurried toward the forest. They soon caught up with the men who were setting up camps and preparing lunch. The women pleaded with them not to cut down the forest and explained what it would mean to the village if they did. They asked the men to return to the village after finishing their meal and wait to talk to the village men. Some of the men seemed ready to respond to the women's pleas, but others had been drinking. One of the drunks came staggering toward the women with a gun. Gaura Devi stood in front of him, bared her breast, and said, "This forest is like our mother. You will have to shoot me before you can cut it down." At this, the sober men decided they had best leave.

Over the next month, rallies were held at the site and a constant watch was kept over the forest. Meanwhile, the mountain women's story caught the attention of the Indian public and created an outcry for the protection of the Reni forest. The government responded to all this with official protests to the Chipko workers and public denunciations of the movement.

But finally Chandi Prasad was called to the state capital to meet with the chief minister. The chief minister agreed to set up a committee of experts to investigate the situation. WTien this was announced, the contractor withdrew his men from Reni to wait for the committee's decision. The committee took over two years to finish its report and its findings were even better than the Chipko workers had at first hoped they might be. The committee said that Reni forest was a "sensitive area," and that no trees should be cut - not only in the Reni forest but also in a larger section of the Alakhnanda watershed that included Reni On the basis of the report, the government put a ten-year ban on all tree-felling in an area of over 450 km². [128]

Since 1975, the Chipko workers have been protecting forest slopes and also restoring bare ones as well. By 1981, over a million trees had been planted through their efforts. Besides the local and immediate benefits, this reforestation has been helping to determine the trees to be planted and what planting techniques to be employed that might work best in the region as a whole.

Plights of the Forest Workers

While the loggers are devastating the forests and enriching themselves in the process, the lowly workers are doing the work but not getting their fair share of the profit. Not only that, their working conditions, housing accommodation do not fare any better. Wages are depressed to the barest minimum. Sometimes the wages are not paid until the timber is sold out and paid for. The waiting period could take months.

Because of the seasonal nature of the work, depending on the seasons of the year, workers are often required to work long hours during the dry season to take advantage of the good weather Often times the workers willingly take the long hours, as much as 16 hours to help defray the expenses during the rainy season.

There is no security of tenure to speak of. The rapid destruction of the forest actually shortened the period when workers will be employed Most of the workers are only casual and there is no real benefit they can expect at the end of their employment. The usual workers who get better pay are the operators of heavy' equipment and truckers. Even then, some of them are hired on a piecemeal work basis.

The work can be dangerous. In a survey in East Malaysia in 1983, it was found that the timber industry has the highest incidents of accidents and death. In 1983 Sabah recorded 153 fatalities and Sarawak 81. By 1984 the industry in Sarawak claimed seven lives for every one million m^1 produced whereas Canada has one death for every three million m^3 produced. Non-fatal accidents involved 1,553 victims in Sarawak in | 1984. (Hurst, 91)

Another survey found that logging in Sarawak has the highest fatal and nonfatal industrial accidents. It accounts for more than 60% and 45% I respectively. Between 1980 and 1984, the logging industry in Sarawak had one fatality for every 136,000 m^3 of logs produced and one nonfatal accident for every 7,000 m^3. In comparison, in 1979, the province of I British Columbia, Canada, had one fatality for every 3 million m^3 and one nonfatal injury for every 31,000 m^3 of logs produced. In the hospital, logging fractures and amputations took up 20% to 30% of the male wards. This high accident rate is attributed to crude logging techniques, lack of education and supervision, together with inadequate or nonexistent safety equipment and a payment system based on log volume produced. Compensation for injury such as permanent disability like leg amputation is compensated with one year's salary and for death, over a year's pay in compensation for the surviving family. [179]

The workers plight is compounded by the minimal compensation the victim or the family receives in case of injury or death. After the tragedy, the unfortunate event is soon forgotten because the lives of the workers are considered cheap, abundant and dispensable. I have heard of workers given only the daily food requirement to keep them working despite the fact that the loggers are making huge amount.

* * * * *

In some earlier cases, not only are the indigenous nations' natural resources stolen right before their eyes, they are forced like slaves to help in exploiting them. This is what happened after the Dutch landed over the West Papua to Indonesia. Not only did the country became a transmigration colony, its natural resources were want only raped without much compensation.[130]

The Anti-Slavery Society branded the Indonesian forests operations in West Papua as exploitation when the people were paid little or no compensation for their efforts. No compensation was paid for the forests as it is considered a "national" asset under the basic law passed in May 1967. Despite that, what ensued was pure exploitation of the workers.

An Indonesian concessionaire PT Kebun Sari commissioned a South Korean firm to harvest the timber. The company paid the workers the equivalent of $ 0.50 per hectare to harvest the log on a 400,000 hectares concession. In turn, the company made $45 a hectare By the time the company exported 24,000 m³ of unprocessed logs, the land had been devastated, its water supply to the villages was polluted and the coastal fishing was damaged.[131]

In another instance, Jakarta-based timber companies used local military, police and civilian officials to force Asmar villagers to go into their own forest, cut down ironwood and mahogany trees, and float them downriver to waiting ships. Although the rate had been fixed at Rp 3,500 per m\ they are often paid on a per trunk basis and have to wait for months before being paid. Even the tools used to get the timber were paid by the workers and deducted from their salaries. All the local officials, who are supposed to protect the interest of the indigenous people, were paid off by the companies. The workers who refused or who protested faced charges of subversion for undermining government development plans.[132]

Mangrove Harvesting

Halophytes are plants that can tolerate salt water In many lowland areas where irrigation water are pumped from deep wells, salt water had penetrated the aquifer spreading salt to land served by this water. This made it difficult for ordinary plants to grow on these lands. However, researchers have found hundreds of plants that can grow on salt water.

One of these is the well-known mangrove trees. There are 33 true mangrove species in the Philippines. They are found along warm waters of coastal areas, salt marshes, and estuaries. Because its wood is hard and heavy, it is used primarily for post, pilings, railroad ties and charcoal. Its bark contains 22% to 33% tannin and is used for tanning leather. The root of the mangrove extends out from the main trunk forming dense thickets that become new plants. The dense tickets provide an irreplaceable habitat for fishes and other sea creatures. They also break up tidal waves and stabilize land around the sea. Like the forests high in the mountains, they are also destined for destruction.

The Philippines was once heavily forested with mangrove trees throughout its coastal regions. From a high of 500,000 hectares early in this century, it has since been cut down to about 38.000 hectares (19%) and continued to be depleted at the rate of 2,000 hectares annually as its habitats are converted to other uses such as aquaculture, beach resorts and development sites.

Mangrove forests, like coral reefs are natural spawning ground for fisheries. In one study, scientists discovered that the destruction of mangrove and coral reefs are costing the nation an additional 960.000 (?) tons of fish yield every year, enough to provide the protein need of the rural people. The output of each hectare of mangrove forest is about SI 1,300 a year.

There is one similarity between natural forests being converted to plantations and mangrove swamps being converted to fish ponds. The natural forests are cut down and planted with a single or two species of tree plants while the mangrove swamps are converted to raise a few species of commercial sea creatures. The diversity of both areas is destroyed.

In 1990 UNESCO declared the entire Palawan area, the only province where its forest cover has been well protected by malaria infestation as a Biosphere Reserve. This protection extends to mangrove forests as the mangrove threats come from the conversion of mangrove swamps into fish ponds, the Rio Tuba nickel mining, and the debarking of mangrove for tannin and "tuba" (liquor) productions. As a result, fishermen are experiencing the decline of several marine resources such as mudcrabs and bivalves.[133]

* * * * *

Mangrove forests have never been widespread. It is now down to about 15 million hectares worldwide from a high of 18.8 million hectares in 1980, according to one study.[134] When the loggers run out of forest timber to harvest, to keep their business going, they resorted to cutting down the mangrove. This is what happened in West Malaysia whose 110,000 hectares of mangroves in the 1970s is being decimated by about 1,000 hectares each year for timber and industrial expansion. As a result, the prawn and cockles industry were greatly affected by the exploitation, flurst, 57)

Mangrove forests are also prime targets for development. They are disappearing at rates exceeding those of tropical rainforests due to farming, harvesting for timber and charcoal real estate development for housing, ecotourism and aquaculture.

* * * * *

Mangroves are natural habitats and one of the most productive wetlands on earth for a diverse marine and terrestrial flora and fauna but many have resorted to exclusively use them for prawn farming. The Environmental Justice Foundation estimates that as much as 38% of global mangrove deforestation is linked to shnmp farm development. Mangrove deforestation is contributing to fisheries declines, degradation of clean water supplies, salinization of coastal soils, erosion due to wind and waves, land subsidence as well as releasing the carbon dioxide to the atmosphere In the Philippines mangroves are cut down for the development of the prawn industry Prawns can bring in an income of $90,000 for a 50 hectare network of ponds with an investment of about $5,000.[136]

New technology from Taiwan on shrimp fanning and the attractivo export prices convinced the farmers to shift from milkfish to shrimp growing. Increase in foreign support for aquaculture development also provided further support to colonize the mangrove forests Because mangroves and other wetlands are considered wasteland, no efforts were taken to protect them. As a result, they were damaged while the shrimp industry collapsed after a widespread outbreak of luminous bactena decimated many swamps of prawns.[137]

Mangrove forests are important as evidenced during the tsunami disaster of December 2004. The forests shielded several Indonesian islands and Malaysia's northwest coastline from the worst effects of the tsunami prompting Prime Minister Abullah Ahmad Badawi to call for their preservation. Its complicated root systems helped to bind the shore together and served as shield against destructive waves.[138]

* * * * *

Other causes of deforestation include coastal development, timber harvesting and flooding. Development of hotels, resorts, and water fronts properties results in the clearing of mangrove forests during construction Many mangrove species are also sought after as exotic woods for furniture and other uses. The construction of dikes, ditches, canals, and causeways also result in flooding that prevents mangrove roots from obtaining oxygen. Pollution from industrial discharges inland and oil spiHs can be deadly to the mangroves. Oil can foul the specialized parts of the tree preventing its growth. [39]

Government Subsidy

Taxation is one way of curtailing deforestation. Buyers refrain from buying expensive wood products while they look to other sources of supply. The Philippine forest charge of $P30/m^3$ in the past for decades was a big bonanza for the loggers. The low tax base served as a government subsidy and was an invitation for forest destruction. With only a small capital, anybody can go into this wasteful enterprise of timber harvesting. At the time when our forest was still covered with trees, sustainable harvesting was never put into practice as loggers tried to extract as much timber as possible. Even when the forest tax was increased tremendously, few loggers really take the duty to harvest sustainably.

The timber trade is seen by many developing countries as their avenue to develop the country. Instead, many not only lose this most important natural resource, the country is often left mired in debt and poverty persists while only a few private individuals reaped the benefits. When it comes to protecting the forests, the governments have always been remiss in their role by subsidizing loggers through tax credits, minimum royalty and rent or tax holidays. Even in the US, taxpayers' money was used to build roads into the cutting areas. The tax holidays in Indonesia were responsible for the rapid exploitation of forest products. Before the incentives, the average log harvest was only 2.5 million m³ a year. With the tax incentives, the volume increased to 10 million m³ in the 1970s and 25 million m³ in 1979. The incentives were given to increase timber harvesting for foreign exchange at the expense of the environment.

Japan's Role in Deforestation

Japan plays a major role in the destruction of tropical as well as temperate forests because of its insatiable lifestyle. Throughout its economic growth, even during recession, it is the largest consumer of timber in the international market. Their conglomerate companies own extensive area of forests in almost all tropical countries in Asia and South America as well as in Alaska, Washington, Oregon and in Canada. They have not shown any high regard for the natural resources outside their own country. What made it incriminating is its wasteful use of a natural resource of other countries that is fueling death and destruction. It is a throw-away society, using very large amounts of paper and plywood in an irresponsible manner. It is the Japanese NGOs, not its government, that have carried the bulk of burden of educating consumers about environmental impact of these unsustainable practices.[140]

They are also the world's principal consumer of hardwoods, at one time accounting for nearly half of all the tropical timber imported by the industrialized world. They are also stockpiling logs from the US Pacific Northwest which they are buying at low prices. The logs are sunk into their lakes and coastline for future use, while leaving their own forest, currently covering about two-thirds of their land untouched. There has been minimal logging in Japan because of strict government regulations even while the forests of the world are dwindling, the assault continued unabated The total forest resource stock of Japan as of 1999 was estimated at 3.8 billion m³ and growing at the rate of 80 million m³ annually. On the other hand its wood demand for the same period was 97.8 million m³ which could satisfy a large portion of its domestic need However, it refuses to utilize its own resources preferring to buy the cheaper logs from abroad without regards as to whether they are harvested in a sustainable way or exported legally.[141]

The government of Japan actually does not care what happens to the forests of the world by not living up to its promises to stop the destruction, clean up the timber trade and fund the protection of ancient forests. It could crack down on the illegal trade of timber products. Greenpeace estimates that around 40% or more of the total plywood supply in Japan is of illegal origin.[142] The timber trade could even be more.

Mitsubishi Corporation, the giant Japanese conglomerate at one time offered to pay off Brazil's entire debt in exchange for exclusive right to the natural resources of the Amazon basin. It is one way of harvesting the timber at bargain price. It is time they reduce their appetite for hardwoods to save the forests instead of using their wealth in destroying the world's greatest ecosystem.

Most of their imports are raw logs. In 1989, Japan imported more than 12 million m of tropical logs. The processing was mostly done in Japan, creating profits and jobs for the importer. Japanese companies control the whole trade chain and have deprived the governments of exporting countries much needed tax revenues by deliberately allowing their invested companies in the tropical countries run at a loss. They also defrauded on timber royalties because sale prices are quoted below the true market value.

* * * * *

The Japanese conglomerates called keiretus are like economic battalions that invade countries in blitzkrieg style, leaving behind barren and desolate landscape No replanting is ever done. The Japan New Guinea Timber (JANTX owned by Honshu Paper Company of Japan started operation in Madang, PNG in 1971 clearing forest for hardwood chips for the manufacture of paper, board and reconstituted wood for the Japanese market. It destroyed more than 50,000 hectares of lowland rainforest without benefiting the owner of the forest or the government. In ten years of operation, they never declared a profit and have nothing to show but barren forest mountains.

As part of the contract, Honshu refused to accept any responsibility for replanting even though it was against the government policy by not doing any reforestation. After the contract was signed did Honshu announce that they intended to clearcut the forest. By 1984, they were destroying 3-4 hectares of forest annually and shipping 20,000 tons of woodchips every month (Hurst, 150-151)

* * * * *

In the three PNG provinces of East New Britain, West New Britain and Madang, Japanese NGOs have created awareness in Japan about environmental and cultural destruction there. They have convinced some local government authorities not to use timber from the tropics but the Japanese central government threatened municipalities who declare bans on tropical log products. The main threat used is that such bans conflict with WTO obligations and are illegal. The Japanese keiretsu had a stranglehold on Japanese economics and politics and they dominate the log imports. It is difficult if not impossible for non-Japanese organizations to affect public opinion in Japan.[143]

The blitzkrieg started first in Asia as early as the 1960s. By 1980, it imported from the Philippines 1.1 million m³, increasing to 1.4 and 1.3 million m³ the next two years, respectively. From there on, the log imports diminished rapidly until by 1989, only 10,000 m³ was imported On the other hand, the import from Sabah with its thick forests started off with 6.3 million nr and peaked at 7 million m³ in 1986 and gradually slow down until almost all the old growth were logged over by 1990s. To compensate the loss in Sabah, Sarawak was invaded with 2.3 million m³ in 1980 and gradually increased that by 1989. it reached 5.6 million m³ and still going strong in the 21* century.[144] In Indonesia, the Japanese started off with nine companies engaged in logging operation. Ten years later there were more than 200 companies. The fall in export is due to the ban on export of logs, but the deforestation continued. (Hurst 16)

Indonesia became the main supplier of tropical logs for Japan in 1971 and peaked in 1974 with a volume of ll.S million m^3 It was made possible by one of the most destructive extraction practices carried out anyw here in the world. Two of the most important trees needed by the orangutans are the teak and the strangling fig. They serve as protection for the orangutans where they access various fruits found in the canopy. These were not spared from the chainsaws as the Japanese, through their suppliers, systematically destroyed the forests.[145]

* * * * *

The destructive way Japanese corporations have been destroying the environment of the world can be gathered from the way Mitsubishi Corporation behaves in its quest for more profit at the expense of the environment of other countries. It is operating in all the countries around the world and in many cases in many destructive ways. This is why the Rainforest Action Network (RAN) is calling an international boycott of the company as the world's worst corporate destroyer of rainforests.[146]

Mitsubishi Corporation (MC) has forest interests around the world where it has been operating for forty years in many cases. It either fully of partially owned with local firms where it operates and has consistently been the number one importer of logs. It is known for its illegal, unethical and unsustainable logging. Despite it bad reputation, it has consistently claimed to be operating under sustainable ways when in fact, all tropical countries have been known to be 95% unsustainable, according to the International Tropical Timber Organization (ITTO).[147]

In the American West, the Environmental Protection Agency (EPA) has branded MC one of the top ten polluters. In Washington and Oregon, it is the top purchaser of whole logs coming from the old-growth forests. In British Columbia, Canada, it is dear cutting the forests to produce pulp for export and is considered by The Vancouver Sun as the worst polluter in the province. Another company engaged in disposable chopstick making is so wasteful that 85% of its timber is discarded because it does not meet its standard. In Alberta, it operates the world's largest bleached pulp mills on a 24-hour basis.[148]

The records of its exploitation in South America are even worst. Not only is the environment worse off, even the indigenous tribes are greatly affected It is the largest exporter of woodchips from Chile's old growth forests. The company owns mahogany logging in Bolivia and Brazil. It has operations in Peru and Colombia. It is also engaged in gold mining and tar sands in Venezuela and prospecting for new mines in Ecuador's Andean rainforest. MC even offered to pay off Brazil's $115 billion debts for exclusive right to gold mining. The list goes on and on.[149]

The destruction of the tropical forests of Southeast Asian countries is reported elsewhere in the book. Suffice it to say that before this new boycott by RAN is called, another NGO, the World Rainforest Movement has also singled out MC for boycott in 1989. Other Japanese corporations such as Marubeni Corporation, C. Itoh & Co., and Nisshop Iwai are being closely monitored.[150]

Six years after the boycott, MC agreed to meet with the environmentalists about protecting and preserving the world's forests, But nothing concrete has been done about its behavior. When two of its subsidiaries, Mitsubishi Motor Sales of America and Mitsubishi Electric, the initial targets of the RAN boycott, were forced to the table and came out with a program to address the environmental issues, the mother company refused to make any assurances to the agreement.[151]

Chapter 4

ILLEGAL LOGGING

As more governments are learning to their dismay that they do not have the luxury of infinite forest resources to sustain the country, many have opted to protect whatever remains by canceling logging permits even those owned by favored friends. This has resulted in rampant illegal logging throughout the tropical world. The timber robbers are only following in the wake of the original licensed loggers who have benifitted immensely. The readily available road networks made their illegal operation easier. Neither are they interested in protecting the patrimony of the nation. They are like the greedy businessmen out to take whatever they can before someone else does. Being illegal, they do not care for whatever ecological damages that may arise.

Illegal logging is a crime against the environment and humanity. The effects of deforestation can transcend boundaries and are known to have caused death and destruction in many parts of the world. But the punishment for wanton destruction that has gone unabated due to greed, survival, livelihood, and lax enforcement of forestry laws has never been meted out. Threat of cancellation of concession has not worked before and will not work today. The need for stiffer penalties like life imprisonment and even death penalty for violators is needed to stem the tide for this kind of criminal act. We need dedicated people whose jobs solely to protect the forests and prosecute the violators.

Many loggers are "cut-and-get-out" lumbermen who do not really care for the welfare of the country and the communities where they operate. They are like "timber robbers" out to take away whatever they can in the least possible time. This attitude cannot be tolerated by the government and the communities in which they operate. Members of the community and the government should safeguard their own surrounding and see that logging and reforestation are done with utmost care. After all they are the most directly affected by the deterioration caused by environmental degradation Another reason is that the government does not have the manpower to check on the rampant violations going on.

Prevalence

There are more reasons why people are getting into illegal logging than getting legitimate licenses to operate. For one thing, a person needs good connections with high government officials and huge amount of money to get a concession. There is no guarantee that after investing a fortune unforeseen events can happen that their license can be revoked. A complaint from one high-ranking officials of the any administration would be enough to get a temporary suspension of the license. Licenses have been revoked only to be released again after interference of high ranking officials or payment of bribes.

Illegal forest practices come in many forms and often difficult to apprehend. Some of these include approval of illegal contracts with private enterprises by public servants; harvesting protected trees by legal loggers, smuggling of forest products such as logs or lumber elsewhere around the country or abroad; logging outside the allocated concessions, etc. All these acts are abetted by the high timber values, low salaries of government workers, broad discretionary powers of local forestry officers, deliberate misguided information, poor regulations, poor dispensation of justice, improbability of punishment, bribery and a host of illegal acts that is often ignored by authorities. I would not be surprised if those who are checking on corruption are the same people who are involved and managed to be bribed after the fact.

With so many corrupt officials running the government, bribes are becoming cheaper. The likelihood of being prosecuted and charged in court is small. It is even more difficult to get convictions in court the way our system of justice is being handled by so many corrupt judge Political patronage system is also rampant that it takes only a "contact" to get things done or quashed. This is the reason why illegal logging activities are so rampant.

Loss of license fees and taxes from timber cutting can be enormous. In Malaysia, 55% to 75% of all industrial wood production is thought to be illegal resulting in a loss of anywhere between $1 billion to $1.8 billion in export tax revenue.[152]

The income earned from illegal logging is much greater than any legitimate undertaking. No taxes are paid. Workers do not receive any benefit, even though they work under poor working conditions. Even in the presence of a total log ban, illegal logging is seldom affected. They have been operating so much under a cloud of notoriety that nothing can stop them except a bald mountain.

Illegal loggers, by virtue of their nefarious activities do not and are not compelled to do any reforestation work. They have no compunction about their illegal activities and its effects on the environment. There is a need to get the local rural communities involved to safeguard the forest, After all, they have more to lose when damages to the ecology will affect their future. There is also a need to share the bounty of the forest and its products with them allowing them to serve as guardians. Care must be taken that they are not corrupted by the system.

* * * * *

Philippine bureaucracy is prone to neglect, patronage and corruption. In 1973, President Ferdinand Marcos issued a decree gradually phasing out the export of logs by 1976. Many firms have no choice but to set up sawmills to process the timber in the event that they cannot export. In 1984, the Bureau of Forest Development officially recorded issuing 189 licenses to major sawmills in the country. The next year, a survey found that 175 of them were processing illegally felled timber Instead of prosecuting all of them in court and canceling their licenses only four sawmills were suspended or revoked of their licenses. After the first EDSA revolution, 150 out of 157 sawmills were cancelled within three months. Instead of selling the logs to the sawmills, the illegal loggers resorted to exporting them illegally. They made use of heavily armed goons to get the timber delivered to their waiting customers. The honest forestry officials were powerless in controlling the flow of timber through the isolated road block. (Hurst, 189) I would not be surprised if they joined them instead of trying to lick them.

There are presently a few licensed big-time loggers after the ban in the 1980s and 1990s when flooding occurred and our primary or old-growth forests have been denuded to less than 3%. Still our forests are being destroyed at an alarming rate of 480 hectares everyday. Most of the illegal cuttings are done on secondary forests left behind by the big-time loggers. Other causes include forest fires from forest clearing and deforestation caused by mining operations.[153]

The illegally cut logs are smuggled aboard Korean and Japanese ships waiting in the high seas. It was estimated to cost the Philippines $700 million annually. Even this amount is very conservative if we consider that smuggled logs often sell at 30% to 40% below market value. This will explain why importers are willing to take the risks of ferrying the smuggled logs outside our ports.

* * * * *

I believe illegal logging would not flourish without the connivance of public officials on the take. There is no way illegal loggers could operate without their knowledge. There are too many sycophants who are only too willing to gain favors from the powerful politicians or public officials and would rat on any wrong-doing. It is also possible that some politicians or public officials are too busy with their own private affair to look into the illegal logging activities going on right before their eyes.

In the Philippines, Congress holds a large part of the purse of other government agencies and local governments. It holds the key to control illegal logging by getting the personnel of the forestry department to be vigilant against illegal logging. If these personnel cannot do their job well, there is no reason for them to receive any salary. In fact, the NGOs are doing a better job than they do in calling the attention of the public. When Congress threatened to withhold the budget for Southern Philippine Council for Peace and Development, the then Governor Nur Misuari of the Autonomous Region in Muslim Mindanao (ARMM) went into action by ordering a total war against illegal logging.

The same act of Congress or whoever controls the purse can threaten to withhold the budgetary allocations of the local government to stop the rampant illegal logging in their locality. I see no reason why this cannot happen unless they are the patrons of the illegal loggers or are on the take.

* * * * *

One of the hardest functions of guarding the country's natural forests is the involvement of politicians, especially those local warlords. Forest guards often turn a blind eye to their illegal activities for fear of their lives. Even media exposures are often whitewashed by succeeding investigations as witnesses are not available to testify for the same reason. They could also be bribed to stay out of any investigation. It is common knowledge that many politicians, especially those in the provinces are like warlords with their band of gun-totting bodyguards protecting their boss from harm and accusations, whether true or not.

As is often the case, corrupt forestry officials are often involved with politicians or illegal timber barons. One of the celebrated cases of crackdown on a gang of illegal loggers happened in Brazil in 2005. Federal agents dismantled a corruption ring involving the federal environment protection agency, Ibama, and arrested 48 of them including a ranking official for allowing illegal logging on some 43,000 hectares of Amazon rainforests over the past two years. Most of the affected rainforests are either Indian reservations or national parks. As many as 1.9 million m³ were illegal cut and sold within the country or exported.[155]

The ranking official arTested was Hugo Jose Scheuer Werle, Ibama's top official at Mato Grosso state that experienced the highest rainforest loss during the 2003-2004 season. He allegedly accepted money ($177,000) from loggers in exchange for documents declaring the wood was legally removed from the rainforest during his two-year stint as head of the agency in Mato Grosso state.[156]

Under the law, Amazon landowners are required to retain 80% of the rainforest on their plot Environmentalists are blaming the state Governor Blairo Maggi, the world's largest soybean producer for the state of the environment. Thirty-two businessmen were also arrested who are connected with the logging companies.[157]

Impact of Illegal Logging

Illegal logging continues to thrive because there is also an illegal international trade of illegal cut logs. This is a major problem faced by many timber-producing countries around the world. According to the WWF Global 2000, 65% of the forested ecological regions are threatened by illegal logging. In some countries in Southeast Asia, Africa and Latin America up to 80% of all the trees are cut illegally. Half of the world's original forest covers have been logged over in the last 50 years.[158] Operators of illegal logging do not care for the environment nor do they pay the proper taxes, royalties and leased payments to the government. According to Worid Bank, $15 billion are lost annually to illegal logging that would otherwise be used to uplift the forest dwelleuj used for reforestation, and other social services in other affected forcstj of the country.

Lives have been lost as a result of rampant logging, legal or illegal. On November 29, 2004, in the provinces of Quezon and Aurora in the Philippines, typhoon-induced flashfloods and landslides killed more than a thousand people and destroyed properties that rendered thousands homeless.[159] Thousands of illegally logged trees left in the fields came tumbling down the mountains along with the landslides.

One year after the tragedy, a number of the logging bans were lifted. The much needed rehabilitation was never carried out but instead illegal loggings continue unabated. The survivors of the tragedy and volunteers plan to form human chains and rally along the office of the Department of Environment and Natural Resources (DENR) on the first anniversary of the tragedy to demand the immediate cancellation of all logging concessions and agreements nationwide.[160]

We cannot seem to learn our lesson or is our population too dense that! people have no safe place to live? Exactly a year earlier (December 2003), in the southern part of I^yte Province, more than 200 villagers lost their lives to mudslides caused by torrential rains and illegal logging Most of the areas affected were near hills and mountainsides.

* * * * *

Importers of tropical timber are also partly blamed for not ensuring that the logs came from sustainable and legally sanctioned forests. Many of them are only interested to get their hands on as much timber for their own consumption without regard to the environmental welfare of the source countries. The wanton destruction of the tropical forests have been called to attention by the NGOs that producing and consuming countries have taken steps to minimize illegal logging through some means such as the tracking of timber trade using certification.

Illegal logging comes in many forms Cutting without a permit is the most common form of illegal logging. Another way of cheating is conniving with slash-and-bum cultivators to cut down the trees in

Forbidden areas and sell them the logs. All it takes is one chainsaw that could cut down tens of trees in a day.

In areas where local permits are required, a new approach is resorted to by loggers. The village leaders are taken to the capital city or abroad for special treatments. They are given special accommodation in luxury hotel, good food and drinks, and even set up with prostitutes until they approve the permit. The rest of the village inhabitants are also bribed to keep the peace. Promises of replanting and other even school houses and hospitals are ignored or delayed as much as possible. (Diamond, 471)

In cases where the permits are granted by the central office, resistance from the local inhabitants such as blocking the logging trucks or threats of burning down sawmills are met with police or military actions. Threats of physical harm have also been resorted to. Some of these publicized untoward events have happened in Indonesian Borneo, Solomon Islands and elsewhere. (Ibid)

* * * * *

In many places where logging had ceased, "carabao logging" is resorted to by enterprising upland dwellers or financed by illegal poachers, Carabao (buffalo) logging operates with impunity in banned areas because these poor loggers are not afraid of being jailed and are helped by the financiers should they be apprehended. There are those who operate independently. They have nothing to lose and the return is much more than they can get from practicing agriculture. It beats the work of shifting cultivators who work for months when they can earn the same amount in a matter of days.

Carabao loggers are usually supplied with chain saws by buyers or sawmill companies to make flitches out of trees. In the 1990s, in the mountains of Quezon Province, there were 3,000 of them. The flitches are usually cut one-inch thicker on all sides and only selected portion are cut and the rest are left to rot. The one-inch allowance is used to offset the crude trimming of the logs as demanded by buyers. Ihis is an txtremely wasteful practice of harvesting timber. As much as 60% of the tree is lost. The flitches are usually sold to sawmills at very low prices Enforcement of anti-fencing law should put a dent on the practice provided honest-to-goodness enforcement of the law is earned out. After all, illegal loggers do not pay taxes to the proper authorities.

In logged over forest, most of the trees felled are less than 30 cm. in diameters, fhe trees are supposed to be left for regeneration for future harvesting. Being illegal, it is difficult to track down poachers in dire need of money. In some cases, instead of flitches, the entire log is dragged to unlicensed sawmills for processing.

* * * * *

Indonesia is the largest exporter of tropical timber in the world and accounts for one tenth of its export earnings. It was able to earn this reputation because of illegal logging. The forest industry is in disarray where logging concessions are concentrated in the hands of a few corporations and individuals. Corruption is widespread and rampant and forestry laws are hardly enforced. Most of the recommendations for the protection of the forests for the past three decades have been disregarded. Priority against illegal logging, restructuring of the timber industry and reform of the forest management system to align with decentralization have made little progress.[162]

At present, the rate of deforestation is about 1.8 million hectares annually. At this rate, the remaining forests could be completely wiped out within 15 years, according to the International Tropical Timber Organization (ITTO). Sumatra, one of the largest concentrations of forests has already lost 60% of its most valuable forest cover, most of it due to illegal logging.[163] The figure is disputed by the Indonesian Ministry of Forestry that reported 43 million hectares of the country's forests have been damaged or destroyed over the last several decades due to illegal logging with an average annual deforestation rate estimated at more than 2.8 million hectares since 1998.[164]

The Indonesian government seems powerless and clueless as to how to deal with the problem. The massive clear cutting and turning the timber into plywood and planks are destined for the US and European markets, according to a BusinessWeek editorial. The largest and most powerful timber trade association in the US, the American Forest & Paper Association 2004 report estimates that 55% of plywood exported from

Indonesia are illegal. The Global Forest Watch 2002 estimates placed illegal logging as the source of 50-70% of the country's wood supply.

* * * * *

Even supposedly protected parks and reserves are not spared. Tanjung Puting National Park is a 415,040 hectare park located in Central Kalimantan. It is one of Southeast Asia's largest protected areas of peat-swamp forest and home to a diverse array of plant and animal species including the orangutan. Around 2,000 endangered animals live within its confines which represent about 13% of die planet's wild population.

National parks are supposed to be protected against logging, but this would not deter illegal loggers from cutting the trees. While authorities have arrested some illegal loggers, no actions have been taken against the powerful timber barons and owners of illicit sawmills. The presence of timber robbers has been a direct result of the political and economic crises confronting the country. Factory closures have forced men to intrude into the forests in search for livelihood and survival. When former President Suharto's cronies with their concessions were revoked, a new generation of timber robbers has moved in to fill the gap. Most of them have even less scruples than their predecessors in protecting the forests. Being illegal, they need to rob as much in as little time as possible.[165]

Illegal logging is also going on in many protected parks in Indonesia. In Aceh's Gunung Leuser National Park, another orangutan refuge, illegal loggers have taken over even after loggings have been banned. The deforestation is getting worst as it involved high-level bureaucrats, security personnel and businessmen who made it difficult to stamp it out.[166]

Before it was proclaimed a park, it was originally planned to be logged over and turned into a padi field. The scheme failed because the regional soil was too acidic for agriculture. The plan was canceled by Suharto's successor, B. J. Habibe in June 1999. This did not take long for illegal loggers to move in. Freelance workers seeking livelihood started to move in. They were paid about $0.60 a day for cutting trees. Some of them are local people, but many came from other islands. They would bring along with them rice and canned foods that would last them for about a month.

Inside the forest, they would build makeshift huts and work from sunrise to sunset cutting trees. The work is not without ordeal from the park wardens. It is like a cat-and-mouse game where they hide deeper in the forest from the wardens. If they are caught, they have to bribe their way out of jail and the wardens would extort money from them.[167]

There are the small-time timber robbers. They usually work independently and sell the logs to middlemen. Once the trees are felled, they would be brought and hooked to a motorized canoe and floated down to a canal or stream and steered to the waiting middleman who buys the logs for about $7 to $10 per cubic meter. These logs are destined to either an illegal sawmill who would then sell the lumber for twice the amount; or loaded to a barge and taken to Kalimantan ports for export which can fetch up to $53 per cubic meter; or sold to the domestic sawmills for local use. According to the Center for International Forestry Research (CIFOR), the East Kalimantan provincial government loses $100 million annually in lost business tax revenue due to illegal legging and unreported timber processing. This does not include the loss of biodiversity and water services nor the future social cost of natural disasters and loss of jobs from forest destruction.[169]

The more daring timber thieves are the big time timber barons. They have built themselves a network of access roads and dug canals to float out the illicit logs to existing streams. They operate with impunity even m well-guarded parks, and in the presence of visiting tourists.[170] Corruption could only be the reason why they are able to get away with these thieveries.

There has been a prior agreement among the local inhabitants with the Department of Forestry to disallow the use of chainsaw in logging operations This is to avoid stirring up the sensitivity of the people on the impact of unsustainable utilization of forest resources and to avoid the giant teeth of the chainsaw into the already disappearing forest cover.[171]

* * * * *

Illegal logging is a crime against humanity in every sense of the word Loggers operate without licenses and pay no permit fees and other taxes. They cut timber in places where loggings are banned either as protected parks and sanctuaries or rehabilitation areas and because there are no private licenses operating there. Unlicensed timber extraction has been responsible for the loss of habitat vital for tigers, rhinos and elephants in Asia, leading to local extinctions of these and other species.[172] These illegal operators are often protected by the military, police or other militia groups, goons or in cahoots with crooked environmental officials to protect their interest as in the ease of one gang of illegal loggers in Brazil.

For over a decade since 1990, a group of illegal loggers in cahoots with corrupt environmental officials were able to cut down and sell $371 million worth of timber until it was busted in the biggest sting operation of its kind in Brazil.[173]

Without taxes being raised, governments have no money for reforestation and they don't even initiate reforestation works for the future generations. Once the protected forests are destroyed, it will lead to more intrusion from upland people who may practice shifting cultivation leading to forest fires, poaching of wildlife, and haphazard human settlement.

They also feast on the greed and corruption of public officials to get with their crime. A culture of corruption is responsible for the proliferation of many illegal activities in other places.

The poor who depend on the forests for their survival may lose their livelihood along with the income needed for the education of the children living expenses.

Most of the timbers sold in the world's market are already depressed in prices compared to the high cost of the ecological role they played. This is compounded by the presence of illegally acquired logs flooding the market. A study conducted by Seneca Creek Associated and Wood Resources International that examined the flow of suspicious roundwood into lumber and plywood found that it has depressed world wood prices by 7-16% on the average, depending on the product. Without the illegally harvested wood in the global market, the study estimates the value of US wood exports could increase by over $460 million each year.[174]

* * * * *

Once in a while, news of confiscation of illegally cut logs hit the newspapers and the media in the Philippines. Most of these illegal cuts logs and converted into lumber came from watershed areas. During a renewed crackdown in Koronadal City in Mindanao, 64 trees were cut down from a watershed area by timber poachers believed to be protected by armed groups engaged in illegal logging. The poor are often blamed for illegal logging, but they are abetted by a clandestine market dominated by timber robbers.

Timber poaching is occurring everyday around the country. A move to stem the flow of illegal logging includes inventory of all planted and naturally grown trees along watershed areas. Roadblocks are set up to intercept illegally cut logs and finished lumber. These measures are always too late as the trees have already been cut down. Only after a massive devastation where deaths have occurred do the govemmenj takes concrete action to charge those involved. This is what happened to the massive landslides that left more than a thousand people dead in Quezon Province. Allegedly, three district officials of DENR connived or ignored the cutting of trees from the restricted areas.[176]

Forestry officials getting involved with illegal loggings is nothing new. It has been going on for decades like officials of other government agencies. There is more money exchanged by conniving with private individuals to sell out the patrimony of the nation than working for a pittance salary given by the government. Few cases have been apprehended like the two truckloads worth of P2.8 million undocumented lumber seized where some DENR officials in South Cotabato were in cahoots with at least 18 individuals in an illegal logging operation.[177] Earlier in the same month, the Army's 7th Infantry Battalion seized two truckloads of freshly cut lumber estimated at 25,000 board feet in Palimbang, Sultan Kudarat.[17*] For every case of apprehended lumber, more than a dozen shipments probably escape the honest forestry dragnet. It would not be surprising if unscrupulous and dishonest forestry officials are involved. How else do you account for the continuing decimation of our forests?

Timber Smuggling

In the Philippines, illegally cut timbers are mostly smuggled out of the country despite government's efforts to stop it. Most of the equipment used in the cutting came from canceled concessions. Cheating and corruption make a deadly combination in fostering deforestation.

During the 1970s, restrictions on log exports were introduced to encourage local processing and to preserve timber resources. But the higher log export prices led to rampant log smuggling and under-reporting of exports. Discrepancies between trade data of Japanese import of logs and Philippine export records have been noted for years, The same situation has happened in Indonesia. Profit is a strong motivation and loggers tend to sell their logs to the highest bidders.

The Philippine criminal justice system is soft of crime especially those committied against the rich and the powerful. The wanton plunder and destruction of our natural resources by unscrupulous businessmen have been going on for decades but no one has been punished for them. Not only is timber smuggling destroying our forests, they illegal loggers are not paying their taxes and salting away precious dollars. Some of them are known government officials or related to them and even protected by high government officials. They ought to be conscionable after reaping off the bounty of the country.

Timber smuggling is a potential threat to the second growth forests after the area is abandoned by the original licensee. In these areas, local politicians, military and forestry officials have been frequently accused of complicity in allowing illegal timber operations by log smugglers and poachers who operate with impunity. The hiring of conscientious foresters is important to reducc timber smuggling. Very- often, logging ships were able to pick up these illegal logs with the connivance of government authorities who release logs through the falsification of log export documents or outright smuggling. There were numerous reports of foreign cargo ships loading logs off the coast of Samar and in Cagayan Valley in the past. Some of these vessels are notorious for smuggling. They change the name of the vessel after each smuggling operation. The DENR people are virtually powerless to stop the smuggling. Corruption and the fear of bodily harm perpetuated by the military/police in cahoots with loggers is one reason.

Log smuggling is not confined to Asia alone. In Guatemala's lush Peten Forest, a 3.4-million hectares of prized cedar and mahogany, much of it over 100 years old were cut down and smuggled into Mexico for sawmilling set up for the trade. The only authority in the region is the military who are the people controlling the logging and milling operations.

Value added products such as plywood and lumber are also subjected to technical smuggling out of the country. Underreporting, undervaluation, and misdeclaration of species from high value to low value logs to avoid taxes, practices resorted to by log experts are adopted by the finished product exporters.

Mahogany is a tree that is difficult to grow on plantations. In Peru illegal loggers are cutting mahogany from protected national parks and watershed areas and "laundering" them to another watershed outside the park boundaries and mixing them with the legal mahogany of another concessionaire to escape detection.[179]

* * * * *

There is currently a move by Great Britain to insist that all the industrialized nations buy timber and timber products from proper managed forests. This was prompted by the Indonesian government ministers saying that corruption in the country was so rampant that it could not do anything about illegal logging and smuggling abroad. They urged the rich nations to cut down on demand. This is being resisted by the US.[180]

The International Union Conserv ation of Nature and Natural Resources (IUCN) is an organization dedicated to monitoring the world's flora and fauna that are endangered of extinction. Those on the Red List are considered vulnerable and cannot be harvested indiscriminately.

Ramin trees are only found in Indonesia and Malaysia and are considered vulnerable species in Malaysia as listed in the IUCN Red List. However, in Indonesia, huge amounts of the remaining ramin has been illegally cut in protected areas, such as the Tanajuang Putting National Park in Central Kalimantan, the last three areas where orangutans exists in viable number. The Environmental Investigation Agency (EIA) and Telapak Indonesia estimate that over 300.000 m^3 of illegally logged ramin were taken from the park each year in 1999 and 2000, then sold out to

Malaysia or Singapore 'legally' to the international market, including Japan.[181]

In a move to stem this form of smuggling, in April 2001, the former Indonesian Minister of Forests issued a Ministerial Decree placing a temporary moratorium on the cutting and grading of ramin. It was later listed in Appendix III of the Convention on International Trade in Endangered Species (CITES) with a zero quota, except for stockpiles and a small quantity of timber certified to FSC.[182] This did not stop the smuggling or some buyers and manufacturers of furniture who are are that it is listed to stop buying.

Timbers are sometimes smuggled out of the country in the form of finished products such as furniture or through an intermediate country as in the above case. According to Greenpeace's investigation, 80% of mahogany exports from the state of Para is controlled by two key players both of which are heavily involved in illegal chains of mahogany supply, some originating in Indian lands. Between February 2000 and August 2001, these kingpins sold Brazilian mahogany to DLH Nordisk which supply the wood to many reputable US and UK furniture manufacturers.[183]

Licensed Loggers

A license does not automatically confer moral legitimacy to the loggers. It would not be surprising to find that many of these licenses were obtained fraudulently through corruption, nepotism, cronyism or to placate rebels. Many of them do not have the capital, knowledge, and experience on how to log sustainably. They are known to be granted special permits or stum page contracts to cut trees for limited period Stumpage contracts are "cut-and-go" operations that are not sustainable because of the short period of operations as long as they paid the forest charges and royalty to the government. They are often awarded to the concessioners without bidding and some corporations were not even unregistered with the Security and Exchange Commission. (Vitug, 43)

Whether it is a timber license agreement or a special cutting permit, one of the conditions for granting the concession is that the permittee should operate the concession and not relinquish to another the operation in return for royalty. This important provision has been violated so often and known to everybody in the field except the authorities. Somehow the loggers were able to get around this provision and managed to cover their wrongdoings by blinding the authorities with bribery. With our dwindling forest cover, it is a wonder how the authority continues to grant these special permits or turn a blind eye to illegal logging.

Even loggers with concessions are also known to cut outside their concession especially when the surrounding areas are public domain. They are also known to cut way beyond their allowable volume. This is possib e with the connivance of the forestry officials. Underreporting of the volume cut is also resorted to. Using the same cutting permit over and over again is also practiced. Some illegal loggers are known to load their logs to waiting ships bound for other Asian countries without the necessary papers. Clandestine operation of sawmills have been known to proliferate by some illegal operators.

Some joggers with just a cutting permit will promote themselves to go into big business. Sometimes these permits are given on the ground of salvaging fallen trees after a typhoon. The permit can be reused over and over again. Underreporting of volume and undervaluation are some ways of cheating the government. This often leads to indiscriminately cutting of trees such as those found on steep slopes or undersized trees and even protected species. Logging outside the given concession is also a common practice.

Some secessionists in the past have been granted cutting permits to bring them back to the fold of the law. They are allowed to cut certain volumes of timber for an allocated time. Without the knowledge and equipment, Aey opt to sell or rent out the license just to get royalty from former loggers Expect these loggers to cheat the government and destroy the forests to get their fair share.

* * * * *

Whether it is legal or illegal, logging must be monitored, especially in areas where there is endemic corruption. Monitoring is best done by third parties, preferably those NGOs from the developed countries with their proven integrity that don't allow nonsense negotiations. Scientific methods such as remote sensing, log tracking, etc. could do more to stem dishonesty than increasing penalty or jailing the illegal loggers. Often times, the real culprits behind the illegal activities are untouchables while these henchmen act as the fall guys.

Satellite remote sensing and Geographic Information Systems (GIS) have become an important tool for monitoring illegal loggings and even forest fires. This up-to-date technology can help forest guardians pinpoint the exact spots where illegal logging is going on and even whether legal loggers are operating outside their concessions. Over-harvesting would be minimized. It should also help in the sustainable management of vast tract of forestlands that would otherwise be difficult to do on sites.

In conjunction with satellite imaging, it is necessary to make an atlas or detailed map on the state of the forest. Boundaries of the country as well as road networks in the forests need to be pinpointed. The atlas will then become an integral part of decision-making processes in the sustainable management of the forest ecosystems. All these work need to be done by experts and there are only a few of them around. One capable group is the World Resources Institute's Global Forest Watch (GFW).[184]

Be periodic study of the atlas any discrepancy can easily be pinpointed and analyzed for any illegal activities. The updating of the atlas will showcase the progress of the ecosystems. It can also help analyze whether legal loggers are doing their share in sustainable harvesting of their concessions. The tool should also be complemented with good governance and rigorous field work.[185]

Total Log Ban

Although concern is mounting over the loss of tropical forest with the loss of biodiversity and the possible climatic change, still some governments continue to lease out extensive tracts of forest lands to timber enterprises. While forestry policies require companies to follow sustainable-yield logging practices, compliances have been inadequate and reforestation work is neglected. On the other hand, corruption has led to over-cutting, and the permanent degradation of many forest lands. Laws for the preservation of forest sanctuaries and parks are toothless because they are not being enforced religiously.

The stage of tropical deforestation may have reached critical proportions. Within the next 30 years or less, there may not be any intact rainforests left except in the remotest parts of the country and well-guarded parks and reserves For decades, most of the tropical and consuming countries have been practicing lip service to sustainable management of tropical forest, and deforestation continues to plague these countries without letup.

Sustainable management of tropical forests is a controversial subject. Some authorities do not believe it is possible to carry out sustainable forest harvesting under the profit system. They may be correct since less than 1% of the tropical timber plantation fall under this category. To top it all, most loggers are not serious about reforesting the areas where they operate.

Total log ban may not be enough to deter illegal logging and smuggling. It must be accompanied by removing the markets for these products. The importing countries must ban all hardwood from selected countries that have decimated their forests to the point of being unsustainable. Concerted political actions among importing countries is necessary to be effective. Likewise, exporting countries should boycott importing countries that entertain or deal with log smugglers. A number of wood certifications have been established but the low prices offered by smugglers are not going to put much dent on the system.

On the local area, all sawmill companies and plywood plants utilizing local forest products must be stopped from operation. Only imported logs can be processed for the local and export market. In the field, it should be made illegal to own a chainsaw. Road networks and bridges used for logging should be destroyed.

Although the logging ban may seem to be the solution to deforestation, it is more important to address the problem of poverty that causes people to convert forest land to agriculture by swidden cultivation. Without strict enforcement to remove this practice, deforestation will continue unabated. Once a concession reverts to the government, it is imperative that forest rangers be assigned immediately to guard the forests from illegal loggers. They abound when the forest become common property Many have resorted to making flitches in the absence of forest guards from the previous concessionaires. This is what has happened to many forest concessions canceled prematurely during the last few decades through out the country.

* * * * *

Political will is necessary when it comes to the total log ban. After the tragedy that occurred during the typhoon that hit Quezon Province, a nationwide total log ban was ordered. But it did not take long for the government to start lifting the ban after representations from loggers and furniture makers called on the government to lift the ban.

The total log ban is difficult to implement because the granting of timber concessions is more a political issue in the Philippines than any other industries. Concessions are often granted, banned or lifted on the ground of political expediency. Corruption probably plays also an important role in winning concessions from high government officials. When Indonesia banned the export of logs in October 2001, they found to their dismay, after doing fieldworks, that it did not put any dent on illegal harvesting exports.

* * * * *

It is well known that there is a correlation with the socio-economic impact and ecological degradation associated with unsustainable logging that has been occurring in many countries. Deforestation is known to increase the likelihood of flooding following heavy rainfall. In 19% and 1997 flood cost Yunnan in China $403 million and $542 million respectively in damages. Severe flooding on the Yangtze River in 1998 affected one-fifth of China's population, killing more than 3,600 people and destroying about 5 million hectares of crops. Economic losses throughout China were estimated at over $36 billion. Soil erosion caused by logging was found to be a contributory factor to the flooding.[186] As a result of this incident, a total log banned was imposed. As of today, it is still being enforced. It is going to take decades of enforcement of the ban for the forests to regenerate.

In 2004 flooding struck the country again in the areas around the Yingjiang County. Landslides occurred in many places and bridges and fulverts collapsed. Sixteen thousand people were trapped in some villages in one of the main logging centers on the China-Burma border. In July of the same year, Burma also experienced the worst flooding in decades.[187]

Nongovernmental Organizations (NGOs)

The serious problem of deforestation around the world has prompt many individuals to set up NGOs to monitor the illegal trade in forest products and help in reforestation efforts through activities such as livelihood programs, reforestation works, certification of forest products and myriad activities. Many of these NGOs were setup in the developing countries where environmental issues do not merit special attention or high priority. Most of these governments are corrupt and heavily indebted that little amount of capital are invested for protecting the environment. They usually operate through the local chapters in many developing countries. One of them is the WWF.

One of the initiatives of the WWF is the setting up of the Global Forest & Trade Network (GFTN) to eliminate illegal logging and improve the management of valuable and threatened forests. By facilitating trade links between companies committed to achieving and supporting responsible forestry, the GFTN created market conditions that help conserve the world's forests while providing economic and social benefits for the businesses and people that depend on them.[188]

NGOs are often powerless in the face of armed goons employed by illegal loggers. They are prepared to kill anyone who stands in their way. To put a stop to timber thieves, Catholic priests have been deputized as forestry officers to apprehend them. This is probably asking too much of them. Two priests who tried to stop illegal logging in their provinces were murdered and another sprayed with gunshots only days after he confiscated an illegal haul of logs.[189]

One of the ways of fighting illegal logging is to spike the trees with nails or other metallic materials on the trunks. This would make it dangerous to cut down the trees using chainsaw It is just as dangerous to cut it using the electric rotary saw in the sawmill. Hie spiking of trees has been done elsewhere but was first introduced here by visiting American green activists and now the former members of the UP Mountaineer, are promoting it. It was first applied in the Bataan National Park in 1994.[190]

* * * * *

If friendly persuasion does not work, more drastic actions can be undertaken. In an authoritarian regime, applying political pressure may not work but in a free-market society, both governments and companies are conscious of their image. The actions taken may be long before concrete actions bear any fruit. Concerted actions by NGOs were able to get some headway in saving the boreal forest of Canada from exploitation. The companies targeted were Mitsubishi, Georgia-Pacific, the Canadian firms International Forest Products (Interfor), and Western Forest Products. Actions taken by the NGOs include chaining themselves to a barge full of red cedar logs, constant barrage of press conferences, petitions and boycotts designed to embarrass logging companies and hurt profits.[191]

Mitsubishi, under a four-year campaign of boycott of its cars, electronics, etc. finally gave a positive response by financing a Japanese forest regeneration project in the Malaysian state of Sarawak to develop methods of helping tropical forests grow back more quickly and selling its majority share in the British Columbia operation. The Canadian timber giant MacMillan Bloedel finally stopped logging on British Columbia's Vancouver Island and sat down with the local Nuu-Chah-Nulth people to plan sustainable management of the company's forest operations.[192]

In 2000, Greenpeace conducted research into the Japanese market to identify customers of Interfor with links to the destruction of the Great Bear Rainforest in Canada. The research identified 229 Japanese companies which had directly or indirectly purchased wood and wood products from it. After releasing the report in March 2001, along with an email-based action against some of the companies, around 70 of them pledged to cancel their contracts with Interfor after realizing that they were fuelling ancient forest destruction by buying its products. The same approach was also initiated in the US, Europe and China markets with success.[193]

War and Insurgency

In ancient times, forests have been decimated to build ships for travel and conquest of other lands. Today, it is a matter of land disputes as neighboring countries fight over lands. The lush Amazonia forest consists of 23.6 million hectares that extends over nine countries has been scenes of several skirmishes and boundary disputes. The fear of losing their territory has forced the governments in the border states to transplant their citizens through transmigration programs to these disputed lands After Brazil annexed Acre in 1903 from Bolivia, the government staked their claim and presence by transporting and settling hundreds of thousand of migrant workers to the area. Peru did the same thing in 1942 by occupying three disputed border areas after defeating Ecuador. This is why countries have been pushing development at all frontiers of the world's largest rainforest.

During the Second World War, millions of hectares of forest were destroyed throughout the European and Pacific countries. In Russia alone, at least 20 million hectares were destroyed in areas under military operation. Today, most of the wars going on are internal in nature that could act like a two-edged sword.

In Southeast Asia, land disputes have repeatedly resulted in armed conflicts between government and separatists movements. The Philippines, Thailand, Indonesia, Malaysia and Burma have all experienced insurgency since independence. These conflicts are usually waged in the forested areas and the casualties are not only the combatants but also the trees being trampled or shattered by bullets and bombs.

It can also be a blessing as in Liberia where the wealthy loggers fled the country, resulting in the stoppage of commercial exploitation of the forests. Continuous warfare like that of Mozambique kept foreign investors uninterested in risking investment in timber harvesting. Conservation measures are often neglected that could lead to rampant deforestation as people find the opportunity to steal without being apprehended. In some occasions, areas such as Vietnam, Cambodia, Laos, Mozambique, and Angola, many land mines were set in the forests that people avoided them. On die other hand, the return of peace could mean more deforestation as new sources of income are needed to pay for reconstruction or service the debts incurred during the war. Damage to properties also required the harvesting of trees for repair.[194]

* * * * *

Modern warfare is particularly lethal to the forests. During the Vietnam War, the defoliation chemical like the notoriously injurious Agent Orange was used by the US military forces to destroy crops and wipe out entire jungles that are offering shelter to the enemies. More than 44% of the rainforests were defoliated while 25 million bomb craters displaced three billion cubic meters of soil, destroying 2-4 million hectares of forests and 36% of all the mangrove forests. Agent Orange is contaminated by the chemical dioxin. A division of "Anti-Forest Rangers" was organized to do the dirty work. (Day, 269)

Another study revealed that close to 16 million tons of munitions were used creating 30 million craters averaging 30 feet in diameter. As a result, the soil has become infertile because of the lack of topsoil. The craters also damaged the drainage patterns of the area It will take decades the damage can be healed.[195]

Another chemical used was napalm. This sticky substance was dispersed onto vegetation and then ignited. It burned similarly to gasoline, and quickly destroyed all surrounding vegetation. Heavy machinery was also deployed such as the Rome Plow. This is a 20-ton tractor with an eleven-foot wide, two and half-ton blade that could plow 1,000 acre of land daily. There were 150 of them plowing and killing massive numbers of animals and vegetation.[196]

Annual US foreign assistance to Latin America increased from $150 million to $850 million between 1980 and 1987. Most of these aids were for directly military and security assistance, and roughly 1% went to environmental protection. This lopsided aid is cause for environmental alarm.

In El Pital, El Salvador's only lower montane forest, once planned as a national park has been reduced to a series of charred remains through bombing campaigns. Counterinsurgency has also turned vast areas of Morazan and northern Chalatenango provinces into virtual wastelands.

In Guatemala, the army carried out a scorched-earth policy against the insurgents by destroying forest, crops, livestock, and at least 440 villages. Between 1982 and 1987 more than one million Guatemalans were displaced from their land. Many refugees have fled to the rainforests of neighboring Mexico where they practiced swidden agriculture and gather firewood.

According to the state-run Honduran Forestry Corporation Honduras lost more than 1,000 square kilometers of forest in 1986 due to US military maneuvers and construction.

* * * * *

Forest trees have become an important source of income by foreign countries in Asia After the Second World War, many insurgency problems sprouted from the newly independent countries in Asia. As a result, many countries started to sell their natural resources to pay for military weapons. In Burma, more than one million cubic meters of the precious teak were cut and sold to Japan and the West. The ongoing insurgency problem is far from over, and the forests are being chopped down with the help of loggers from Thailand. Today, China is helping the country decimate the forest.

Forests have become a place of refuge for armed dissidents, a source of funds for the insurgents, and food for the fighters. Inside these ecosystems can also be found valuable natural resources waiting to be mined aside from the poor and the marginalized people who are ripe for recruitment. Many developing countries such as Colombia, India, Indonesia, Nepal. Pakistan, Ivory Coast, Uganda and the Philippines and a dozen countries suffer from civil war or insurgency problems. Together they cover over 40% of the world's tropical forests.[197]

Insurgency in the Philippines can be found in almost all the forested areas throughout the country. Their roles have inadvertently aided the destruction of the forests. Some have resorted to illegal logging to augment their income for food, medicines, and weapons in the war against the government. In places where legitimate logging operations exist, a system of taxation has been devised based on the equipment used by the loggers. In almost all logging areas where insurgents proliferate, some concessionaires were charged for each chainsaw, bulldozer, stripper, trucks, etc. These expenses are passed on by the loggers to the end users and to the trees through careless over-cutting and tax evasion. Some of the insurgents have gone into business by making flitches for the sawmills.

According to a 1992 report of the Armed Forces of the Philippines (AFP), the NPA may have received about PIoo million annually from the concessionaires in Luzon and Mindanao. The "taxes" are based on the equipment and machinery used and the volume of logs felled. (Vitug, 134)

Funds that could be used to uplift the lives of the poor or used to protect the environment have to be diverted to buy weapons to fight the unnecessary war. Forests are affected directly and indirectly as a result, Governments are forced to sell the nation's patrimony such as granting logging permits to cut down trees or set up cash crops plantations to pay for the needed weapons. In some cases, die military have direct interests in logging concessions or the production of cash crops.

* * * * *

During the height of the Moro War in the Philippines, President Marcos used the carrot-and-stick approach to the rebels. He would grant the ex-rebels "special cutting permits" to fell and sell trees for limited period, usually one year. In one year alone, Marcos issued more than 12,000 permits not just to the Muslim rebel returnees. Some of the concessions were taken from legitimate holders and given to the rebels. The problem is that no one bothers to do any replanting as there is no incentive for the future. Because most of them do not have the capital and equipment, the returnees would sell their rights in return for royalties. (Vitug, 14-15) This added monetary burden could only be countered by wanton destruction of the forests which is the normal case. Loggers are out to make money at the least expense without regard to the welfare of the forests.

* * * * *

War can be destructive or good for the forests depending on each individual circumstance. Local dissidents have used the forests as a source of income by extorting money from the loggers or the forest dweller to prolong the war. In Cambodia, the Khmer Rogue was heavily dependent on timber sales. In Colombia, the drug lords use the forest to cultivate and process illicit crops such as coca while carrying out anti-government activities. To control the conflict, international agencies have imposed sanctions on timber sales to keep them from financing the purchase of arms In rare cases, war carried out in the forests can sometimes be good as it discourages logging and mining activities. People are fearful of getting killed by mines or being kidnapped for ransom. As a result of years of conflict, Colombia has more forest cover compared to past years.[198]

In another case in the Philippines, the rebels of the New People's Army (NPA) were forcing concessionaires to reforest and to pay workers higher wages. The rebels would threaten to bum down the reforestation sites unless they complied. The forests have served the rebels well for decades as shelter and training ground against government forces. This is also true in many countries infested with freedom fighters against the sitting governments. (Vitug, 128)

Paradoxically, some claimed that the forest cover has actually diminished as American war on coca production using herbicides has forced many cultivators to move deeper into the Amazon highland forests. This constant push on peasants has led to the clearing of over 1.75 million acres of rainforest.[199]

The return of peace to the land inevitably fueled the forest destruction. In a number of countries the push for rapid post-war economic recovery has led to excessive logging. Governments routinely use forested areas as places to settle demobilized soldiers and war refugees who are likely to take up destructive farming and resource extraction practices. The international community would be wise to invest heavily in forested areas during post conflict periods since such spending can do double duty by preventing a recurrence of fighting and protecting the forest itself.

* * * * *

In some countries with internal problems such as separatist movements, the military always plays a pivotal role in forest degradation. In Indonesia, the government has to play a subordinate role to the wishes of the military to prop up the bureaucracy. The military, especially the generals, is given a free hand to augment its budget from the operation of mining and forest exploitation. They range from contracts to guard large foreign mining operations, usually paid by mining companies to outright direct illegal logging and mining in league with corrupt local government officials In the conflicting areas of Aceh and West Papua, a region rich in natural resources, the military has provoked conflict in order to justify their continued presence.[200]

Even Vietnam, the once communist country has been blinded by the green bucks. Even its world renounced World Heritage Site of karst landscapes did not escape the long arm of the exploiters. Limestone is the main raw material in the manufacturing of cement. In 1998, a new cement plant under a joint venture between a Swiss cement company and a local company started operation. A loan of $30 million was provided by the International Finance Corporation (IFC). A year later, due to protests from the local and provincial authorities, an environment assessment was undertaken. After four years of study, no report was still forthcoming, although an officer of IFC promised a report soon. A source close to the study reported that the Vietnamese Army ordered that the limestone hills being exploited be excluded from the study. The provincial government soon refused to allow the study to continue. In the meantime, the company continued to quarry 4,000 tons of limestone a Day.[201]

In the Philippines, the military has intruded into the forests in the fight against the insurgents. Whereas before, government officials and influential family clans are the only ones in control of most of the forests, today, much of the remaining natural forests are now controlled or owned by high-ranking military' officers. The forests are being used as a reward for the loyalty of the military officers to the government. As one Agtas, a Negrito of the Sierra Madre mountains laments, "We no longer have a place to go. Every place we find, government projects or plantations follow. We are like swine that are being hunted down, scrounging around in ever decreasing number of places. Will we die like this? Will we die in the land of our birth like this, without a measure of dignity?"[202]

Sometimes the retired military personnel were given concessions as rewards for their loyalty. This is the case of the Veterans Woodworks and its affiliates, Tropical Philippine Wood Industries. They are in the plywood and sawmill businesses respectively. (Vitug. 17) The fate of these two concessions is an interesting case of disputes over cronyism and loyalty involving forestlands.

Government Sanctions

Despite the alarming loss of forest covers in many countries governments continue to be complacent or are in complicity with logging companies or buyers in selling their patrimony for personal gain. This is the case at Burma's Kachin State rich ecosystem being depleted of its forest timber for export to China. The forest of Kachin State is one of the most bio-diverse and rich temperate areas on earth that suffered from one of the highest rate of deforestation. The scale of logging this area and the associated illegal cross-border timber trade is undermining the prospect for future sustainable development in Burma's northern border areas.[203]

There are no serious efforts to stop the illegal logging because a minority of those under the SPDC Northern Command consists of soldiers who have enriched themselves at the expense of the forest destruction. Two-thirds of the export to China came from illegal sources. In 2003, 96% of the imports of logs and sawn wood amounting to 1.3 million cubic meters were illegal. The destruction of the forest and die illegal timber trade took place with the full knowledge and complicity of the SPDC.[204]

In 1984, there were four logging companies based in China along the border of China and Burma. In 2005, there are now 100 despite a nationwide logging ban in China in 1998. The reason is that their business is being sustained by the illegal logging operations going inside Burma.[205]

Revenue generated from the cross-border timber trade with China has funded conflict in Kachin State that led to human rights abuses and increased poverty. Competition over territory between armed opposition groups, business interests and others, seeking to control the trade is a proximate cause of violence, and a source of instability that has the potential to transcend the border. The trade has led to increased factionalism, corruption and cronyism. It has also intensified ethnic tension between Kachin subgroups, entrenched power structures that created conditions under which local warlords have thrived. This will make any attempt by the relevant authorities to manage the resource and subsequent revenue flow all the more difficult.[206]

Burma is the second largest producer of opium after Afghanistan. Since the collapse of the communist party of Burma, the heroin trade, like the logging trade expanded rapidly. Drug traffickers have invested heavily in logging businesses as a means of money laundering.[207]

* * * * *

War has a way of disrupting the operation of logging and deforestation in many countries This is the case with Cambodia as civil unrests allowed the forest cover to occupy two-thirds of Cambodia in the 1970s. Once peace reigned, logging companies moved in to remove as much timber as possible in the least possible time. Evidence of rampant deforestation forced the government to call a temporary moratorium on logging and transport of timber in January 2002.[208]

The London-based Global Witness was hired by the Cambodian government to monitor corruption in the forestry business upon the insistence of foreign donors in 1999 as an independent monitor. A team was sent to monitor and record any evidence of illegal logging Eva Galabru and two of her two colleagues marched deep into the Preylong Forest to track down any illegal activities. They discovered fresh evidence of commercial logging despite the moratorium. They documented violations by companies linked to top Cambodian officials who operate in view of forestry officers. Confronted with mounting criticism, Prime Minster Hun Sen moved to sue Galabru for slander and fire the group as the country's official forestry monitor.[209]

Threat to withhold two World Bank grants worth $20 million did not seem to deter the C ambodian officials. This is because the money to be made in forestry is so large and the gains are not distributed very far beyond a small group of government ministers, senior military officers and the prime minister's relatives.[210]

* * * * *

Accountability is sorely lacking in many personnel in the forestry department. Instead of being disciplined for any wrongdoings, they are often promoted. There are numerous cases of Forest Service employees in the US being promoted after being caught for illegally selling 20 timber sales in California in order to try and skirt the application of certain environmental laws. The timber sale contracts are cancelled and millions of dollars in damages are paid to the timber companies by taxpayers. In another case, a forest supervisor stole firewood from the national forest that he manages and was caught. Instead of being dismissed or charged in court, he was promoted to the regional office and put in charge of overseeing the most important wildlife conservation plan in US history.[211] Cases of these natures abound a]so in our country. Foresters who allowed loggers to get away with violations of environmental laws are often promoted through the intercession of the loggers or rewarded with expensive gifts. Those who insist on enforcing forestry laws can end up dead.

* * * * *

The saddest part logging, whether legal or illegal is that only a few favored clients are benefiting while they lay the rest of the country's landscape in waste. A logging concession is like a license to rape the patrimony of the nation. Many unscrupulous loggers used their concessions as collateral to borrow money from government institutions often with the approval of the higher authorities. Some used their concession to borrow money for the sole purpose of absconding with it with no plans for repaying the loans. Others have known all along that their projects are not feasible but they serve as a way of wringing money out of the government lending institutions.

During the regime of President Marcos, state banks lost billions of pesos in loans to crony loggers who borrowed heavily. Most of them have violated forestry' laws and never punished but penalized with fines for their wrongdoings. Many of these concessions were later abandoned, foreclosed or sequestered by the government. While the country was going bankrupt, these loggers, awash with dollars, were looking to the Asian neighbors to invest in logging operations and prided themselves for denuding the landscapes. The sad part of it all is that many of these loggers were able to invest in foreign lands using dollars salted from the Philippines at the height of the log export ventures.

Under the present setup, it is almost impossible to get conviction against big-time illegal loggers. They are not only well-funded, well-connected and influential they are always willing to bribe their way out of any problem. Cases of tampering of evidence, ignorance of the laws by judges, inadequate funding and lack of vehicles for out of town cases, etc. have hampered the enforcement of forestry laws. Political pressures are often exerted on the law enforcers not to procced with the cases and even on judges to dismiss the cases brought before their courts. In one case, the judge dismiss the case because the accused argued that the word "lumber" is not covered by the phrase "forest products" by which he was charged. In another case, the accused could be arraigned as he was out of the country and could not be available for hearing, according to his lawyers. The prosecutor asked the court for two days to check on the information with the immigration bureau. Instead of allowing the gesture, the judge took the words of the lawyers for the defendant and consigned the case to the archives. (Vitug, 118) Cases of these natures are not surprising.

Chapter 5

AGRICULTURE

Since the Neolithic revolution 10,000 years ago, more forests have given way to farms and pastures than to any other use. The spread of agriculture is still the most important cause of forest clearing today, especially in the tropical countries where the growing populations need to be fed and housed. Most of the nations around the world were once at least modestly tree-covered until population pressures took over the forest to feed the growing population. In India, for example, the expansion of cash crops or commercial agriculture had resulted in the deforestation of the 70% of all land between 1951 and 1976. The same thing is happening to Indonesia, China, Brazil and countries too poor to import food for their growing populations and need to grow them locally.

It is inevitable that the encroachment will result in deforestation. Agriculture is one of the leading causes of deforestation and one that is a necessity for an exploding population that need to be fed. Yet many of these plantations were planted to cash crops that were exported to the rich countries without benefiting the local masses.

As in other human activities concentrated on forestlands, unique ecosystems are being destroyed especially the flora and fauna. The lives and livelihood of indigenous people are disrupted, including their culture. Indigenous people are threatened with eviction from their ancestral lands to make way for agriculture. Sometimes they are even threatened should they refuse to move out as they fight for their rights.

All these destruction on the fragile forests were made possible through the loans provided by the domestic, international financial institutions and even government-to-government loans and grants. Sometimes these loans are extended despite protests from international and national NGOs in clear violation of their own safeguard policy related to forestry. It took a long while before these lenders realized that the damages have been done. Or is it their deliberate intent to exploit the natural resources of the topical countries that they extended the soft loans to?

Shifting Cultivation

Shifting cultivation or more commonly known as slash-and-burn cultivation is one of the most wasteful practices. In this farming method, the trees are burned down to release the mineral and nutrients within into the soil to enrich it. Unless taken into by the new plants, everytime the rain comes, some of the nutrients are washed away and after a while the soil can no longer support growing the crops. Unlike in ancient times where forests are plentiful and populations in the forests are not so congested allowing the long fallow period to thrive until the next harvest; and burning down the forests meant the trees are lost forever.

Slash-and-bum agriculture can only support crops for a few seasons before they must be left to fallow. The fields are generally excellent for the first year, dropping by 30% the second year and 50% by the third year due to the loss of many nutrients through leaching by the heavy tropical rains and the removal of others in the harvested crops. What makes it objectionable is that more forests are burned down to get a few years of rich nutrients and allowing the rest to be eroded by rainfall. This is a waste of resources. More often than not, burning a forest has a tendency to get out of hand.

During fallow, a secondary' forest usually regenerates at the site, and plant nutrients are brought up from the subsoil by deep-rooted trees. It will take from six to twenty years to regenerate the soil depending on the local conditions. Population pressure often reduces the fallow period making it difficult even for secondary forest to survive. Where governments are unable to provide the techniques, training and equipment needed by farmers, the land becomes degraded and eventually is abandoned. The farmers then clears more forested land for cultivation. In ancient times many lands were once fertile and supported large human populations; today they are barren and barely produce enough to the small populations.

Though conditions vary widely, often at least fifteen hectares of land must be available for each dependent person if shifting cultivation is to be sustainable over time. Growing population density make this practice difficult once a threshold point is reached at which farmers return to a plot before its fertility is fully restored. A dangerous cycle of degeneration begins, unless skillful and painstaking measures to recycle nutrients and organic matter to the soil are carried out. The only way to stop further burning is to subsidize the farmers with fertilizers.

* * * * *

According to the Food and Agriculture Organization (FAO) unsustainable agriculture is the main cause of 90% of deforestation around the world. There are several reasons why people are driven into the forests to practice shifting cultivation. They are driven into the forests by national and international forces with different interests. Their lands are often taken over by government and corporations that force them to move into rainforest areas or those already there into deeper rainforests. In some Third World countries, forests are used as a safety valve to avoid social upheavals when people are being dispossessed by the rich and powerful landlords. The government would offer the forests as free land, even promoting road projects to help the new forest dwellers.

The inability of the government and the private sectors to provide jobs and the inequalities among the rich and poor especially on land tenure policies forced many to look to the forests for their livelihood, Government has promoted transmigration as a solution to the problem of unemployment and failure of land reform. At times, the forestlands have been logged over with the available road networks that made it easy for farmers to move in and practice their trade.

In Ecuador, the government encourages fanners to migrate to the forest by granting titles to the forest. Provisions for land titles for plots of 45 to 50 hectares for willing migrants are given provided the lands are developed. The only way to develop the land is agriculture and it necessitates the destruction of forests by burning them down and practising slash-and-burn cultivation.[212]

Many farmers in the tropics still depend on forest trees to restore fertility to the soils that they farm. These people who occupied about 30 million sqauare kilometers live by practicing shifting cultivation. The fallow period ranges from 8 to 12 years in tropical rainforests to 20 to 30 years in drier areas. This is a stable and productive practice if the population density is small and stable. But if the populations keep growing which is the usual case, there is no chance for the forest to regenerate. Wide swatches of otherwise productive forest lands are destroyed to keep up with food production for the growing families and to supply the needs of the nations.

Two-thirds of the upland forests are under unsustainable cultivation and will result in uncontrolled soil erosions unless remedies are undertaken in the form of terraces. Mechanized farming methods are not possile because of the difficult terrain to operate. Furthermore, most of them cannot afford them anyway.

In the Philippines, 55% of the country's total land area is upland forests. About 12 to 20 million indigenous and migrant settlers live inside states owned forestlands. The problem is exacerbated by the large landless families seeking forested areas for livelihood. The presence of logging roads made it easier for them to invade the upland forests.

Cash Crop Agriculture

Timber is one of the most precious commodities in the world. In Amazonia and Indonesia, where timber harvesting is difficult to remove trees from the forest, the farmers resort to burning down the forests and allowing the nutrients from the trees to fertilize the soil. This wasteful practice is adding carbon dioxide into the atmosphere and changes the composition of the air. This is beside the many ecological damages that often result from destruction of the forest.

Sometimes the government abet in the destruction. In Guatemala, the government used to build roads into the forest and then encourage the farmers to move there to grow cash crops such as coffee, cinnamon, cacao, and rubber. The timber that are cut down to make room for these crops are generally burned or left to rot instead of being harvested, compounding die waste of potentially valuable resources. In Honduras, it has been estimated that forests with a commercial timber value of $320 million are squandered annually this way. (Ang Trees, 28)

In countries where governments persist in allowing this practice, loggers should be allowed to harvest the timber before turning over the areas to cash crop plantations. At least, the timber could be used productively to keep off carbon dioxide from the atmosphere. There are actually far more degraded land, those that have been harvested of timber that can be utilized for cash crop plantations.

Intercropping and crop rotations have been replaced with monoculture farming in many parts of the world. These could cause great potential ecological dangers associated with monocropping on the crop and the soil. It is an unfortunate invitation to the growth of weed and insect pests that attack the unchanging crops. This in turn leads to the well-known cycle of increased use of pesticides to control resistant pest populations, followed by more harmful chemicals.

Many islands in the Atlantic and the Caribbean, as well as areas on the American continents, faced severe soil degradation problems in the 18th and 19th centuries as a result of the introduction of large-scale sugar, potato, and tobacco production by European colonizers. The same problem exists in many developing countries today where farmers are producing mainly cash crops for the international market. Any unforseen problem could leave the country susceptible to natural disasters such as blight or insects affecting certain crops or devastating natural calamities.

* * * * *

Commercial agriculture or plantations are usually operated by multinational companies with a ready market back home. Through concession agreements and even outright purchases of land, the companies take over the land with the intention of converting it for planting cash crops. These crops include sugar cane, tobacco, cassava, soybean, oil palm, maize, rubber, pepper, benzoin, nuts, coffee, cocoa, etc. Others are engaged in the planting of tropical fruits such as coconut, banana, pineapple, papaya and other citrus fruits. Dunng the colonial days, the western countries colonized many countries to supply these cash crops for their home consumption.

There are two ways how deforestation is carried out by commercial agriculture. One way is to take over the fertile and best located agriculture valleys from the poor farmers who are engaged in the planting of staple food such as rice, wheat and com. Others are forcibly ejected from the land by the landlords who sell off the land. Other small time farmers are often induced to sell out with tempting offers. This forced them to seek new pasture in the forests to continue their livelihood. Some countries have never been self-sufficient in staple food production as a result because food production for home consumption is neglected for its low price while the cash crops have higher values and available foreign markets.

A more direct way of deforestation is what happened in Indonesia where plantation owners encroached on the forestland to plant oil palm for their international market. In central and south America, the cash crop is soybean, financed by international financial institutions. The experiences of these countries are repeated many times in other countries.

Most cash crops are planted by big landowners with encouragement from the government to export and earn foreign exchange to pay for their foreign debts. These cash crops tend to take up the best land and use crop inputs such as fertilizer, weed-killers and pesticides that are degrading the land and harmful to the workers. Furthermore the pesticides also kill other organisms that are beneficial to mankind.

* * * * *

Cash crops are subjected to pesticides used to control pest infestation. Most of these pesticides are banned in the places of their origins because of their cancerous and other ill effects on human health. Even the use of pesticides is not well regulated and those who are tasked to do the spraying are seldom protected. Monoculture plantations are prone to pest infestation.

Bitter Sugar

The rise of sugar consumption caused deleterious effects on health. Until the 16 century foods were sweetened by using honey or maple syrup and consumption was at a very low level. The development of sugar plantations across the world increased production and consumption. By 1750 sugar intake in Europe and North America had risen from negligible levels to about 1.8 kilos per capita and is now up to 55 kilos.

Sugar can be found in many of the food and drinks we consume daily. It has been implicated in many diseases such as heart disease, diabetes, obesity, candidiasis, hypertension, mental illness, and a litany of other maladies. No wonder it is called one of die worst additives in the world. Substitutes like synthetic sweet such as Nutra Sweet are available that do not destroy the ecosystems.

Sugar is the first widespread tropical monocrop planted and harvested that deforested the forests of South America during colonial times. The Portuguese, after taking control of coastal Brazil in 1530, leveled large tracks of forests, replacing them with sugar plantations. Sugar planting requires highly intensive labor, but indigenous people unwilling submitted to do the work. This gave rise to the use of enslaved labor from Africa to do the work.

By 1600 Dutch entrepreneurs took sugar production techniques from Brazil to their Caribbean colonies. These island ecosystems are even more fragile than continental systems which are partly responsible for the deterioration of the land. Consequently, sugar harvest radically impoverished the vegetation of major Caribbean islands during the early 1600s and 1700s. They were followed by the English planters in Barados and nearby island. Spain followed suit in Cuba in the 1700s where the rich lowland soils of the Mat an/a plains were cleared of both mahogany forest and old grasslands. Cuba became one of the world's biggest producers of sugar - its chief export. When die Americans took over the island in 1898, major investors from Boston and New York built factories to convert the cane into sugar. To feed the refineries, the central were supplied canes from a rapidly expanding acreage under production with newly American-built railroads linking the countryside. By 1930, the transformation of Cuba into an export monocrop landscape was nearly complete with the felling of the last tropical forest. Even Fidel Castro's revolutionary regime after 1959 was unable to diversify Cuban agriculture. Sugar's ability as a cropping system helped assure that more varied vegetation does not return to the island.

The extension of the European control of the Third World agriculture and cultivation of cash crops for export has for centuries affected the forestlands. In the Philippines, during the early Spanish era, about 90% of the country was covered by old-growth forest. Since 1844, sugar has become a leading export crop. When the US colonized the island, most of the sugar were exported to the US at a preferential price. In the late 1980s, the Philippine quota for the US market was reduced due to the production of substitutes such as sugar beet and high fructose com syrup prompting the sugar barons to sell it at the world market at prices below the production cost. As a result, many of the lands lay idle that forced the workers to move upland and clear the forest for planting cash crops.

Wetlands have to be drained and grasslands irrigated for the same purpose.[213]

In Negros Island, where 60% of the sugar were produced, the drop in the world's prices have forced out many workers to move upland, infringing on the rights of the indigenous people. Forests were destroyed for shifting cultivation. From 30% of the total forest cover in 1980 it declined to 5% in 1992. Overall, the Philippines cultivated upland areas increased from 582,000 hectares in 1960 to over 3.9 million hectares in 1987. Soil erosion was estimated at about 122 to 210 tons per hectare annually for newly established pasture compared to less than 2 tons per hectare for land under forest cover.[214]

The development of the sugar plantation resulted in extensive deforestation to provide land for planting sugar cane and fuelwood gathering for sugar processing. The same effect can be found in Brazil as demand for sugar for consumption and as fuel for gasohol increased. (Ang, Trees, 71) The Philippines have the distinction of having over 5,000 people killed in November 1992 during the Oimoc, Leyte deluge as a result of deforestation and the planting of sugarcane. Since the 1950s, the watershed area around Ormoc had been planted to sugarcane which is a poor absorbent of flood water. Only 10% of the mountain range was still forested at the time the tragedy struck. A DENR study points out that had there been adequate forest cover, the flood would not have risen above four feet that overflowed the fragile banks. (PCU, 33) In the same year, another great flood struck the province of Nueva Ecija where less than 12% of the 14,000 hectares of forests remain. Much of the watershed has been converted into sugar plantations.[215]

* * * * *

Haiti is one of the poorest countries in Latin America. When it was colonized by the French in the 1600s, tens of thousands of acres of virgin forests were cut down to make way for sugar cane and in a short time Haiti became the largest sugar producer. To process the sugar canes, sugar mills were constructed and they are run on fuel based on wood. More trees are cut down to fuel the mills even while entire forests were shipped to Europe to make furniture from mahogany and dyes from cam peachy. The rest are turned into charcoal which supply 71% of the energy.[216]

In 1950, some 25% of Haiti was covered with forest. The relentless cutting reduced its forest cover to about 1.4% in 2004. In May 2004, a torrential rain left 700 people dead with another 1,000 missing and presumed dead. Light rains can turn deadly because of the flood caused station.[217]

Coffee and Tea

Many South American countries have coffee as their chief export crop. It has been responsible for widespread forest destructions. The heavy use of pesticide in coffee plantations has resulted in water pollution. The development of coffee plantations in Brazil, the world's number one coffer exporter, from the late 18[*] century wreaked further damage to the land because these were normally planted on deforested slopes, leading to very high rates of soil erosion. By 1900 the subtropical hills of Brazil's Sao Paulo state dominated world coffee production for the international market. Cultivating coffee requires well-drained, rich, and fertile soils. This had by the 1960s, denuded great tracts of the Sao Paulo hills under unsustainable cultivation because of the seemingly unlimited forest available. The forests are gone and the soil has been degraded, New lands from the forests are needed because restoration cost is too expensive for farmers to undertake.

Medical researches have shown that coffee contains 2,500 ingredients with 16 of them cancer-causing agents. One of its ingredients is caffeine, known to have profound effects on fetal development if ingested in large quantities. In one study, spontaneous abortions, stillbirths, and premature births are more frequent in families where the father's caffeine consumption was high. This suggests that caffeine could have some kind of mutagenic effect. Another study of more than two hundred women shows that they have significantly higher birth defects among offspring of heavy coffee drinkers. It also reduces a woman's chances of becoming pregnant. Even decaffeinated coffee may not be safe. Coffee is decaffeinated with a solvent called methylene chloride, a cancer-causing chemical. It has no nutritional value and alternative decaffeination methods are available.

* * * * *

The production of cash crops in Asia began in the 19th century. Tea, originally restricted to China and Japan, has spread quickly to Assam and later Ceylon and India Many tea plantations were established by clearing the forests. In Assam, foresdands once owned by the indigenous inhabitants have continued to diminish over the last century and a half due to the invasion of lowlanders and the establishment of tea plantations. In 1871, 280,000 hectares of foresdands were cleared for tea plantations. By 1900 there were nearly 800 tea estates established and most of the 400,000 workers were hired from outside the area. Between 1930 and 1950, more than 600,000 hectares were taken over by the settlers.

Cutting down the consumption of coffee and tea with the exception of herbal tea will reduce the pressures to plant more land for cash crops. Like tobacco, they displace large tract of forests without any health benefit. Coffee processing causes chronic water pollution while the making of instant coffee is one of the most energy intensive processes used by food manufacturers.

Children should be taught early not to drink coffee, tea, coca and cola. These products come from nutrient-draining crops that could otherwise be used for food production instead. Large scale plantations have forced peasants to move to marginal land where slash-and-bum agricultural practices by the people have resulted in clearing large rainforest.

Soybean Connection

Soybean is a legume containing one of the cheapest and most important edible seed that could provide vegetable protein for millions of people and ingredients for hundreds of chemical products. It has been used as food and as a component of medicine in China for 5,000 years. The US is the number one producer of soybean and 98% of it is used as livestock feed in the form of soya meal Tliis is followed by Brazil and China. (EB, v II, p. 59)

Soybean is traditionally grown in temperate and subtropical regions of the world. It is expanding into the tropical regions as high-yielding tropical soy varieties have been genetically modified for the tropic. Brazil and Argentina continue to increase the area for soybean production at the expense of the forest or as in the case of Argentina at the expense of other agricultural crops.[218]

Since the outbreak of the foot-and-mouth disease in 2001, soybean has become increasingly important as the basic ingredient for cattle feed in Europe and the US, and large volumes of Brazil's soybean production are exported to Europe. In 1940 the land allocated in Brazil for soybean production was only 704 hectares. By 2003, there were 18 million hectares devoted to its production of 50 million tons.[219] The export represents 6% of Brazil's gross domestic products. The Brazilian government estimates that its total soya production will reach 63.6 millions in 2005 with the simultaneous increase in the area of production by 50% in the past four years, from 14 million hectares in 2000 to 21 million hectares in 2004. The WWF estimated that nearly 22 million hectares of forests and savannah land in Latin America could be destroyed by 2020 as a result of soya agriculture.[220]

The cultivation of soybeans in the Amazon has been the root of increased direct deforestation of the cerrado in Brazil where soya production is concentrated, and of increased indirect deforestation of the Amazon through the displacement of land-based activities from the areas taken over by soya. Soya has become the country's biggest farm export, equal to about $10 billion in 2004.[221] As explained by Philip Feamside, "Soybean farms cause some forest clearing directly. But they have a much greater impact on deforestation by consuming cleared land, savanna, and transitional forest, thereby pushing ranchers and slash-and-burn farmers ever deeper into the forests frontier. Soybean farming also provides a key economic and political impetus for new highways and infrastructure projects, which accelerate deforestation by other actors."[222]

The expansion of soya plantations in Brazil is partly the responsibility of Blairo Maggi, the so-called 'King of Soya,' the governor of the province of Mato Grosso as well as die CEO of Grupo Amaggi, the company responsible for die soya business. In his quest to expand and expedite the gathering and delivery of soybean to the market, he proposed the paving of the BR-163, the soon-to-be superhighway linking Mato Grosso to Santarém, major port on the Amazon River. The 1,600 km road would cut through a 10 million hectares swath of land through the region. He was unrepentant about the project saying, "To me, a 40% increase in deforestation doesn't mean anything at all, I don't feel die slightest guilt over what we are doing here. We are talking about an area larger than Europe that has barely been touched, so there is nothing at all to get worried about."[223]

His expansion was made possible through the loans provided by International Finance Corporation (IFC). Two loans were awarded, one in July 2002 and another in 2004 totaling S30 million. The first loan was provided to support the incremental working capital needs of Amaggi such as farmers' advances and inventories of soybeans and by-products. The 2004 loan was for the establishment of additional soybean collection centers and silos and to further help meet its working capital needs.[224]

Even protected parks are being invaded, helped by local politicians up for election. The Iguacu National Park, with an area of 185,000 hectares on the Brazilian side and 55,000 hectares on the Argentina side is a designated UNESCO World Heritage and home to the monumental Iguacu Falls that straddle the Brazilian-Argentina border is being invaded by hundreds of farmers. Illegal roads are built with the aid of local politicians. An existing dirt road used for light traffic and tourism has been widened and a barge system to help vehicle cross a river was installed. A court ordered the intruders out but in January 1998, there was a second invasion. The government is considering evicting the locals by force after receiving reports of heavy trucks carrying agrochemicals going into the park, presumably for the soybean plantation.[225]

* * * * *

Argentina has lost 70% of her 105 million hectares of forest, leaving only 33 million hectares. Most of the northern and central regions are the ones greatly affected by deforestation. A major part of these destructions is attributed to the advance of soybean production that started to be developed 30 years ago. Half of the land was used to plant soybean and in the 1990s, the drop in the international prices forced the farmers to expand the coverage for more soybean production to compensate for the monetary value. Forests were burned as the quickest way to colonize the forest and bulldozers moved in to remove the stumps.

Thousands of hectares of the millenary old forest at El Impenetrable (Chaco) were once logged for decades by logging companies and are now being logged by soybean companies. Public lands covered by Chaco forest are involved, very often the ancestral property of the indigenous peoples. Since December 2003, a new law promoted by the Chaco government made logging in the native forests even easier. Social and environmental organizations have warned that if things go on this way, in ten years time no forest will be left. For this reason they submitted a petition to the local Courts of Justice against law 5285 that the Chaco government passed last December, modifying forest Law 2386. They agreed that the previous law was not a good one, but that the new legislation is even worse. According to the complainants, the law is unconstitutional because the indigenous peoples were never consulted as established in the National Constitution and ILO Convention 169. They also claimed that it will facilitate destruction of the native forest.[226]

The continuous sale of public land is taking the Chaco forest away from whe Wichi, Cuom and Mocovi indigenous peoples. The indigenous communities are losing their territories forever. The disappearance of forests where they used to obtain their food and natural medicine are gone and the number of sick people and deaths is increasing.[227]

Bababa Connection

The banana industry has made some Latin American countries so dependent on it that they are called banana republics. The main tragedy is that forestlands are deliberately cleared for banana plantations, but the monocrop is inviting counterattack from nature. In the early 1920s, the Gros Michel banana was host to two epidemic diseases, Panama Disease and *Sigatoka*, which destroyed whole plantations. The only alternative was to move the plantations every ten years and the only lands available were often cleared from the forests. By the 1930s, large tracts of what had been Caribbean coastal rainforests were virtually deserted, and the companies set up a second generation of clearances on the narrow Pacific lowlands.

After World War II, banana plantations continue to expand at the expense of the lowland forest under pressures from the MNCs. The NMCs, with their huge investment portfolios had managed through threat and intimidation to move their investment from one uncooperative to a cooperative country, forced countries to clear forests for plantations.

Ecuador was a prime example. With cooperation from the Quito government, the MNCs cleared large areas of the Pacific coastal lowlands so that by the 1950s Ecuador was one of the world's major banana exporter, but at great cost to its previously rich forestlands. What makes this practice abhorring is that subsistence foods were often relegated to marginal production, along with the indigent people who grew them. Only the rich investors grew in wealth at the expense of the forests and its inhabitants.

In Central America, especially in Guatemala, Honduras, and Nicaragua, the early 20th century saw large areas of specie-rich rainforests turned into banana plantations. The banana republics created by the United Fruit Company are responsible for much of the tension in regional politics today. TTiis is turn led to further destruction as landless peasants are pushed into the rainforests. Consuming less bananas may reduce the demand for more banana plantations to alleviate the pressure of the forests.

In India, the Modhupur National Park, a public forested area is a protected ecosystem but it did not survive the onslaught of the commercial and industrial plantations. Its 62,000 acre has been reduced to 3,000 acres. Even this small area where a protective 60,000 feet of concrete wall is being erected could not survive. Laborers were hired by plantation owners to cut down the trees inside and converting them into banana pineapple and papaya plantations. They called their acts "social forestry." These destructions are repeated in other places and these plantations are owned by the local Union Council Chairmen.[228]

Banana is susceptible to pests and fungal infections and declining soil fertility. Some of them are incurable such as the fungus that caused Panama Disease. Numerous agrochemicals and fungicides are used in banana production to enhance the success of these crops. Fertilizers are needed to accommodate the declining soil fertility and herbicides to keep the ground free from other vegetation. These chemicals and fungicides are applied 45 to 50 times per growth cycle. Many are these, sprayed by airplanes have great potential of polluting air and water. Some of these agrochemicals are banned in industrialized countries and applied ten times more than required.[229]

The excessive use of agrochemicals and pesticides has contaminated the soil that future use of the land for agriculture or reforestation is almost impossible. Not only that ground and surface water are also contamininated that could have adverse effects on the animal and human lives. During the 1970s and 1980s, 10,000 Costa Rican banana workers were sterilized due to the use of Di Bromo Chloro Propane (DBCP), a nematicide. The chemical was not banned in Costa Rica until 1987, ten years after it was banned in the US. Accidental poisoning, negligence and illiteracy are other causes of poisoning.[230]

* * * * *

Ecolabeling of agricultural products are becoming a vogue in many farms in an attempt to stop deforestation. At present, the largest ecolabeling is the Better Banana Project (BBP) and managed by the Conservation Agricultural Network, a coalition of Latin American conservation groups and the Rainforest Alliance. Farms that wanted to use its trademark, ECO-O.K. must meet strict environmental and social standards. To date, more than 150 farms have been certified in Ecuador, Colombia, Panama and Costa Rica with more than 74,000 acres certified. Their production accounts for about 10% of the bananas produced in Latin America and the Caribbean. In Guatemala and Honduras, dozens more farms are enrolled in the program. They need to make changes to conform with die set standards.[231]

It normally takes 15 months for a farm to meet the standards to win certification. Nine guiding principles to promote environmental sustainability and social equity were adopted. They include zero tolerance for deforestation, conservation of water and soils. Other standards to be met are good wages for the workers, proper safety equipment, improved housing for workers and their families, schools for their children, training for adults and medical care and the rights to organize unions. Pesticides use is steadily reduced and the most dangerous chemicals have been outlawed entirely. Soil conservation and waste management programs are in place. Wildlife is protected and watersheds are reforested. Inspectors also make surprise visits and every farm is audited on an annual basis.[232]

Chiquita Brands International is one of the first companies to apply for ecolabeling. In 1992, it set out to follow the standards with two farms which took two years to get certified. Gradually others farms were transformed to meet the standard until all of Chiquita's 115 company-owned farms in Latin America were certified in 2000.

Cotton

Cotton is one of the most important sources of fiber for the textile and chemical industries. The long fibers from the bolls are used for numerous textile products such as cordage, twine, bags, and industrial thread. The shorter fibers called 1 inters are an important source of pure cellulose for the production of rayon, plastic, explosives, film, paper and other products. The cotton plant is also a v aluable source of oil.

Like most of the other cash crops, cotton plantations have their origin from forested lands. In Central America, clearing land for cotton has contributed to widespread deforestation and severe soil erosion. All parts of the cotton plant are susceptible to pests and diseases. One well known insect pest is the boll weevil which is responsible for most of the damage. The insecticides used are well known for their toxicity to humans also, such as benzene, dieldrin, TEPP, chlordane and toxaphene, to name a few. The heavy applications of these chemicals often lead to soil, water and food contaminations. In India, 50% of all pesticides used in the country are applied to cotton, as in many other countries. Water used for irrigating cotton plantation resulted in massive wastage and destruction at its source as it did to the Aral Sea in Russia.

Numerous chemicals are also used in the processing of cotton lint to textiles. Unless care is taken, they can be a health hazard to workers causing brown lung disease. The chemicals used to bleach and dye fabrics are a major source of water pollution in some countries.

* * * * *

Cotton growing is a well-subsidized industry in the West. This placed many African countries depending on the cotton for their livelihood at great disadvantage. Not only that, many African countries are experiencing deforestation because of this cash crop. Cotton need plenty of water, soil nutrients and open space. After a few years of cultivation, the plantations have to move on because the soil nutrients have been exhausted. Wherever they move, the shade trees have to be cut down because cotton need plenty of sunlight. This has resulted in deforestation amounting to 100,000 hectares annually for a small country like Benin that depends on cotton for 80% of its export revenues.[233]

Oil Palm

Oil palm is native to Central Africa, where millions of natives rely on it as a staple crop. But elsewhere it is planted as a cash crop in large plantations. There are many uses for palm oil which is a vegetable oil derived from it and has many uses such as shampoo, chips, frozen foods and cosmetics.[234]

Between 1990 and 2002 the global-planted oil palm area increased by 43%, mostly in Indonesia and Malaysia. In Indonesia, the total area planted more than tripled from 1.1 to 3.5 million hectares. Plans were underway by the private sector to increase the area under cultivation, According to the Indonesian Palm Oil Research Institute (IOPRI) it is estimated that 3% of all oil palm plantations are established in primary forests and 63% in secondary forests and bush, making up 66% of all currently productive palm oil plantation involving forest conversion.[235]

Since the 1997-2002 monetary crisis in Indonesia, the plantation owners became disinterested in planting oil palm. They are more interested in the timber stands. Around 70% to 80% of the new oil palm projects are allocated in production forests with a high forest stocking which provides a pre-start up bonus in the from of sale proceeds from the timber stands, After taking the timber stand, many companies abandoned the project altogether. In the province of Jambi around 800,000 hectares of forest cleared to set up oil palm plantations were abandoned after the timbers were sold. In Landak district, West Kalimantan some 300, 000 hectares have been neglected.[236]

Between 1997 and 2001, a company in Berau carried on clearcut operations on 9,000 hectares of forest without planting a single palm. It then failed to pay the district government most of the $90 million in taxes owned on the timber it cut down. For all of East Kalimantan, according to the Indonesian daily Kompas, fictitious oil palm schemes caused the state to lose $400 million in 2004.[237]

Some of the oil palm plantations were illegal forest conversion by encroaching outside the designated areas. In Riau, Sumatra, a subsidiary of the Indonesian Indofood Sukses Makmur group, is in the process of clearing a peat-swamp forest outside its concession boundaries. In the Lake Sentarum National Park in West Kalimantan, the oil palm plantation area grew from 3,000 hectares in 1994 to 94,000 hectares in 2000. According to newspaper reports, the total forest area decreased from 528,300 hectares to 323,000 hectares. Other areas affected are Mount Meratus in South Kalimantan, and national parks such as Tanjung Putting, Bukit Puluh and Gunung Leuser National Park.[238]

Death and destruction followed these palm oil plantations. Aside from the forest destruction, loss of biodiversity, collapse of indigenous culture, dozens of people have been killed in land tenure and labor related conflicts while hundreds of deaths can be attributed to the environmental impact. The workers are poorly paid and exposed to danger and unhealthy working practices. Pesticides pose a real health risk to the mostly female workers.[239] The devastating smog caused by the forest fires that ravaged Indonesian forests in 1997 was due to forest clearing by fire to make room for oil palm plantation.[240]

* * * * *

The economic recovery since 2004 has spumed a rush to expand more plantations to growing oil palm trees. Exports from Malaysia and Indonesia, which comprises 84% if the worldwide palm oil production, have brought in $11 billion in export revenues for the two countries. This has raised alarms among environmentalists, fearful that old growth forest where important wildlife habitat for orangutans will be cut down. There are already in existence many illegal loggers operating in the regions and efforts to stamp them out have proven to be futile.[241]

In Malaysia, in 1975, there were only 642,000 hectares devoted to oil palm plantations. By 2004, it has expanded to nearly 4 million hectares, much of which were taken from the primeval forest and home to the endangered orangutan and other wildlife. Doubts have been raised whether it is possible to have sustainable planting and wildlife protection for these new' plantations. This has prompted some environmentalists to brand the oil palm as "cruel oil."[242]

Cocoa

Cocoa is an agricultural product primarily used in the production of chocolate. The primary supplier of cocoa is C6te d'Ivoire (Ivory Coast) which supplies about 40% of the world's need. The cultivation of cocoa started in 1912 to supply the French markets when the country was a colony of France since the 1880s.[243]

Cocoa is planted on large scale plantations and by individual farmers, and has affected heavily the tropical rainforests of the country. From 12 million hectares, the Ivorian humid tropical forest has decreased to some 2.6 million hectares nowadays. The area of cocoa plantations has increased from 500,000 hectares in 1975 to some 2 million hectares. At present these have contributed to nearly 14% of the deforestation in the country.[244]

* * * * *

The case in Ghana is almost similar. After Great Britain colonized the country, timber rights were given to the various chieftains as a way of foresting their loyalties. In turn these rights were promptly sold to loggers or cleared and replaced with cacao plantations. After the country was granted its independence, the government claimed ownership of all forestlands and sold most of them to loggers. Cocoa farmers followed the loggers, settling in the newly cleared areas. Although cacao farmers tried to conserve the forest cover to protect the cocoa trees which grow better under the tree cover, the trees were cut down by the logging companies. This is compounded by bad forest policies and a corrupt forestry department. Government officials often received kickbacks from the loggers by setting extremely low royalties on logged trees and failed to collect most anyway. Booming foreign demand in Asia combined with new timber mills financed by the World Bank plunged the timber sector into crisis.[245]

The farmers never received any compensation for looking after the trees and instead were left with mined fields and even get blamed for the state of the environment. Similar scapegoat happens in Madagascar, Senegal and other countries across Africa. Even the fertilizer companies are blaming the slash-and-bum farmers and offer to sell fertilizers to raise productivity on existing land to stop destruction of forestlands.[246]

Tobacco and Cocaine

Not every crop is good for the health. In fact some plants are bad and restricted while those addictives are banned by governments. Some of these products are tobacco that causes cancer and prohibited drugs such as cocaine and other derivates.

A large portion of forestlands in Central and South America and Asia have been converted into plantations for illicit drugs. Many of these illicit plantations are located inside the jungle to avoid detection. In Peru, the demand for cocaine has led fanners to clear more than 200,000 hectares of virgin forests to plant coca leaves.

The plants of these prohibited drugs use a far greater amount of nutrients than those used for food production. They are usually well-guarded, well-fertilized and cared for. The processing of these leaves into high grade drugs has caused pollution to the sunounding areas. The worldwide drug problem is costing the addicts and governments billion of dollars trying to control them. The money could have been used to improve the living standard of the poor rural people and alleviate the pressure on the forests where some of these drugs are produced.

* * * * *

Cigarette industry is one of the most profitable businesses and one of the most wasteful in terms of human health with no beneficial return for the users. The report by the Center for Disease Control (CDC) released on January 1996 found the direct medical cost of smoking in the US totaled $50 billion nationwide, more than twice the $21 billion in revenues paid for tobacco growing and manufacturing.

Tobacco crop is very demanding of nutrients and rapidly degrades the land that would otherwise be used for tree plantings. It requires eleven times the nitrogen and thirty-six times the phosphorous of a food crop and therefore exhausts the nutncnts in the soil quickly in three to four years. The growing size of tobacco plantations is also reducing the size allocated for food crops. Farmers in some European countries are being subsidized a billion dollars a year just to grow tobacco. The money could be put to better use subsidizing reforestation or tree plantations in developing countries.

In connection with smoking, the use of 10 billion pieces of matches is responsible for the felling of 4 million trees annually. These matches contain sulfur which causes acid raui and zinc oxide, a metallic contaminant. Substitutes like lighters can be used instead.

More than 5.5 trillion cigarettes literally go up in smoke every year and with it all the paper used in cigarette rolls, cartons for packaging, moisture-proof cellophane used to preserve the freshness of cigarette between manufacture and use, and the energy spent in the manufacturing and transportation of these products to the end users.

* * * * *

The introduction of tobacco as major cash crop in many Third World countries has had a devastating impact on the forests because of the amount of fuel required to cure the tobacco leaf. In Tanzania, the wood from one hectare of forest is required to cure the tobacco coming from the size of forest lands. During the 1970s, more than one million m^3 were used. It is estimated that about 12% of all timber cut down is used in the tobacco industry.

In a survey of Thailand's tobacco industry in the 1980s, 44,000 hectares have been devoted to tobacco harvesting. The acreage may seem small but if one were to consider how much firewood is required to cure the tobacco leaves from one hectare of tobacco, the amount of wood could be staggering. It is also estimated that one hectare of forest is required to cure tobacco produced from one hectare of land. (Hurst, 224) The continued growing of tobacco means new forest lands have to be exploited even if the acreage is not increasing in area.

Sustainable Agriculture

Due to the increasing population and the dwindling forestland, it has become imperative for swidden farmers to adopt new innovations in their farming practices. Farmers have started to manage their land by planting fruit trees for long term consumption and food crops for home consumption. Irrigation is being put in place and widely practiced. Rice paddies are erected as new markets are made available to them. They have learned to experiment and discover the most ideal crops for a specific weather and soil conditions. Farmers have learned to rotate crops while maintaining gardens for different plants with their own uses. Landscape is modified to stop erosion by the terracing of steep slopes. Farmers are also planting according to the intraseasonal variations, changing economic circumstances, demand and marketing opportunities. They have learned to adopt scientific information whenever available and feasible. This changing pattern of farming is commonly known as agrodiversity.

Agrodiversity or crop diversity is the systematic use of a number of different species of plants by farmers in the new approach to sustainable agriculture in the face of diminishing and overlapping lands and short and diminishing fallow period. They have learned to make do with the use of choice crops and the diversity of the environment such as land, water, and biota as a whole. Farmers have learned to plant trees through root nodules that can fix nitrogen to assist recovery of soil fertility after cultivation.

The Lawa tribe of northern Thailand grows 120 crops which include crop for food, medicine, or d6cor, and those used for weaving and dyes. At least 20 different rice seeds, each with its unique characteristic were planted according to the different soils, humidity and soil fertility.

The Hanunoo tribesmen in the Philippines have planted 150 species of crops at one time or another. Surrounding fields are planted to asparagus and legumes such as sieva beans, hyacinth string beans, and cowpeas. Toward the center are the tree crops, root crops and other staples. Through centimes of practical agricultural experiments, some indigenous tribes have practiced sustainable agriculture without modem inputs that are destructive to the environment.

Land Reform

Agricultural lands in tropical countries have always been treated like a pawn between government and rich landowners. The few rich people owned most of the best lands while the poor are forced to the mountains to make a living. Most farmers do not have a secure control over the lands owned by the state. This gave rise to insecure tenure that limits the incentives for farmers to make long-term commitments such as trees planting for timber that will ensure income in the future. With titled land, the farmers can obtain credit easily to make investments in their own land such as using the money to purchase fertilizers instead of resorting to slash-and-burn-cultivations.

Land reform plays an important role in the problem of land tenure and tenants rights. It is the key step to break the vicious cycle of poverty, Émphasis should be given by the authorities that only low-lying areas can serve for land reform to stop them from clearing upland forests in the hope of securing ownership. Otherwise more forests may be inadvertently destroyed with the prospect that they may someday own the cleared land. By giving the slash-and-bum farmers land intended to be titled to them in the future to cultivate, forest clearing will be greatly minimized. It will also minimize the use of firewood for heating since the low-lying areas are generally warmer than the forested area.

One problem plaguing the land reform program is the difficulty in supplying enough land to the landless. The sheer number of landless families could mean each family can only own a small plot that can hardly afford a subsistence living. In the Philippines, the per capita arable land has been declining and stood at 0.18 hectare in 1975 to 0.14 hectare in 1992. This was brought about by urbanization, where agricultural lands were converted to urban use. The net effect of this trend is that forestlands will have to be converted to agriculture to keep pace with food production.

* * * * *

Land reform can be given to a community instead of isolated families. When the farmer or community as a whole is given an incentive or goal to accomplish in return for free land, there won't be a lack of candidates, It is an opportunity of a lifetime.

The Gandoca/Manzanilla Wildlife Refuge of Costa Rica created in 1985 was the recipient of a land titling project. The local NGOs helped the farmers by identifying ways to make a living without damaging the forest. In one year, twenty five community nurseries to support reforestation have been set up. More than 1.5 million trees were planted by 1,200 farmers. To facilitate more tree planting, the imposition of a conditional land titling is the requirement that a section be set aside for a successful tree farms. Only lands previously cleared are included in the program.

* * * * *

The problems of poverty and uneven land distribution in rainforest regions should be addressed without delay. On the average, 73% of the households do not own the land they till nor will they be able to do so in the foreseeable future. Landless people are apt to rush to the rainforests and practice swidden agriculture or cut flitches to make ends meet. Land must be made available through land reform instead of promising them boggy ram forestlands unsuitable for agriculture or ranching. In Brazil, 4.5% of the landowners own 81% of the farmlands while 70% of rural households are landless.

In the Philippines, the combination of land concentration and population growth contributed to a large increase in landless workers. From 1975 to 1980, the percentage of landless workers in the agriculture sector grew from 40% to 56%. Over 60% of them were employed in the sugar and coconut farms at less than subsistence wages. A close connection existed between landlessness and upland migration. Between 1980 and 1983, more than 60% of all upland migrants were landless. It has only led to more deforestation. In many places insurgency problems exist in over 80% of the provinces. Giving inexpensive forestlands may be cheaper and easier than sharing some of the vast tracts of valuable land that are available.

Efforts to help communities and small stakeholders share in the benefit of forest products have been a failure. Many of these community-based forest management agreements granted by the DENR are under review for dismal performance mostly due to failure to comply with the terms of the accord. This is partly due to the lack of funds to sustain the poor forest dwellers. They need more sustained outside support that the government cannot afford to grant. An NGO, the Philippine Tropical Forest Conservation Foundation Inc. (PTFCF) hopes to change the situation with an initial P45 million grants to help eleven other NGOs engaged in forest protection and restoration activities.[247]

Agroforestry

Agroforestry is the combination of farming and forestry in one venture. It is an important sector that should be encouraged to promote sustainable development. It is also an effective and direct solution to help stop deforestation on a large scale, due to the large number of people that can be harnessed. Some 40% of the global employment and 50% of the world's assets are associated with these two businesses. Most of the wealth of nations can be found in the soil and the natural resources around and beneath them. It is the primary source of subsistence for the most of the world's inhabitants.

Trees are grown not only for wood but also for food, forage, fertilizer, while providing ecological functions. It is particularly attractive because it offers potential for reducing the forest loss rate to shifting cultivation and other opening of forest margins for more intensive food production, The upland dwellers should be taught the high value of agroforestry and adopt it as part of their livelihood.

It is a practice that has been utilized for many years and is now widely promoted as a land-use approach that yields both wood products and crops. Trees and crops may be grown together on the same tract of land in various patterns and cycles. The trees may be planted around die perimeter of a small farm to protect crops from livestock, provide fuelwood and to serve a windbreak or shelterbelt. They may also be planted in alternate rows of trees and crops until the trees' crown cover the penetration of sunlight. The extensive use of agroforestry will greatly diminish the demand on the forests and provide jobs for the rural people. It can be a year round undertaking providing employment instead of farmers being idle until harvest time.

Agroforestry has been proven to be effective in many undertakings in the tropics. Helping farmers achieve increased intensive crop production on their limited lands reduces the need for them to clear additional forestlands. Woodlots for firewood as part of the project will hopefully take over the role of firewood gathering in the forests.

Integrating multi-purpose trees with agriculture where land is scarce is one of the major challenges of agroforestry. Increase in productivity can result from growing trees that have multiple purposes such as trees that can be planted to contain livestock, act as a windbreaker, produce fruits for consumption, add nutrients to the soil and protect it at the same time. They also provide fuel wood and fodder as well as act as an ecological stabilizer of the environment. Agroforestry can create employment for the rural workers in places where there are only a few employment opportunities.

* * * * *

Agroforestry need not be confined to planting agricultural crops for food or forest trees for fuelwood and even for sale m the future. Small-time livestock raising and animal husbandry have been an important part of agroforestry. In South America, iguana has been raised as a traditional protein source. Although they grow slowly, they are efficient fool converter. Their eggs are prized not only as a source of protein but as a powerful aphrodisiac. In Central America, a mere 15 kilos of beef are produced annually from a hectare of grazing land. By comparison, the same area given to iguanas could produce more than 220 kilos of meat a year without degrading the land.

Beekeeping for honey is very old, dating back to ancient times. Honey was the source of most of the sweets in the early civilizations before sugarjanes were cultivated. At one time it was considered the food of me gods. Beekeeping is an easy venture and not much work need to be done before harvesting.

Bees have played an important role in the pollination of many plants. Without this vital role, our once lush forests would not have been the way they were. Honey harvesting docs not even affect the bees in their ecological functions.

Beekeeping for honey and beeswax is a good potential source of livelihood and income. In the northwestern province of Zambia, some 10,000 beekeepers own about 500,000 hives and produce about 1,000 metric tons of honey and at least 100 tons of beeswax annually. Half or the honey is exported while 80-100 tons is sold on the local markets with the rest used to brew a local beer called mbote. The price of honey is going up as more companies enter the business.[248] While sugar has taken over the role as a sweetener, honey is mostly used in the baking industry because of its special characteristics. It is also better than sugar for our health.

Buttery collection is an important hobby for some collectors because of the different and beautiful designs on their wings. Butterfly farming has great potential because of the well-established market throughout the world. The market was estimated at more than $200 million in 1985.

Butterflies can easily be bred by providing a habitat where they can propagate prolifically. Research has shown that it is impossible to overharvest them because it is virtually impossible to catch all the butterflies in an area. Each species has a preferred food plant for its caterpillars. By planting certain species in small plots in the forest many more butterflies can be raised without affecting the population.

Papua New Guinea is the only tropical country to have a constitution specifying insects as a natural resource and to have a government agency solely dedicated to the insect trade. The Insect Trading and Farming Agency buys insects for export from village collectors all over PNG. Since it was established in 1978, it has exported $250,000 annually.

There is big money in butterfly trading. Some butterflies species are protected under the US Endangered Species Act. When three poachers in the US were captured for commercial trading in butterflies from natural parks and forests in California, the 2,375 specimens recovered were estimated to be valued at $307,642.

* * * * *

Orchard planting is an important part of agroforestry. It is a profitable business venture that has attracted even urban dwellers. Part of the agricultural land used for planting crops can be set aside to plant orchards for its fruits.

In 1983, Balbir Mathur, a naturalized American from India organized Trees for Life to feed the hungry people of the world with fruits from the trees planted. Since then, millions of trees have been planted and millions more of the seedlings were distributed in India. His most ambitious project is a drive calling on the US and the old Soviet Union to join a move to plant 100 million fruit trees in developing countries.

Urban city dwellers with vacant lots or gardens can help case the problem of food shortages through orchard planting. Public lands can also be devoted to orchards. They serve as shade and recreation and when fully mature can supply us with fruits and nuts. For home with ample space for landscape, planting fruit bearing trees can provide families with fruits in the future and help reduce global warming. In Pangasinan, the one-time governor Oscar Orbos once initiated a program to plant 500 mango trees everyday.

* * * * *

Reforestation requires a lot of seedlings and plant nurseries are the ideal site to propagate them. To ensure higher survival rates, sapling instead of seeds are supplanted in the wilds. These are first grown in nurseries located near the forest for easy transportation. This gives rise to a kind of agroforestry business that is much in demand for countries with severe deforestation problems. The rural areas can serve as a good source of plant nurseries to minimize the cost of transporting them to the denuded areas.

Since 1984, the government of Uganda and CARE-USAID have co-sponsored a project which involves planting trees in the nursery farms for fuelwood. A network of small, community managed nurseries was established that became attractive to rural workers and especially women. In three years, the project supported 274 nurseries producing three million seedlings a year. The augmentation of income will reduce pressure on the forest.

* * * * *

The destruction of the forests has not brought prosperity to the Brazilian indigenous people. It continues to be one of the world's largest debtor nations. It has not solved the unemployment and housing problem although it is endowed with rich natural resources that are being destroyed daily. People are still invading the forests seeking fortunes and livelihood. The millions of rubber trees can be tapped by the unemployed without cutting down the trees. For decades the rubber tappers were exploited by the rubber barons and companies that pay low prices for latex and charge them high prices for their supplies. It is time we give the rubber tappers a break by paying a fair price for the natural rubber before they turn to slash-and-bum agriculture to augment their income.

Although rubber can be manufactured synthetically, natural rubber is still important to the transportation industry fhe tires we use for our automobiles contain 20% natural rubber while heavy equipment and aircraft tires must be 100% natural rubber. All in all they still account for a third of the world's needs.

Originally native to South America, the tree *Havea brasiliensis* is is now mostly planted in plantations around Southeast Asia, Liberia and Nigeria. Forests have been decimated to plant rubber trees because of the huge demand caused by the increasing number of automobiles on the road.

There are an estimated 100,000 rubber tappers and 300 million rubber trees scattered through the Amazon and Orinoco River basins. Rubber trees grow up to thirty-nine meters high and ninety centimeters in diameter and live for two hundred years. They are ready for tapping five to seven years after planting and can continue to be tapped for 30 to 40 years. Each tapper can tap only 400 trees a day and at this rate it will give employment for millions of indigenous people without destroying the forest. A typical family needs 200 hectares to survive with an income as rubber tappers.

Hydroponics

In places where the soil is infertile, saline, or harmful due to contamination, planting can be done completely without using soil. This process is called hydroponics cultivation. It is the practice of growing plants with liquid on sand and gravel supplemented with the necessary nutrients. The sand and gravel are used to support the plants at the root, The nutrients are consumed by the plant roots together with the water, oxygen, and the essential mineral nutrients in soluble form. Sometimes the plants are hung in the air.

Operating a small plot can be very expensive, but the cost gradually diminishes as the area enlarges. During the Second World War, the US armed forces often used hydroponics cultivation in growing vegetables because of the infertile and disease-bome soil in the Pacific bases where human feces were used as fertilizer. Today, hydroponics is confined mostly in greenhouses throughout the world for the cultivation of vegetables and flowers. The practice can be extended to planting ings for reforestation projects.

NASA has been experimenting with hydroponics cultivation for its planned space station to provide food and oxygen for the crew. Plants will need sunlight to produce food and oxygen while taking in carbon dioxide from the crew, striking a balance between man and nature in space.

Closely related to hydroponics is aeroponics. In the latter system, the plant roots are suspended in highly oxygenated nutrient solution allowing easy inspection and pruning of roots. The nutrients with oxygen and water are pumped to the chamber enclosure to maximize the growth.

Chapter 6

FUELWOOD

Since man first walked on planet Earth, wood has been the source of energy for cooking and heat. It is still the principal fuel for cooking in Africa, Asia and South America and many parts of the world. It also makes it possible for man to live in some of the closest and remotest regions of the world. In many places, it is free for the picking but in others, it is so scarce that people have to walk for hours just to gather the fuelwood.

It is the primary source of energy for the vast majority of rural households and small-scale traditional industries in developing countries. Demand has been made in mining areas deep inside the forests. Where iron ore is mined and processed, charcoal consumption can be staggering. Wood used for heating in cold climate has been substantial. More than three billion cubic meters are harvested worldwide as fuel; more than half of it in the tropics. It accounts for about 80% in some areas in some developing counties.

Today, half the world's population depends on wood and half of the supply of wood is used as fuelwood w'hile 2 billion are facing firewood shortages.[249] Some wood are turned into charcoal for use in most industrial processes. In 1850 wood accounted for 90% of the US fuel supplies and half the nation's iron today is still produced using charcoal.

The high cost of petroleum products such as natural gas and kerosene for cooking have forced many poor households and small businesses in the rural areas to once more resort to using charcoal or firewood for their energy needs. Haiti, one of the poorest countries in the Americas has become a desert of 28,000 square km as a result of fuelwood gathering and charcoal making. Less than 2% of its forest covers remains. The 8.5 million inhabitants, of which 80% use biomass such as fuelwood and charcoal is expected to wipe out the remaining forests unless some drastc measures are undertaken.[250]

Unabated Demand

Today, no less than two billion people in developing countries derive at least 90% of their energy requirements from fuelwood, while another billion meet at least 56% of their energy needs in this manner. By the middle of this century, there will not be enough firewood for 90% of the tropical inhabitants unless something is done immediately. There is already a large section of society in many tropical countries that lack the resources. In 1988, India is already in dire need of 133 million tons of fuel but only 33 million tons are available. Thailand needs 25 million m³ but only 16 million m³ are available.[251] All these shortfalls can only come from illegal sources which mean deforestation. Part of the solutions adopted is planting firewood plantations. This is only a partial solution to a big problem.

The removal of trees has many disastrous social and ecolgical ramifications, often beyond the boundaries where they are gathered. It many parts of the world, it is the only readily available source of energy. The depiction of the world's oil and gas reserves, and the high cost of oil and other alternative energy sources, guarantees that this demand for wood will not abate in the years ahead.

Wood as fuel is a low density form of energy but nevertheless it is important and may be the only source available for the poor. The demand is expected to continue as the growth in human population is outracing the growth of new trees. An average user in Africa bums as much as a ton of firewood a year and a family of five will consumc all the fuel available on one hectare of woody steppes annually. With over 100 million people depending on wood in the region, as much as 25 million hectares per year are being destroyed, and these areas are potential deserts in the making unless reforestation is started immediately. The results of huge demand and dwindling resource are soaring wood prices, a growing drain on incomes and physical energies spent in gathering in order to satisfy the basic fuel needs.

The situation is worst in semi-arid regions where trees are subject to drought. Africa, which has the highest birthrate in the world, is particularly hard hit on its northern and southern margins. As a whole, African consumption of firewood and charcoal rose from 250 to 502 million m³ from 1970 to 1994 and is expected to increase another 5% by

2010, according to FAO.[252] Ethiopia has most of its forests gone and other African countries have rates of demand for firewood many times the sustainable yield of their forest. Firewood is now so scarce in the Gambia that gathering it takes 360 worn an-days a year per household, Children are often used to gather wood instead of going to school to the detriment of their education.

The processing of agricultural products such as grain drying and food processing, tobacco curing, and rubber production require large amounts of fuelwood. Many other activities that require the use of wood and substitutes are cither not available or too expensive for the rural folks to purchase.

The demand is so acute in some African countries that young trees are being cut down before they are fully matured. With so many people hewing trees for their energy needs faster than they can grow back, there is a need to protect young trees from being cut down. It has been declared illegal to cut young trees for whatever purposes in many areas, Enforcement must be strictly applied. Iliere is a need to start a woodlot plantation even while firewood is still available to guarantee supply in the future and that the trees planted today will have enough time to mature before they are gathered.

Community Woodlots

Community woodlots are the response to the expanding demand for fuelwood and its diminishing supply in many parts of the world, Woodlots are introduced to provide fuelwood, lumber, and other forest products. For convenience and practicality the plantation must be near the community for easy access and security and large enough to meet projected demand on a sustainable basis. Planting fast-growing softwoods can initially take care of immediate demand. The Leucaena or ipil-ipil is one of the fastest growing trees. It can grow up to 15-20 meters in six years and provide 35-50 tons of wood per hectare. Its nitrogen-fixing roots also replenish the soil with nitrogen. Another shrub, Euphorbia can yield 80 tons per hectare even in arid or semi-arid lands. The flowering shrub *Calliandra calothysus* produces dense wood that burns well and is good for cooking. Strong popular support, participation, planning and sharing of benefits are also needed.

Successful community woodlots have been implemented in many regions of the world. More are needed because of the continuing demand.

A largely overlooked alternative is the *Prosopis*, a shrub native to the arid regions of several countries. Some 40 species are used for firewood, fodder and food for the rural people. It can grow up to four meters in one year producing a hard, slow-burning fuel. It thrives without irrigation, is nitrogen fixing and can help enrich the soil. The fine-grained wood can also be used to make furniture, and the pods can produce high protein or high sucrose depending on the species.

* * * * *

Massive planting involving millions of people planting trees in and around their farms and villages throughout the countryside is one economically feasible solution to the rural energy crisis in many parts of the world. The cost to the rural folks would be minimal but the result will be beneficial for all. Even in areas with available firewood for gathering, firewood plantations provide economical and social values and act as guarantee against future shortages. Excess firewood could be sold to other communities. There is no compelling reason to harvest the trees. The longer the trees are allowed to live, the more valuable they are in the long term.

In parts of Africa and Asia where firewood are not gathered for free, fuelwood can be a source of income and employment opportunities. Unemployment plagues many tropical countries. In these countries, forestry-based activities can be a major source of off-farm employment in the rural areas. Many rural, non-wood-based industries such as tobacco, pottery, sugar refining, bakeries often depend on wood for fuel. Local residents can earn income from growing, harvesting, and selling wood to these industries. Often, the survival of industries and jobs depends on the available fuel woods from the local community forestry activities. Investment is small but the return can be enormous and rewarding.

* * * * *

Government support may be necessary in some cases especially when no private entrepreneurs are willing to join in the venture. A successful businessman will need capital, will power, and community cooperation to succeed. Many village households in Changbaek, South Korea had problems gathering firewood after vast areas have been deforested. The deforestation caused flooding and soil erosion that prodded the government to launch the Village Fuelwood Program. The villagers started planting different species of trees for multiple uses. Within five years they planted two million hectares with 235,000 of them allocated for fuelwood in twenty thousand villages. More than three billion seedlings were grown and planted.

In Minas Gerais, Brazil, a private commercial wood energy plantation that extends over more than 200,000 hectares provides the bulk of the energy for the iron and steel industry. Firewood is a cheap and renewable energy source and is readily available in thickly forested areas. But to provide a constant supply for years, especial firewood plantations may be necessary.

In Rondonia, Brazil, another private company is using fuelwood to generate electric power for the city of Ariquemas, which is isolated from the national grid. In the Philippines, which like Brazil is heavily dependent on imported oil, a "dendrothermal" program was launched around 1980 to produce electricity from fuelwood. This program also aimed to stimulate rural income by contracting small farmers to gather fuelwood. It would have provided the farmers with a guaranteed market at reasonable prices. Under the National Food Authority (NFA) 16 dendrothermal projects were lined up. It was envisioned by proponents that the millions of hectares of denuded land could be planted with fast growing ipil-ipil, acacia or gmelina that could be harvested in 2-3 years for burning in turbines to generate electricity for the remote villages. In a few projects, it was realized that there is not enough woody stems to make the projects worked as planned and only two projects were operational. The other problems plaguing the projects were the insurgency problem, lack of funding and the proponents lack of interest after they have collected fat commissions from the purchase of imported and expensive turbines.

The attractiveness of the commercial plantation as an energy source varies considerably from country to country, depending upon the energy options available and the relative long-term costs of different energy sources. One thing for sure is that it is one of the renewable energy resources that will be in demand as long as the planet exists. The only misgiving about burning trees for energy is that the carbon sequestered by the trees will be released back to the atmosphere.

Charcoal

Charcoal making is a waste of energy. Half of the energy is lost from converting wood into charcoal using the primitive method of conversion. In the rural areas where this method is used, charcoal is produced by stacking wood on piles and then covering them with earth, leaving a small opening on the top through which a fire is lighted. The wood is then left to smolder for around 10 days. The hole is then closed, the fire smothered, and the charcoal is ready for collection. It is possible to improve the efficiency of charcoal production using improved charcoal stoves like the Lakech of Ethiopia which increase efficiency by 35%.[253]

Charcoal is used as domestic fuel for heating and mostly for outdoor barbecue cooking. Because of its low sulfur content, it is used to replace coke in the metallurgical processes. Charcoal is also used for making black gunpowder, for carburizing steel in the production of calcium carbide, sodium cyanide, and carbon tetrachloride, and for making are electrodes. It is also used as absorbents for poisonous gases and for the removal of colored impurities in oils and syrups.

Before the advent of coal, charcoal rather than wood was the main fuel throughout the developing world and even today. To extract the iron from the ore, extremely high temperature is required. The most convenient way to produce such temperature is to burn charcoal. (Collins, 45) Charcoal for industrial uses requires many laborers and voluminous amounts of wood. In the 15th century, the iron industry in the Oberpflaz district of Rhineland employed more than 8,000 workers to cut and transport nearly 20,000 tons of wood to produce about 10,000 tons of charcoal annually. At present, the firm Acesita in Brazil uses about 480,000 tons of charcoal a year for steel smelting. More than half of it came from charcoal made by eucalyptus.

In Europe and England, during he same period, charcoal making was chiefly responsible for felling of the trees. In Brabant the forest areas were settled by the Franks in the 6A and 7th centuries and later became the center of charcoal production where large part of the forests were destroyed.

A bauxite mine in Amazonia produced eight million tons of aluminum a year for the Japanese market and came from an estimated 18 billion tons of iron ore from an iron-smelting plant. The iron industry was fueled by cutting down 4 million hectares of rainforest to make charcoal every year.

Another grand project, the Grande Carajas Project will have thirty mines digging for iron ore. It will require 10 million tons of wood from the forests for charcoal to produce the pig iron. The price tag of the project is $62 billion.

Charcoal production is an integral part of the process of clearing forests for agriculture. The best candidates for making charcoal are the unwanted and so-called "useless" species that are not in demand. They can be cut down as a way of thinning the forest for the benefit of the hardwood species in demand.

Settlers support themselves during the first season by producing and selling charcoal from the trees they cleared. There is a need to use alternatives to charcoal to minimize demand for wood from the forest, Substitute raw materials such as animal bones, com cobs, rice hulls, and other biomass can be used.

* * * * *

The presence of convenient transportation such as railways through forested areas can contribute to deforestation. When a railway was constructed in the remote northeast region of Thailand, it opened up the forest of timber harvesting. First, large quantities of timber where cut down to construct the railway. Then the forests were intruded by people who go into business with the forest products supplying the market. The forest products such as timber, wildlife, and charcoal were traded on an increasing scale. At one time, the villagers were producing five railcar loads of charcoal for Bangkok each day. (Hurst, 232-233)

Other activities that required huge amounts of wood were set up in a short time. They include housing projects, sawmills to process the wood into lumber, tobacco plantations requiring wood for curing, and plantations for cash crops. (Ibid, 233)

Biomass

Oils are made up of hydrocarbons and so are many plants. It should not come as a surprise that some trees and plants can provide us with fuel energy like those coming from coal natural gas and oil. These underground fuels were formed from decaying plants about 300 million years ago through solar energy by photosynthesis. These are not renewable but trees are renewable and inexhaustible if we only learn how to take care of them. The raw materials for biomass include maize, sweet sorghum, beet, potato, cassava, molasses, etc. But the most ideal are those coming from the trees. In fact, half of the energy needs of the developing countries came dircctly from firewood.

The high cost of petroleum has led to attempts to "grow" gasoline. There are at present three ways of converting biomass into fuels. The first method is called biomethanation which produces biogas, fuel composed of methane and carbon dioxide. The second method is fermentation to produce liquid fuel in the form of an alcohol called ethanol. This is mixed with regular gasoline at about 20% to reduce consumption of imported oil and is becoming widely popular today. The third method is growing certain plants and converting them into fuel by a process known as pyrolysis or destructive distillation. This method utilizes thermal decomposition of carbonaceous materials in a closed container and heated at high temperatures to produce hydrocarbons in the form of gases, solids and liquids that are collected. (Myers, 248-249)

One suitable plant species is the legume ipil-ipil, a native of Central America but has been supplanted in many countries and is widely grown in the Philippines. The National Electrification Administration (NEA) has launched a fuel-from-wood program in 1984 precisely to harness. ipil-ipil with the hope of saving $30 million per year in oil import bills. Under an ideal condition, a 12,000-hectares plantation can produce the equivalent of one million barrel of oil a year. It is an attractive species because it grows extremely fast. There are actually many more uses for this versatile plant such as forage and industrial and commercial uses. (Myers, 252) One pioneer project in Pangasinan encountered so many problems such as lack of funds and political instability coupled with the insurgency problem forced the project to shut down.

An experimental ipil-ipil plantation in Hawaii was harvested after four years when the trees reached about 12 cm in diameter. Giant mowing machines chopped off the trees at a height of about 15 cm above the ground level so that the stump can regenerate by coppicing. The foliage is mechanically sucked out of the chips and dried for use as animal feed. The harvested materials of about 250 tons of wood per hectare are fed into boilers to produce about 18 million kwh of electricity. This is equivalent to about 18,000 barrels of oil or diesel fuel worth $80,000 at the price of $50 per barrel. (Ibid, 253)

Another way of "growing" gasoline is done by growing plants that secrete latex, an emulsion of the hydrocarbons and water. One well-known latex is rubber. There are about 30,000 species of plants that produce latex and some 5,000 promising species are from the family of *Euphorbia* that are rich in hydrocarbon materials. (Myers, 256) Experiments have shown that one hectare plot can produce as much as 14,000 liters of oil per year at a cost of $20 per barrel (1995). The Amazon's *Copaifera Langsdorfia* is a rapid growing tree with a unique sap that is so similar to diesel fuel it can be used directly in truck engines. (Collins, 30) The hydrocarbon can be tapped in the same manner as rubber being tapped for latex through its bark without cutting down the tree. A single-cap bore tapping can yield between 10 and 20 liters of hydrocarbon fluid within two hours. The yield may be small but through selective breeding and genetic manipulation, the yield can be increased several folds. (Myers, 257)

Another plant that merits attention is the guayule rubber that is estimated to produce 6,000 kg/ha latex or an equivalent o(10 barrels of oil per hectare. The Euphorbia lathyris is said to produce ten times more latex than guayule or 100 barrels per hectare.[254]

During the Second World War, the Japanese were using a certain "petroleum nut tree" in the Philippines for fuel for their tanks. The tree yields a highly volatile oil and is ideal for household use. A mere half-dozen trees can produce 300 liters of oil annually. The oil contains hydrocarbons of a type rarely found in nature, and is sometimes so flammable that freshly picked nuts can be lighted with a match. The tree can also thrive in secondary and disturbed forests and ideal for the Philippines where most of the forests have been disturbed. (Ibid, 258) The petroleum nut is locally known as apisang, abkol, abkel, and langis in Benguet; dael and dingo in Mountain Province and sagaga in Abra. They are also found in the Bicol provinces, Palawan, Mindoro, Nueva Ecija and Laguna provinces.[255]

* * * * *

Biomasses are plant materials that can be converted into energy. It can be converted to methane, methanol, or gasoline at a fraction of the current cost of oil, coal, or nuclear, according to Jack Herer, a long time hemp activist. One of the promising plants is hemp. This plant is illegal in some places because of its connection with marijuana. In his book, *The Emperor Wears No Clothes*, he wrote, "Hemp stems are 80% hurds (pulp byproduct after the hemp fiber is removed from the plant.) Hemp hurds are 77% cellulose - a primary chemical feed stock (industrial raw material) used in the production of chemicals, plastics and fibers... an acre of full-grown hemp plants can provide from 50 to 100 times the cellulose found in cornstalks, kenaf or sugar cane."[256]

According to his research, only 6% of the US acreage planted to hemp crops would provide all of American's gas and oil energy needs. Each acre of hemp would yield 1,000 gallons of methanol. Fuels from hemp, along with the recycling of paper, etc. would be enough to run America virtually without oil.[257]

Industrial hemp harvesting is allowed under Canadian laws but farmers are required to undergo the necessary criminal record check before they are given license to grow the alternative crop for its seed. The farmer is required to submit his field's global position system co-ordinates so it could be inspected at any time. The hemp is also tested for delta 9 tetrahydrocannabinol (THC) levels by Health Canada. THC is the ingredient in cannabis that causes psychotropic activity. Industrial hemp cannot exceed 0.3 milligrams of THC.[258]

There are plenty of grasses that can be harnessed to produce electricity. One of these is the switchgrass, a perennial warm-season grass native to the prairie hills of southern Iowa and northern Missouri. Ground switchgrass can be burned in a coal-firing energy facility, displacing a small amount of coal used. It could also be used to produce ethanol.[259]

Another grass called Miscanthus is showing signs as a potential energy source. Like switchgrass, the crop can be mixed with coal and burned to generate electricity. It is a renewable source and therefore the net effect on atmosphheric CO_2 is zero.[260]

* * * * *

Probably the most useful energy sources that can be gathered from plant wastes left behind from the residues of cash crop milling. They include rice husk from rice milling, bagasse from sugarcane, coconut husk and shell from the coconut, etc. It was estimated that in 1996, biomass consumption for energy accounted for 72 million barrels of oil equivalent.

The disposal of rice hulls has been a perennial problem because of excesses. There were plans to use rice hull coming from the rice mills for generating heat and electricity. Three power plants were under construction: one in Bulacan for a 40 MW plant developed by Cypress Energy, a US company and two units by the Philippine National Oil Company located in Cabanatuan and Aurora, Isabela each with a 2 MW capacity.

Bagasse is the fibrous residue left over after the juice has been extracted from the sugarcane. It has been used as a fuel for cogeneration to produce electricity and heat for the industry. At present, there are about 39 sugar mills operating in the country. They are mostly located in Negros and each mill can generate an average of 4,600 tons of sugarcane, Most of these wastes are disposed by incinerator. Improvement and construction of new boilers can generate an estimated additional 100 MW for sale to the private sector.

Animal Dung

Loss of tree cover can drastically reduce the land's capacity to support life due to loss of soil fertility. In India, Pakistan, Bangladesh, and Nepal, cow dung whose energy is mostly methane has been used as substitute fuel due to firewood scarcity. Cow dung is hand molded into pyramids and left to dry in the sun. Every year 400 million tons of animal dung were used in Asia, Middle East and Africa as fuel, robbing the soil of fertility and reducing the grain harvest by about 20 million tons, enough to feed 100 million people. This is a serious matter for many Third World farmers who cannot afford to buy fertilizers. It is also practiced in the treeless Andean valleys and slopes of Bolivia and Peru, where the dung of the llamas has been the chief fuel in some areas since the days of the Incas.

Methane is a greenhouse gas whose molecule is 25 times more effective in reflecting sunlight than carbon dioxide. It would be ideal therefore to bum off the methane which is an inexhaustible energy that is often allowed to evaporate into the atmosphere. Burning the sludge left behind is much better than manure when composed and used as fertilizer.

The process of biogastification has been in use as far back as the 1910s in China, and much attention has been given to this technology for producing fuel for cooking. For decades, China has promoted a rural biogas program employing concrete digesters that convert animal and human waste sludge for fertilizer and as a methane-rich gas for cooking Some five million digesters were in operation in 1989.

Bio-Gas of Colorado, Inc. has built a manure-to-methane facility that converts one ton of manure from 75 to 100 heads of cattle daily to 7,000 cubic feet of natural gas. Preliminary investigation has shown that approximately 30 million cubic feet of methane daily can be produced from feedlot waste throughout California. Other utility firms are also looking into this source of energy for cooking and heating use.

* * * * *

When forests are denuded of trees, it is a matter of time before all the nutrients are lost to soil erosion. Another solution is to use chicken manure as a fertilizer substitute for cow dung. It has low heating value and therefore cannot be used as fuel for burning. Chicken waste contains the vital nutrients of nitrogen, phosphorous and potassium, all essential to tree growth. It also contains boron, iron, zinc, and molybdenum. Each chicken can produce two kilos of manure each year.

Another substitute for fertilizer is pig mature. In a single year, an average pig generates 300 kilos of manure, enough fertilizer to increase grain output by 100 to 150 kilograms. The output of 20 to 30 swine would be equal to that of one ton of ammonium sulfate.

Cooking

The main source of energy for the rural people is firewood. This makes it important to have a working knowledge of fuelwood in order to maximize its use. Pound for pound every species of wood produces about the same amount of heat. Hardwoods are denser and therefore contain more heat value because they are slow to bum. Softwoods on the other hand burn fast and hot and are often used to banish morning chill. They are used primarily as a kindling fuel to start off the fire. Easy to chop up, softwoods are great for warming up the place but they do not produce long-lasting energy needed for cooking.

More than determining the kind of fuelwood to use, wood seasoning is probably more important. A freshly cut wood contains about 25% to 50% water. These woods are difficult to light, bum poorly and tend to smoke and hiss when burned. The white smoke produced is largely steam from the boiled water. For each kilo of water evaporated from the wood, more than 2,300 BTUs is lost.

The process of seasoning is done by the sun and the air. The sun's heat provides the energy needed to evaporate the moisture while the wind carries the moisture away. Stacking the wood for more efficient seasoning can reduce the time required. Seasoning or drying usually takes 6 to 18 months, and it could be improved by splitting the wood to smaller pieces. Wood sacking is also important to minimize the flow of air within the pile of wood.

* * * * *

Cooking is a necessary part of human existence. In die rural areas the traditional three-stone cooking is still much in use. With only 6% energy conversion rate, it is out of place in this age of diminishing firewood. With growing demand and difficulties in gathering firewood in many places, it has become necessary to maximize the use of the available firewood. A more efficient use of cookstove is necessary to minimize wastage.

A cookstove is a device located in the kitchen or outside the home where fuel is burnt for cooking purposes. The cooking of food indoors using biomass or wood often leads to excessive levels of indoor air pollution. Women and children are mostly affected. The ordinary cookstoves have to be improved if the biomass burning efficiency is to increase. Improved cookstoves deserve special consideration because the use of efficient stoves can achieve significant savings of fuelwood and charcoal. Cookstoves can reduce injuries from bums, which are widespread among small children, and reduces the number of lung, eye and ear ailments associated with excessive smoking in the living room. Other ailments include acute respiratory infections, chest pains headaches, giddiness. Smoke in the home from cooking on wood, dung and crop waste kills nearly 1.6 to 5 million children.[261] Studies in China found that smoke was a strong risk factor for lung cancer among non-smoking women. In Gambia, it was found that girls aged under five had six times higher risk of lung cancer.[262] Traditional cooking in the open air is a waste of fuelwood.

The latest cookstove in use in Kenya and neighboring countries has an efficiency of 25 to 40%. It is made of metal with ceramic liner to reduce heat loss. Called the Jiko, it can save up to 600 kilos of fuelwood a year. Another benefit comes from the reduced exposure to particulates from smoke that is often 20 times the level that WHO considers a serious health risk. Almost one million households now use it instead of the traditional metal stove with 10 to 20% efficiency.[263]

The cost of the ceramic Jiko is about $5 and beyond the affordability of many poor families. A cheaper version has been developed called *Maendeleo*. It borrows the insulating element from the ceramic *Jiko* without the metal outer covering. The ceramic liner is set down in the middle of the open fireplace; it is then reinforced with mud and stones. A pot placed atop the stove heats almost as quickly as one on a Kenya ceramic *Jiko*. Indoor smoke is reduced considerably through more efficient combustion. The stove is usually placed near a wall of the hut so that smoke can climb along the wall and exit easily.[264]

In Nepal where 80% of the energy comes from firewood, the Improved Cookstove (ICS) is much in use. It is made of local materials and do not need any change in cooking patterns. It is made of 3-part mud/earth, 2-part straw/husk and I-part animal dung. The whole structure is plastered smooth with the same mud mortar. ICS has two fire openings for cooking pots, one behind the other. There is no need to blow the fire. It utilizes the heat generated by burning fuelwood, more by the deflection of the flames and heated air inside it which travel to the second opening with the help of an in-built baffle located just below the second opening, before the hot air exits out of the chimney, which is made of unbumt clay bricks that are abundant in the village. The iron plates are fitted on the potholes for pots. The potholes are round in shape, and the pot bottom fits tight on them. It can be made in different sizes and capacities to suit the family size and the pot size. It can have one or more openings for pots/pans.[265]

There are several advantages such as 30-35% saving in fuelwood. They are also easy to make and operate, produce no smoke in the kitchen, cause less soot, and lessen the chances of household fire or children getting burned.[266]

A new stove designed by Bemabe Paita for the IRRI is widely used in Burma. More than 15,000 have been sold there since the stove became available. It is fueled by rice hulls, an abundant waste from rice milling. Called the *Ipa-Qalan*, it heats efficiently and produces little smoke. The stove could reduce pressure on forests in the amount of at least two tons of wood a year for a family of six. This can translate to about one hectare of forest saved from fuelwood gathered annually. Like most Asian countries where people are rice-eaters, it could mean millions of hectares of forests that can be saved from the axemen.

A program of public education on the many ways of saving energy in the rural areas can help protect the trees. Whatever the success of reforestation projects have achieved, an alternative energy source for wood can also contribute greatly to a solution of the firewood problem, A shift from wood-burning stoves to those running on natural gas. coal or electricity has indeed been the dominant trend for the past decades and has greatly reduced the use of wood for cooking.

* * * * *

Solar energy is particularly interesting and has many uses especially in tropical countries because of the year round sunlight available. Solar dryers for agricultural products such as grain, meat, fish, and tobacco have proven to be cost effective substitutes for wood fuel. The use of wood in one fishing center in the Sahel region of Africa for drying 4,000 tons of fish consumes 130,000 tons of wood every year. Deforestation in many areas extends to 100 kilometers around.

Therefore solar energy is a good alternative to firewood. The solar box cookers produce no smoke and no pollution. It can be used to pasteurize drinking water by heating water to 65° C for six minutes. It could also save millions of hours for women and children gathering wood for fuel. At least half a million solar box cookers are already in use mostly in China and India. It is also easy to make and simple enough for a 10-year old to build without tools in less than an hour.[267]

In Kenya, Dr. David Kammen of Princeton University under the sponsorship of UNESCO has examined windmills and solar power to help in reducing firewood as the main source of energy. His invention was a solar oven using direct sunlight. A typical oven incorporates walls with a reflective coating such as aluminum foil and a metal floor plate to absorb sunlight The energy is then re-radiated within the box as infrared heat, which does not escape because it is blocked by the glass. Pots on the bottom metal plate can heat water or food to more than 300 degrees in under an hour. The ovens are mostly used for crackpot-style cooking. The cost of each unit is about $20 to $40 and too high for most households.[268] More than 100 countries around the world use ovens in a diverse range of styles.

Chapter 7

CATTLE RAISING

Livestock are important sources of meat and milk and cattle are the most important of all livestock. Cattle alone supplies half of the world's meat and 95% of the world's milk while their hides produced 80% of the leather used for the production of shoes, bags and other leather products. Today, there are over 1.3 billion of them, grazing on 24% of the land and consuming enough grains that could have fed millions of starving people.

Livestock are overpopulated and number about two billion heads today, They are growing faster than the human population and are diverting and degrading precious resources such as fertile land that could be used to grow grains for human consumption.

In order to supply the demand for livestock especially beef in the world market, vast areas of forestlands have been converted into pasture. The process is still undergoing despite the knowledge that it is destroying the natural ecosystem of the place. The result is that only a few capitalists are benefiting from these ventures to the detriment of the indigenous people who live in and around the areas. Many of these projects are funded by the World Bank and international financial institutions, sometimes in clear violation of its forest policy. When big corporations and institutions are involved, the forests are at their mercy.

One of these corporations is the IFC extending a $300 million loan to Bertin of Brazil for cattle raising. It was a violation of its own policy, the Natural Habitats Policy (OP 4.04) where one of its provisions is "The IFC does not support projects that, in the IFC's opinion, involve the significant conversion or degradation of critical habitats." When it extended the loan, it claimed in its own opinion that the soya expansion projects it has financed and the cattle ranching project it is proposing to finance do not involve the "significant conversion of these critical habitats. Yet time and again these activities have proven to be disastrous to the ecosystem of the fragile rainforest."[269]

Cattle Ranching

In spite of their usefulness as food and raw materials, their large numbers have proven to be disastrous to the environment by the way they are being raised. Cattle ranching have many similarities to shifting cultivation. It is sustainable only for a few years and has to move on to allow the land to fallow before the land can be productive again. Deforestation caused by cattle ranching is mostly confined to the Brazilian Amazon and in Central America. The reason is the demand for beef by the rich countries in the developed world, especially North America, Europe and Japan. Many in the developing countries are also finding a taste for beef, driving up the likelihood of destruction of the tropical forests. The high cost of beef production in the developed world compels them to look elsewhere for cheaper means of producing beef.

In Central America, the amount of tropical forest converted into pasture for cattle ranching doubled in twenty-five years from 1950 to 1975. Once converted, it stays that way for several years before it becomes unproductive and is abandoned to nature, migration or development. Many of these large scale cattle ranching are financed by the Inter-American Development Bank, the World Bank, and the UN Development Program.[270]

During the eighties, two factors led to the increased exports of beef from the tropical region of Latin America with the consequent aftermath of accelerated deforestation of the Amazon. On one hand, increased consumption of beef in the countries of the north, particularly for fast food chains in the US, and on the other, lower prices of land and labor in the tropical countries of Latin America, made the final product cheaper. As an example in 1978 the price of a kilo of beef imported from Latin America averaged $1.47 compared to $3.3 a kilo of beef produce in the US.[271]

In the years 1993 and 1994, the US imported over 200 million pounds of fresh and frozen beef from Central American countries. Today, it has grown to 300 million pounds annually from Central America alone.[272] Two-thirds of their rainforests have been cleared for raising cattle precisely to meet the demand of the US food industry. At present, there is no w ay to ascertain the origin of the beef once it is inspected by the US Department of Agriculture (USDA) inspectors. It is not labeled.[273]

* * * * *

The relationship between cattle ranching and deforestation was called the "Hamburger Connection." Brazil was not part of this connection, but it did not take long for Brazil to cash in on this venture. By far. most of the cattle ranching are done in the Brazilian Amazon where 80% of the land has been cleared not for timber but for cattle ranches.[2'4] Instead of harvesting the timber, the easy way to clear the huge tracks of forests is to burn them down. Between 1966 and 1978, 80,000 km^2 of the Amazon forests in Brazil were converted into 336 cattle ranches to support six million heads of cattle under the auspices of the Superintendency for Development of Amazonia (SUDAM). Hi ere are also some 20,000 smaller ranches established throughout the Amazon and the likelihood of conversion is expected as demands continue to rise.

During the 1900s, deforestation accelerated making Brazil one of the biggest producers of beef for the international market. Between 1990 and 2001 the demand of Europe's processed meat unports from Brazil rose from 40 to 74%. Russia and the Middle East have also joined in meeting the growing demand. In 1995, Brazil exported less than $500 million and this jumped to $1.5 billion by 2003, according to data from the USDA. Between 1997 and 2003, there was a fivefold increase, from 232,000 to nearly 1.2 million metric tons.[276] The number of cattle more than doubled from 26 million in 1990 to 57 million in 2002 and 164 million in 2004. The IFC has been very recently involved directly both in the expansion of soya and cattle ranching in Brazil.[277]

There are several reasons for the increase in demand of Brazilian beef. Some of the reasons are the devaluation ol the Brazilian currency, the fear of importing beef from countries afflicted by mad cow disease, foot-and-mouth disease and possibly the fear of avian flu forcing people to to beef.[278]

From the 41.5 million hectares lost in 1990, it has since increased to 58.7 million hectares by 2000. The loss is expected to increase as there is a new demand for another product - soybeans for the international market.[279] The total area devoted to soybean cultivation in 2002 was only 4.9 million hectares and most of them are planted in once deforested areas of Mato Grosso and little are newly cleared forestland. The overwhelming majority of the forest areas lost in the Brazilian Amazon eventually became pasture. According to the most recent census available, the area of land devoted to crops in 1995-96 amounted to 5,608,000 hectares while the figure for pasture was 33,579,000 or a ratio of 1:6 in favor of pasture.[280]

Brazil supported the role of cattle ranching in the hope of developing and boosting the economy of the country and pay off its huge debts. As early as 1966, owners of large cattle ranches were given long-term loans, tax credits to cover investments, tax write-offs, tax holidays, and 75% subsidies. Unfortunately, cattle ranchers took advantage of the generosity of the government without making deliveries. Only 9% of the projected output was delivered and the ranches were used as tax shelter rather than boosting the economy. The government has since stopped supporting new cattle ranches, but continued to subsidize existing ranches and costing the government more than $2.5 billion in lost income.[281]

* * * * *

The Tehuantepec Isthmus of Mexico is home to one of the most megabiodiverse places in the world. It is also the only natural bridge between tropical subhumid and humid forests of the Pacific and the Gulf of Mexico coasts where water is accessible and plentiful.

The government had the area and its surrounding opened up for conversion into pasture to raise cattle for export. Nearly half a million hectares of medium and high-altitude rainforests in the Tuxtlas-Acayucan-los-Choapos zone was also totally transformed into pastures for large cattle ranches. With additional funding from the World Bank, in less than four years between 1974 and 1978, 200,000 hectares of high altitude forest were cut. This has resulted in the marginalization of large indigenous and campesino populations.[282]

Once the region was opened up, further developments were in the offing. Other megaprojects include the construction of four-lane highway and two-way railroad system for the bullet train that will transport merchandise in containers. A strip of "maquiladoras" was proposed to transport raw materials from logging and mining. Plans were underway for converting the forests into monoculture agroforestry plantations by planting eucalyptus, sorghum, etc. for the international market.[283]

Hamburger Connection

Most of the beef imported from South America end up as hamburger for the consumers in the US. The price of one quarter pounder in the Philippines costs a little more than a dollar and twice that much in the US. But the real cost to the environment is more difficult to quantify. However, one estimate puts the destruction of McDonald's Quarter Pounder at 55 square feet of rainforest. This small plot of land contains an average of one giant tree, 50 smaller trees, 20-30 different tree species and over 100 species of insects, as well as birds, mammals, and reptiles.[284] Other estimates put the cost of destruction of about five square meters of forest lands whose trees would be releasing about 200 kilos of carbon into the atmosphere. Each cattle raised in the field releases methane to the atmosphere that adds to the greenhouse effect. There is also the possible loss of genetic stock and genn plasm and biodiversity.

Whether in the factory or bred in the ranch farm, cattle are subjected to unusual amounts of antibiotics, hormones, pesticides and other unhealthy additives. The meat and dairy industries not only feed us deceptive, false, and misleading nutritional information, they also feed us with four times more of these additives that we consumed in 1960. Animal meat carries high concentration of toxic chemicals. (Ang, Trees, 86)

A study made by the US Food and Drug Administration (FDA) found that fast food hamburgers, including buns, condiments, lettuce, and tomatoes contain 113 different pesticides residues, representing fourteen different pesticides formulations. Some of these pesticides detected are BHC, DDT, dieldrin, heptachlor, lindane, parathion, etc. They are also found in beef frankfurters. Ground beef is also saturated with pesticides. Eighty-two industrial chemicals and pesticide residues were also detected, representing eleven formulations. Most of these chemicals are carcinogenic. (Ibid)

* * * * *

One of the hard-hitting organizations, the Rainforest Action Network (RAN) launched a nationwide boycott of Burger King in 1985 to demand that it stop importing cheap beef from tropical rainforest countries. After two years of persistent boycott, Burger King stopped the importation after suffering a business loss of 12%. It canceled thirty-five million dollars worth of beef contracts and agreed to stop beef importation from the rainforest.[285]

However, we must be wary of claimants that they are no longer buying beef from tropical countries until such claims can be verified. In some cases, cattle raised in a tropical country are imported live to the US and slaughtered there. This allows hamburger chains and other meat processors to claim they are using American beef. Only a total ban on imported cattle and beef will ensure that cattle ranching is reduced enormously. The people of the tropical countries need the protein more than overweight people of the developed countries.

* * * * *

A kilo of beef provides us with 1,100 calories but it uses 44,000 calories of fossil fuels to produce the grains used in feeding them. Corn alone uses 40% of all the fertilizers used in the US. The same kilo of beef uses 5,500 gallons of water. Half of all the water used in the US has been for growing grains and used for livestock production. Water sources from the underground aquifers are diminishing and are not being replenished quickly by rainfall.

Far more controversial and dangerous to human health is the use of antibiotics and hormones in raising cattle. Hormones speed growth and produce leaner meat, earning additional income for the farmers. These hormones often contain estrogen and androgens that can be cancerous to humans. One synthetic hormone, diethylstilbestrol (DES) has been outlawed, but farmers are still using them illegally.

Other questionable drugs that are potential human carcinogens include ipronidazole, cabadox, and dimetridazole. In fact, more than 90% of the nearly 30,000 animal drugs now in use have not been approved by the government.

* * * * *

At present about a quarter of the earth's surface is used for livestock grazing while only 11% is devoted for food production. The reverse could mean more than twice the grain to feed the hungry millions. The cost of a kilo of cattle for beef requires about 8-16 kilos of grain. Where 22,000 kilos of potatoes can be produced on one hectare of land, only 185 kilos of beef can be produced from the same size area. This is wasteful practice in the face of millions of hungry people around the world.

More than 50% of the current tropical rainforest destruction in South America is directly linked to livestock raising especially cattle. Virtually all of the imported beef used in the US is "lean" (grass fed) beef. Because of this beef lacks the "marbling" preferred by American consumers, it is rarely used for steaks or roasts. Instead it is used to manufacture frankfurters, sausages, canned stews and soups, frozen dinners and pet and baby foods. However, its use for hamburgers and ground beef accounts for 25% of all beef consumed. If we continue to destroy the forests in these biodiverse regions at the present rate, there may not be any forest left standing and up to 500,000 plant and animal species will become extinct.

Greenhouse Gases

In producing the feeds for cattle, vast amount of energy' is used. Whatever cash crops such as corn, soybean, oat, wheat, sorghum are produced, they produce a lot of agricultural wastes that are often burned, Every year, the burning of these biomasses and grasslands emits millions of tons of carbon into the atmosphere. Their production is also linked to the greatest soil erosion in most countries than any other crops. In some areas in the US, the topsoil losses are greater than during the Dust Bowl.

In the West where agriculture is highly mechanized, a sizable amount of fossil fuel is burned to run these farms. Unfortunately, these grains are not used to feed people but livestock. The US devoted 70% of their gain production as livestock feed. It takes about a gallon of gasoline to produce a pound of grain-fed beef in the US. Aside from the fossil fuels, there are the fertilizers needed that also emit the greenhouse gas nitrous oxide. Nitrous oxide released from fertilizer and other sources accounts for 6% of the global warming effect. (Rifkin, 225)

Besides deforestation, cattle are also helping in the global warming by emitting methane from their guts. Methane molecule is able to trap 20 to 25 times more heat from the sun than each molecule of CO_2 and can exacerbate the global warming now besieging the world. More than 500 million tons of methane are released to the atmosphere every year for which 60 million come from the cattle. Methane is responsible for about 18% of the global warming. (Ibid, 225-226)

The burning of forests, grasslands, and agricultural waste worldwide released an additional 50 to 100 million tons of methane into the atmosphere. Even more methane is released by the growing numbers of termites that feed on the felled timber of the tropical rain forests once they are razed for grazing. Live trees produce substances such as alkaloids and terpenes that help check the growth of the termite populations. When the trees are cut down, the termites can feed on dead wood chips without getting killed. This has resulted in increases of termites by a factor of ten in cleared forests. The termite population is suspected of contributing additional millions of tons of methane to the atmosphere. (Ibid)

Chapter 8

FOREST FIRES

Forest fires contribute significantly to forest denudation around the world. It is not only a widespread problem but it is accelerating. Fires have altered the face of the land most profoundly and extensively in Africa, Amazon, Indonesia and in the temperate zones. At least a third of the continent in Africa is covered with savanna grassland, many of which would be forested had they been left unmolested by man-made fires, Centuries of burnings by hunters, herders and tillers have created an enormous new ecological zone between the remaining forests and the natural grasslands.

A large raging forest fire is an awesome and feared phenomenon. Fire is no respecter of mankind and nature and occurs in all kinds of forests. Large forest fires have destroyed many plants and animals, immeasurable amounts of soil and timber. Most forest fires are the result of man's carelessness, ranging from activities such as camping, smoking, and debris burning. The other causes like spontaneous combustion due to continuous drought, simmering weather and lightning are also common, Trees of all species may be damaged even by small fires because the fires cause wounds that provide prime breeding access to damaging insects and fungi.

The first thing a forest fire does is to destroy the trees and vegetation through its flame and heat. Even a 120° F prolonged heat exposure could destroy the tissues while any temperature above the 147° F could be fatal for most trees. Others that may be killed along the raging fire are small plants, bacteria and fungi that could be beneficial to mankind. Unfortunately, some wild and endangered animals have also been killed.

As if nature is not doing a great job, humans have deliberately burned bn rainforests as a way of clearing the land for cattle ranching, settlement, and slash-and-bum agriculture. Brazil and Indonesia are two Wthe great wanton forest burners.

Causes of Forest Fires

One of the unfortunate destruction inflicted on the tropical forests is the way they are being cleared through the use of fire. This is practiced not only by swidden cultivators, but also by cash crops plantation owners in a hurry to remove the thick underbrush. The burning often gets out of hand until conflagration results in more areas being burned down.

Rainforests have been burned down repeatedly in the past nevertheless the farmers have not learned their lessons. In Brazil, up to 1987 the official estimate was forty-five fires per year but satellite photos showed that there were more than seven thousand fires all over the valley. An area of about 20 million hectares of forestlands went up in smoke. The fires sent up more than 500 million tons of carbon, 44 million tons of carbon dioxide, 6 million tons of particles, 5 million tons of methane, 2.5 million tons of ozone, a million tons of nitrous oxides and other substances.

One of the biggest fires to strike tropical forest occurred in 1983 in East Kalimantan. It destroyed 3.6 million hectares of old-growth forests. While drought is partly to be blamed, illegal logging wastes facilitated the spread of the wildfire. The illegal harvesting had been linked to militaiy personnel.

The Foreign Ministry of Indonesia was even elated with the destruction. Fire had cleared the land intended for a large transmigration settlement without cost to the government. This short-sightedness only encouraged the inhabitants to destroy the forest by burning. The enormous wealth of the timber should have been harvested. It could have supplied the timber needed domestically with leftover for export. The millions of tons of carbon could have been contained.

The Philippines have been fortunate to have suffered fewer forest fires probably due to its dwindling stock. The only province able to survive the onslaught of loggings is Palawan. During the El Nifio drought and dry season of 1998, it was hit by fires that destroyed more than 5,000 hectares in the southern part of the province. The fire continued to spread for days because there were no firefighting equipment available.[286]

Frequency and Effects of Forest Fires

Forest fire is far more common in temperate countries than in tropical countries. In a typical year, over 9,000 forest fires occurred in Canada destroying about 2.5 million hectares. Two-thirds of them are caused by people and the rest by lightning. Even that varies from some parts of the country. Western Canada and the Northwest Territories experienced about 50% fires from lightning while only 10% visited the Maritime provinces. As much as 85% of the destructions caused by lightning occurred in the West and North which are inaccessible to firefighters.[287]

Fires are sometimes beneficial in the temperate zones. Forest fires remove the mature trees in the forest that are most susceptible to insects and diseases. Surface fires remove accumulated materials on the forest floor, promoting the growth of new seedlings. Some species of frees even rely on fire to open their cones and release their seeds to regenerate. However it is not positive for all species. Many birds, mammals, and insects are dependent on old growth forest and are displaced by fire. Several species of trees such as white spruce, balsam fir, and white cedar need longer intervals between fires in order to reach reproductive maturity and will not survive in an area that bums too frequently.[288]

* * * * *

Every year hundreds of millions of tons of carbon dioxide is spewed out of the burning forest in the Brazilian Amazon. It has made the country one of the top greenhouse producers in the world. The term "lungs of the world" originally coined for the Amazon is no longer applicable as it is burning more oxygen than it is producing, laments American ecologist Daniel Nepstad.[289]

Burning down forests does not only release carbon dioxide, but also other greenhouse gases such as methane, ozone and nitrous oxide into the atmosphere. While the Earth has a defense mechanism against these pollutants called "trace radicals," gas molecules interact against these greenhouse gases to make them harmless. They are very limited. As more greenhouse gases are released, the trace radicals are overwhelmed and used ug making it difficult for the earth to stabilize the atmosphere.[290]

Burning down forests causes large amount of water to evaporate into the atmosphere This may partly account for the costly damages due to typhoons, heavy rains and flooding being experienced by countries in other parts of the world. Not only that, each huge tree burned can only be compensated by thousands of young saplings for the carbon it holds.

* * * * *

Tropical forests are usually too moist to propagate wildfires, but once it has been subjected to burning, it becomes susceptible to future fires. Once the canopy is opened up, the sun and air movements increase the drying of the forest floor adding more fuel for burning. Hie subseqent fires can bum faster, longer and more intense. Initial fires have been demonstrated to kill no more than 45% of trees over 20 cm. in diameter, whereas in recurrent fires, up to 98% of areas are liable to be killed.[291]

After a forest fire, most stems remain standing, even though they might be dead. Forests can recover after a fire, but they remain very sensitive to further disturbances. The reason is that regeneration processes are slowed down by repeated disruptions. For the forest to recover the seeds in the soils, remaining trees must be allowed to germinate without disturbances. Salvage logging in burned areas with its heavy equipment can do great harm to the sprouting trees.

Amazon

One of the great tragedies of the 20* century is the destruction of the Amazon in Brazil. The largest South American country embraces half of the Amazon. Amazonia contains the largest known tropical forests and biodiversity in the world. The government's destructive forest policy of allowing migrant farmers and cattle ranchers to torch invaluable forest trees have been condemned by environmentalists and govenments around the world. This has led to loss of biodiversity for the sake of a few years of fertile agriculture or cattle ranching. On top of that, carbon dioxide is emitted that has aggravated the global warming.

Since the 1970s and 1980s, loggers and farmers have cut down or burned vast stretches of the forest. Only the condemnation by the international community prompted the government to take action. Even so destruction continued unabated. In 1995 alone, 11,200 square miles of rain forest were razed in Brazil mostly by loggers, cattle ranchers and shifting cultivators. About 13% of the 2 million-square mile Amazon is gone as a result.[292] The figure is almost the same as that released officially.

The Brazilian side of Amazon seems destined for total destruction. In 1955, burning and logging destroyed more rainforest than in any previous year, according to the figures released by the country's National Space Institute. The area lost 29,059 square kilometers (13,350 sq. miles), almost twice the area deforested in 1994. High rainfall reduced the damage in 1996 to 18,161 square kilometers, and the Brazilian government says it expects the 1997 figure to be lower still, at around 13,000 square kilometers. But observers are skeptical of the claim because of the large number of fires spotted in the Brazilian Amazon by the US 's NOAA-12 satellite earlier that year.[293]

As of 1995, 4% of the Brazilian Amazon forest is under protection while another 16% is protected as part of the Indian reservation. With the cooperation of the World Bank and the WWF, it hopes to protect 10% of its forests by the year 2000 at a cost of $84 million and $156 million.[294]

In 1997, the US government's NOAA-12 satellite spotted more than 24,000 fires in the Brazilian Amazon between early August and mid-September, the height of the burning season. This is a 28% increase on the previous year, the satellite's first year on fire watch. The blaze has also spread to neighboring Colombia.[295]

Many of the fires in Brazil are set to clear the rainforest, although some occur accidentally when farmers bum pasture, according to one scientist, One reason the 1997 fires were so extensive is that forests were very dry, a consequence of the El Niiio, a periodic climatic oscillation, which is also strong that year.[296]

Burning season in the Amazon runs during the dry season from July to January. In 2004, government satellite images of the forest registered 165,440 "hot spots," fires whose flames can shoot as high as 100 feet and push temperatures beyond 2,500 degrees. That year, Brazil lost an estimated 10,000 square miles of forest, the second worst year on record and the same amount as the preceding year.[297]

Many ecologists and environmentalists doubt that the title of the "lungs of the world" should still be applied to the Amazon. Even without the massive burning, the popular notion that the Amazon is a giant oxygen factory for the rest of the planet is misguided, scientists say. Left unmolested, the forest does generate enormous amounts of oxygen through photosynthesis, but it consumes most of it itself in the decomposition of organic matter.[298]

Indonesia

Most of the fires that took place in Indonesia are caused by the deliberate burning for the establishment of plantations for palm oil or pulpwood. The burning of forestlands has been a government policy of land clearing for the sake of monoculture plantations. Some of them are burned down to cover up tracks of illegal logging while others are burned down after legitimate loggings were done. Still others were burned by farmers over land disputes or have been taken over by plantation owners as part of the government development projects.

During the 1982 and 1983 fires in East Kalimantan, 3.5 million hectares of forests went up in smoke and with it 20 million m³ of primary frorests and 35 million m³ of secondary forests with an estimated cost of $5.5 billion. The fire could have been caused by careless logging where debris left behind became fuel for fire. The fire was abetted by the drought caused by El Niflo then. (Hurst, 36)

It seems that the government as well as the commercial business adventurers, in their insatiable greed cannot wait to harvest the timber before burning it down. The 1997-1998 burning season was the worst 50,000 km² of forests were reported lost to fires but officially it was reported only 6,000 km².[299] The fire was unfortunately burning at a time when the drought effect of the El Nifto was affecting Indonesia. The fires was finally doused by the December rains.

The main fire allegedly caused by plantation owners clearing land occurred in the island of Sumatra and in Kalimantan on Indonesian side of Borneo. These produced the haze that blanketed the tiny city state of Singapore and much of the Malaysian peninsula and other neighboring countries including the Philippines. Others are burned by slash-and-burn cultivators. It was compounded by the industrial pollution and the drought in Indonesia. The thick haze caused the crash of an Indonesian Airbus killing 232 on board and a ship collision that divided a cargo ship in two, Besides that, hundreds of people and countless animals were roasted to death. In Sarawak alone more than 5,000 people have to visit the hospitals while 20 million Indonesians have been affected with eye, skin and respiratory problems. There were also cases of starvation because rescue planes were not able to fly rescue missions.[300]

A million hectares of peat in Kalimantan that the govenment is draining for a massive rice-planting project was also in fire including the ditches meant to remove the peat. With the fire, the chances of rice production are greatly diminished because a silicon layer impervious to water could be created that could affect future irrigation vital to wet rice planting. Not only that, the carbon dioxide emitted into the atmosphere could be more than all the emissions of power stations and car engines of W'estem Europe in one year. By the time the fire died down, one billion tons of carbon would have been emitted.[301]

Russia

The vast forests of northern Russia are one of the last great wilderness areas of the world. They are the lungs of the northern hemisphere, soaking up the carbon dioxide emissions that float across Siberia on the prevailing winds from the industrial regions to the west. Yet they are also under threat from an unprecedented surge in the number, frequency and scale of forest fires.[302] Every year 15,000 to 30,000 forest fires covering 5,000 to 30,000 km² are registered. The volume of timber, according to remote-sensing data exceeds 500 million cubic meters annually.[303]

The Siberia forests are the largest in the world. Twenty years ago forest fires destroyed about two million hectares of Siberian forest. In 2004, 22 million hectares were burned. The tenfold increase is expected to rage out of control this summer 2005. It often starts illegally and deliberately in the Russian Far East by rogue timbers firms who plan to buy the licenses of the timber merchants and logging companies cheaply because of the damages done already by the fire to the concessions. Licenses to log healthy forest are very expensive. The government is helpless in fighting the raging fires because it has neither the money nor the equipment to stop them as experienced in the past .[304]

In 2003, one of the hottest summers in Europe, 22 million hectares of spruce, larch, fir, Scots pine and oak were destroyed, charred, scorched or in some way affected by fire. On one day in June of that year, a US satellite recorded 157 fires across almost 11 million hectares, sending a plume of smoke that reached Kyoto, 5,000 kilometers away.[305]

Part of the reason for the forest fire getting worse, increasing in areas under risks is due to global warming. Global warming is the result of "more extreme droughts, greater droughts, longer droughts, and more frequent droughts," according to Dr. Anatoly Sukhinin, head of the forest fire laboratory at the Sukachev Institute of Forest.[306]

Health Risks

Fire is not only killing trees and animals within the confines of the forestlands, it can affect the people far away from the destructive fire. The smoke, smog, haze and airborne matters are known to travel for thousand of miles blown by the wind. Smoke is made up of a c complex mixture of gases and fine particles produced when wood and other organic matters burn. The biggest threat from smoke comes from fine particles. These microscopic particles can get into the eyes and respiratory system where they can cause health problems such as burning eyes, runny nose, and illnesses such as bronchitis.[307] Persons susceptible are those with respiratory problems such as asthma, emphysema, chronic obstructive pulmonary disease, and bronchitis and those with chronic lung and heart diseases.

People who have not experienced or have been diagnosed with lung or heart disease may begin having problems in smoky conditions. Symptoms of potential lung and/or heart problems include chest tightness, chest pain, shortness of breath, or sudden, overwhelming fatigue. People who experience these symptoms should consult their health care provider.[308]

When the air quality is unhealthy, precautions should be undertaken. People who live near the fire-stncken areas are advised to remain indoors and keep windows and doors closed to avoid inhalation of smoke, ashes, and particulate matter, according to the American Lung Association. Specially designed dust masks with true HEPA filters are recommended to filter out the fine particles. However, this is difficult to use for people suffering from lung disease.[309]

When using air conditioners in the home or in the car, set the air in the recycle or re-circulate mode to keep out outside air. Avoid using wood and gas stoves and candles at home. Avoid smoking or exercising inside the house. Medication should be available for those suffering from lung the heart ailments. They should drink plenty of water to keep the airways moist.[310]

Children are more susceptible to smoke and pollutants because their respiratory systems are still developing or not yet well developed. They also breathe in more air per pound of body mass than adults.[311]

* * * * *

The smoke haze of July to October 1997 caused by the burning of the forest in Kalimantan and Sumatra affected several countries in Asia, Right within the region, schools and airports have to be closed. Visibility was reduced to the length of the width of the street. At times the pollution index reached over 1500, 15 times more than what is considered safe, and the hospitals were clogged with people suffering from respiratory problems. At least 75 million people suffered from smoke-related medical problems, and the economic cost of the fires has been put at $3 billion.[312]

Other countries particularly hard hit was Singapore because of its close proximity to Indonesia. The Ministry of Health that monitored the situation came out with the following findings. It showed that there was a 30% increase in outpatient attendance for haze-related conditions. An increase in PM_{10} levels from 50 $\mu g/m^3$ to 150 $\mu g/m^3$ was significantly associated with increases of 12% of upper respiratory tract illness, 19% asthma and 26% rhinitis.[313]

Supplementary findings from scanning the electron microscopic sizing of the haze particles showed that 94% of the particles in the haze were below 25 μm in diameter. There has been some conccm because particles smaller than 2.5 μm in diameter can easily bypass normal body defense bolism and penetrate deeply into die alveoli of the lungs. During the same period, there was also an increase in accidents and emergency attendance for haze-related conditions. There was no significant increase in hospital admissions or in mortality It was considered a mild smoke haze.[314]

Mitigating the Forest Fires

Forest fires that start at the forest floor are just as devastating as those that bum above the crown of the trees. There is a better likelihood of spreading and engulfing larger areas because of the rich fuel found on the floor. The long hot summers that often accompany forest fires are worsened by the debris left behind by logging. Logging also opens up the canopy allowing sunlight to dry up the debris. The debris serves as a huge pile of kindling fuel made up of branches, barks, treetops left behind after the timber is removed. Under the hot sun, it is always possible to spontaneously cause fire to bum out of hand. Therefore it is always prudent to remove the debris or bum them on guarded sites.

Forest fires can be mitigated by thinning to remove the fuel load. This is accomplished by removing new growth in the forest floor and the dead trees. Hazards can be reduced with firebreaks.

In privately owned forest, the owner must be required by law to clear the forest of debris to help prevent fires. Owners are encouraged to keep a few- goats and sheep to consume the unwanted scrub vegetation. Aircraft and helicopters are also used for fighting the fires. Sophisticated vehicles capable of traveling steep slopes have been developed to get firefighters, equipment or water to the scene of fire. The earlier it is put out, the less likely it will engulf a larger area.

Chapter 9

OIL AND MINERAL EXPLORATIONS

The continued spiraling cost of oil and minerals in the world's market has spurned a desire for oil and mineral exploration throughout the world. Many of these natural resources can only be found deep in the rainforests of some of the poorest tropical countries. The big companies are everywhere the possibility of oil and minerals can be found. It is another great threat to the large portion of the rainforests. Furthermore, one of the saddest parts of the exploration of our natural resources is that the national interest as a whole does not benefit except individual vested interest. After a century of plunder of our forests, the people as a whole still remain poor and neglected.

In the case of oil exploration, some of the biggest names in oil companies can be found exploring in and around the rainforests. Conoco Inc., Occidental, and British Petroleum have been active in the Yasuni National Park in Ecuador. Chevron is exploring in the southern highlands of Papua New Guinea. Shell is exploring in Nigeria while Exxon is involved with Colombia.[315]

Many tropical countries, in trying to get the multinational companies to invest in the country have repealed laws and regulations protecting the environment for the sake of development. Even environmental laws protecting national parks and protected areas have been lifted to accommodate the selfish interest of corrupt politicians, the greed of industrial investors and the rich consumers of the wealthy nations addicted to the good life.

Mining of whatever kind have been proven many times to be deleterious to the health of the people with their toxic effluents and the cause of many ecological disasters in many places where these companies operate. Often times, it is only when tragedy strikes that we become aware of the problem, but the truth is that the damage is affecting us everyday when we are least aware.

Mining

The Philippines is said to contain Si trillion worth of unexplored mineral resources waiting to be exploited. But like all explorations, not only are the land being degraded, the workers as well as the surrounding are also exploited. Mining can be just as destructive to the forest as logging. Logging roads have to be constructed leading to the site. Timbers have to be cut not only for shoring up the tunnels and the dug up caves, but also to provide housing and other facilities needed for the operation.

Then there is the problem of the mine tailings. Mining have been known to damage the water resources around and past the site of operations. The mine wastes and tailings have to be impounded somewhere and it often leads to soil erosion which in turn leads to siltation of important water systems such as rivers and lakes where indigenous depends on their livelihood of fishing. Forests and crops are destroyed and people are displaced from their ancestral lands. Once the mines are abandoned, we are often left to clean up the environmental damages. If chemical processes are required, additional environmental problems are expected. According to a World Bank report, it cost the Philippines roughly P15 billion annually by the mining industry. These include the damage to the environment, deforestation, and catastrophes such as landslides and flash floods, not to count the lost lives and anguish suffered by the people.[316]

There is also the big problem of pollution as these ores are treated and refined and the effluents have been known to be toxic to the environment and the residents. These toxic wastes are often allowed into local streams and rivers polluting the water system and the surrounding lands. Even if impounded, it could still leach into the groundwater or worse like what happened to Guyana in August 1995.

The toxic waste pool where the mine tailings were impounded overflowed or broke releasing over one billion gallons of cyanide-laced waste water into a tributary causing widespread die-offs of aquatic and terrestrial plant and animal life and the poisoning of floodplain soils used for agriculture. It also contaminated the main source of drinking water for thousands of people and the destruction of the ecotourism industy. At first those mining companies tried to cover up the spill by burying the fish carcasses. When they were discovered, the Guyana government was informed. But because it was strapped for cash to service its debt, instead of punishing the companies they granted them a new concession.[317]

Mining consumes a lot of energy and wood is often the only available source of energy. They are turned into charcoal to fuel the ovens in processing the ores. If other facilities are needed such as ports, dams, villages, small generating plants, etc., trees are cut down and turned into charcoal for the needed energy. This is what happened to the state of Minas Gerais in southeastern Brazil where pig-iron production consumed nearly two-thirds of the state's forests.

The following article is typical of other mining operations utilizing open cast mining. Bauxite mining is the second largest foreign exchange earner in Jamaica, after tourism. It is also considered the number one culprit in the deforestation of its forest. The reason is the way the mineral is extracted - by open cast mining which requires the complete removal of vegetation and topsoil. At the same time, access roads are required to pass through the forests and into the mining area. Once access roads are opened up, loggers and coal burner yam stick traders move in, taking the trees in and around the mining areas. Therefore mining is responsible for extensive deforestation far beyond the mining areas.[318]

In recent years, deforestation has led to the deterioration of more than a third of Jamaica's watershed, drying up streams and rivers and rendering cities and towns suffering from lack of water. The diversity of plant and animal life is also threatened by the destruction of forests, leading to the loss of traditional ways of life, the knowledge about local plants and their medical and other uses. [319]

* * * * *

The Supreme Court (SC) recently came out with the decision upholding the law opening up the mining industry to foreign investors. In its decision, it claimed that mining has nothing to do with deforestation, Obviously, the SC must be basing the decision on mines located in deforested areas where there are no more trees to be cut down. Otherwise, there is no way that forests can remain untouched as history has time and again proven to be deleterious to the forests here and abroad.

Environmental groups, NGOs and even members of the influential Catholic Bishops Conference of the Philippines (CBCP) are up in arms against the government opening up the Samar Island Natural Park for bauxite exploitation by two multinational companies. Two mining permits have been granted by the DENR to Bauxite Resources Inc. and Alumina Mining Philippines Inc. under the mineral production sharing agreements (MPSAs). The estimated value of the mineral is put at $21 billion.[320]

The park has been declared a forest reserve by two presidential proclamations which is said to contain 70% old-growth forest. The destruction caused by the Pyrite Mining in Barangay Bagacay, Hinabanga, Samar, must be fresh in the minds of the oppositors. Once opened up for exploitation, it is a matter of time before destruction set in.[321]

Fear has been voiced about the possible pollution of the 25 river systems situated in the forest of Samar that provide water for domestic agricultural use of some 1.5 million inhabitants and the possible pollution of the fishing grounds. These are the livelihood of most of the people living there.

* * * * *

Most of the communities in the mining areas are against the exploitation of their mineral resources because it will disrupt their way of life and their livelihood. They are fearful of the environmental degradation and the tragedy that follows after the exploitation. No wonder many communities are against the mining firms and are being assisted by armed groups such as the New People's Army of the communist Party and even the militant Cordillera Peoples alliance in Luzon.[322]

The environmental groups and the Catholic Church have joined forces to gather one million signatures to oppose the operation of foreigners in the exploitation of our natural resources. The hostility against foreigners exploiting the natural resources probably stems from the tragedy of the spill caused by the Marcopper Mining Corp. operated by the Canadian mining giant Placer Dome. The spillage contaminated the Boac River in Marinduque and left the river dead and caused diseases among the local communities.[323]

Another area of conflict involved another Canadian company, TVI Pacific. This time it involved a sacred altar that belong to the 2000-strong Subanon tribe of Zamboanga del Norte, whose ancestors have inhabited the place since the 17* century. Members of the tribe even went to Canada to plead for their case not to disturb the area.[324] This would probably be ignored as TV I Pacific has been known to organize armed group to protect its interest. In one incident, a group of 50 Subanons who tried to block a road into their ancestral territory were attacked by an armed group and beaten with gun butts and canes. They were trying to prevent TVi from bringing drilling equipment and cyanide used in processing the ores. The tribesmen have long been suffering from dispossession, first from other settlers, then the loggers and now the foreign nationalists who claim to own the land. The Mining Code of 1995 allows foreigners to own the land they are mining. The TVI is laying claim to 2.9 million acres of land at more than 20 sites in the Philippines.[325]

On December 27, 2002 one of its buses was ambushed by heavily armed men believed to be members of the Moro Islamic Liberation Front killing 13 men in a gold mine in Canatuan that it was exploiting, Notwithstanding all the problems with the local inhabitants and militant groups, the foreign companies are expected to continue mining here and the government is adamant about letting them operate here because of the conomic and fiscal problems faced by the nation.[326] The government expects $6-$7 billion investment in the next ten years coming into the country, P57 billion annual tax revenues and $800 million exports, However, the benefit may be canceled out by the cost to the environment as well as the economic and social costs. The WB estimates it costs the government $2 billion annually due to environmental degradation And this includes only damage from water pollution, mismanagement of fishery resources and air pollution in four urban centers It also excludes social costs and the loss of quality of life.[327]

According to an NGO, Movement against Mining Globalization, Plunder and Resources, there are 857 abandoned mines in the country. They continue to bring environmental havoc to the environment and endanger the health of the communities.[328] It is a common practice for companies to abandon the exploration sites once they have served their purposes and Te communities are left to fend for themselves.

Gold Mining

Gold has been used as hedge against inflation for centuries and has been kept hoarded. So far, the world has extracted about 125,000 tons of gold from the ground which is enough for industrial and ornamental uses and do not need the gold being mined today. There are now 35,000 tons of gold lying in the vaults of central banks. Still the glitter of the gold continues to hound people greedy for its beauty; 90% of the gold are used in the jewelry industry.

To extract gold from the mines, mercury is used to separate the metals through a process called amalgamation. The toxic properties of mercury have been knovn since the Middle Ages when they were used in the extraction of silver. (Hecht, 161) Although most of it can be recovered, still losses due to dumping and evaporation do occur. The spent mercury is causing a lot of problems for people downstream who come into contact with this poisonous heavy metal. Once discharged, it can bioaccumulate in the tissues of living animals until it reaches the top predators and people who consume them.

Mining projects are scattered through out the world. Some have been more destructive than others, but until recently they have destroyed comparatively small areas of forests. But the continuing demand and explorations have unfortunately found most of these minerals deep inside the tropical forests.

The gold mine at Serra Pelada in the south of Para, discovered in 1980, has drawn much attention because whole mountains have been divested to remove one of the richest gold deposits ever discovered. Nuggets as hefty as seven kilos have been unearthed. More than 50,000 prospectors labored by hand clinging to their tiny claims of only four square meters mining the metal and putting the lives of natives at risk. As the mining progressed, more forest lands were under siege. The Yanomanis, a tribe of 9,000 Indians are fighting for their lives in the territory of Roraima. The miners have flooded this remote rainforest bringing with them diseases that the tribesmen do not have any immunity. The miners have also carved out more than 100 airstrips out of the rainforests. All the gold is sold to the government which is counting on the region's mineral wealth to offset a ponderous forcing debt. (Ang, Trees, 134, 215) By 1986, only a pit 360 feet deep is left.[329]

Throughout the Brazilian Amazon, there are some 500,000 gold miners called *garimpeiros*. They came from all walks of life trying to seek their fortunes and hope to strike it rich. Gold prospecting is hard work and dangerous. Many have been poisoned by mercury. The dumping of mercury into the water ways is also spreading the toxic wastes where dams are in operation affecting everyone downstream. What was once crystal water where women washed and children gamboled has become an oily turgid flow, thick with waterborne diseases and more subtle and deadly mercury. (Hecht, 161)

* * * * *

The Cordillera Mountains in Northern Luzon were once heavily forested, When gold was first discovered early last century, underground mining was used to extract the gold by Benguet Mining using trees to shore up the tunnels. Thousands of hectares of pine trees were cut down annually. No sustainable reforestation and harvesting were introduced so that before long the great demand far exceeds the regeneration of the pine timber.

When gold was discovered in June 1989 in Kematu, South Cotabato, hundreds of tunnels were indiscriminately dug up even on sloping areas which easily eroded the mountains of Kematu, home of the T'boli tribe made famous by Manuel Elizalde of PANAMIN. Siltation of the Banga River has been exacerbated by the gold mining. Accidents due to landslides and cave-ins have killed hundreds. But the biggest problem is the improper use and disposal of mercury in gold processing that contaminated water supplies which can kill innocent people far from the mining areas.

* * * * *

Ghana, a poor African country is under assault by the multinational companies for its gold holdings in the rainforests. The country has been under assault for its once rich forest that has been reduced from 8.3 million hectares to only 1.2 million with only 2% old-growth intact forest today. Now the rest are being invaded for gold mining. It is Africa's second largest gold producer and the mining operations have displaced more than 50,000 indigenous people without just compensation. They employed less than 20,000 Ghanians, burned villages, illegally detained activists, raped women and denied them their local culture. It is being abetted by the World Bank, International Monetary Fund and its government.[330]

The mines are located m the forest reserves and formal request to the World Bank not to support the mining projects have remained silent. The gold mining companies have gone ahead with processing the permits to some of these reserves. In the meantime, a Canadian company, diamond explorer PM1 Ventures have been exploring for diamonds in the Ashanti II Gold Plate located in the southwestern Ghana.[331]

Nickel Mining

Open pit or strip or open-cast mining is the most dangerous aspect of mining to forest trees. Wholesale removal of forests is necessary to get to the mines. Not only that the topsoil will have to be removed and more often than not, it is lost forever. Regeneration is impossible without the topsoil. One form of open pit called leach mining requires the application of chemicals to separate the metal from the rest of the minerals. The chemicals depend on the metal to be removed. Sulfuric acid is used in the case of copper or cyanide and sodium in the case of gold to obtain a higher rate of recovery. In this method, other heavy metals are released that can contaminate the surface and groundwater.

Governments in dire need of foreign investments almost always opt for the opening of mines even in protected areas to the detriment of the indigenous tribes. Hidden costs to the environment are often neglected which is often much more expensive than the benefit brought by the mining. Whatever benefits promised to the indigenous people for exploration of their ancestral lands are too little and too late and even not fulfilled.

Rights of the indigenous people are often ignored. l ake the case of the Mangyans of Mindoro Occidental. A nickel/cobalt mining project was initially awarded to a Norwegian company, Mindex Resources Development The company was later acquired by a Canadian company, Crew Development Corporation after it acquired 97.7% of Mindex. The 9,720-hectare concession was located within the ancestral domain claim of the indigenous tribe of Mangyan communities. The large-scale mining is expected to destroy the livelihood and displace the people. The Pre-feasibility Report of Kvaemer Metals, a consultancy firm hired by Mindex, reported that the project poses a threat to the forest habitat due to massive clearing, bulldozing and temporary stockpiling of the topsoil in the mine site. No amount of mitigating measures can be done to reconstruct a wildlife habitat massively destroyed by a mining operation.[332]

The project is also expected to destroy the watershed areas around four major rivers and two main irrigation systems that provide water for the lucrative rice fields and fruit tree plantations. Deterioration of the mountainous slopes is expected to carry silt and flooding leading to the contamination of the fertile land valley devoted to these plantations. The mine tailings are also expected to contaminate the ground and surface water used for drinking, irrigation and livestock.

The local inhabitants, supported by the churches, students, environmentalists, etc. strongly opposed the project. Even under the law protecting the indigenous community, no permit can be granted without their consent. An ordinance was even passed by the provincial council of Oriental Mindoro declaring a mining moratorium. But this did not deter the government during the term of President Estrada from granting a mining permit in December 2000. When the regime fell, the permit was revoked in July 2001. However, on March 10, 2004, the Office of President revoked the termination/cancellation oermit earlier issued against the MPSA and granted the mining permit.[333]

The project is expected to push through despite the many peaceful protests and dozens of resolutions expressing resistance to the mining projects submitted to the DENR from different institutions, organizations, churches, and other local government units.[334]

* * * * *

In another nickel project in Palawan granted to the Rio Tuba Nickel Mining Corp is under fire. This open pit mining is largely funded by Sumito Metals of Japan. The hydrometallurgical plant is designed to extract the low-grade ore that was once mined more than 20 years ago. It proposed to produce 10,000 metric tons of nickel using massive amounts of sulfuric acid, a highly toxic chemical used to produce nickel. The chemical will be imported from Japan at the rate of 270,000 metric tons annually for the next 20 years.[335]

During the exploration, other metallic mineral such as mercury, cadmium and arsenic are expected to be dug up and may settle in the water system that may cause further toxicity to the environment. The methanol, sulfuric acid and sulfur gas to be used in the processing are all deadly substances, according to Dr. Romeo Quijano, a toxicologist from the Philippine General Hospital. Part of the operation also involves limestone quarrying on Mt. Gotok, a sacred place for the people, and is expected to wipe out old growth forests harboring some of the precious and endangered plants and animals, some on the verge of extinction, according to Senator Edgardo Angara. [336]

The area covered by the project is 5,265 hectares. During the lifespan of more than 20 years, the firm is expected to move a mine waste of 35 million metric tons and this voluminous earth containing many toxic mine waste have to be impounded somewhere. Safety features posed by the nickel processing facility were mostly ignored.[337]

In 1969, a mining corporation talked with the elders of the inhabitants and asked for permission to build an airport on the land. The elders agreed in exchange for houses, a hospital and schools along with education for the children up to college. Other promises include employment, water and electricity, roads and to provide help if there were any adverse effects from the mining operation. After 20 years, the promises have yet to be fulfilled.[338]

Oil Explorations

Most of the unexplored oil today are found in forested areas, The consequences are new settlements where people need to be housed. Subsistence agriculture for food, firewood gathering for cooking and light, and timber felling for housing are the initial impacts on the forest. Airfields are sometimes hacked out of the jungle for oil exploration. Many of these oils are located in the fragile forest of PNG, Indonesia, Ecuador. Venezuela and Colombia Once established more migrants and unemployed workers will add more pressures on the forest.

Oil was discovered in Ecuador in 1972. When Texaco and Gulf pushed the first road to Puerto Francisco de Orellana on the Napo River, 100,000 landless farmers came down from the slopes of the Andes to wrest a new life in the forest. For weeks, thousands more came to find employment and those unemployed are forced to sustain themselves while they wait with shifting agriculture in the forest.

The site is located within the Yasuni National Park, Ecuador's largest protected area and one of the largest parks in the world. Covering an area of about one million hectares, the lowland tropical forest is designed to protect one of the most biologically diverse spot on Earth. Because oil income accounts for half of the country's revenues, this has made it vulnerable to the destruction of its ecosystem to take out the oil. The inaccessible jungle is often reached by plane or cars. Construction of airport and road networks is therefore necessary.

During its twenty years of operation. Texaco spilled over 18 billion gallons of oil in the Ecuadorian Amazon and is responsible for a multibillion dollar toxic cleanup bill that affected communities, Indigenous nationalists have had to pursue in US courts since the rian government was not interested in resolving the issue.[339]

* * * * *

Once oil is found, getting the oil out is another problem. Getting it out will require pipelines across forest routes to deliver to the coast where oil tankers are waiting or to cities where refineries are located. In the case of Ecuador, a new route was proposed that would cut through seven protected areas including the Mindo-Nambillio Reserve in the Andes-Choc - the first and largest community protected forest that holds the world record for avian biodiversity. In the three years since February 1998, fourteen oil spills resulting from the ruptures of existing pipeline have dumped over 100,000 barrels of oil in headwater rivers on both sides of the Andes. The communities affected have not been compensated and cleanup is expected to take decades.[340]

The proposed new pipeline is expected to transport a minimum of 350,000 barrels of crude everyday. The government allowed the pipeline consortium to choose the route of the pipeline although there is an existing pipeline route that could have been used without destroying new forests. The reason is that it is more convenient and cheaper to use the new route.

Future Oil Prospect

An important and useful energy can only be found only in the form of oil. With the continuing high cost of oil, many alternative forms of producing oil from crops and other energy sources are being feasible. Many researches for conversion of alternative sources have been channeled toward converted wood wastes, bovine mature, and municipal organic refuse into oil. With the rising population and the increasing garbage, mostly organic matter, being generated with nowhere to dispose, the transformation of these wastes into oil has been undergoing rigorous research since the 1970s.

The process involves using cellulose from the plant kingdom, wastes from the cattle feed lot and chemicals. By reacting carbon monoxide with the wood wastes in the presence of sodium carbonate solution as a catalyst at temperature of 700° F and up to 4000 psig. Carbon monoxide reacts with sodium carbonate in the presence of water to form sodium fomate which, in turn, reacts with cellulose in the wood wastes to form oil and regenerate sodium carbonate.[341]

Chapter 10

DEVELOPMENT PROJECTS

Many governments of tropical countries with large forest areas look to them to alleviate poverty among the people by opening up vast lands to development, taking the risk of destroying the forests in order to help the people attain a better life. Many of these megaprojects start with the building of huge highways crossing the vast expanses of forestland. This is followed up with projects such as dam building, exploitation of natural resources, railways traversing through the rainforest, resettlement areas, etc.

Most of the projects are huge and need to be financed from outside sources. As a result, many of the tropical countries are greatly indebted to the international financial institutions, or are beholden to governments willing to extend the loans. Unfortunately for most of these countries, the cost of these development projects only keeps piling up without so much benefiting the country as a whole. A lot of the money extended ends up in the pockets of corrupt officials.

There are many grassroots NGOs trying hard with projects intended to save the environment such as helping to stop deforestation and assisting the indigenous people to survive the onslaught of greedy loggers and consumers. More funds should be channeled toward improving their livelihood and restoring the degraded land.

Sustainable development is needed to prolong and make it possible for all mankind to enjoy the bounty of the natural resources But for decades, this has been only rhetoric. At present, many of the financial assistance being given to the tropical countries seems to be channeled toward more destructive projects instead of helping save the rainforests and the indigent people who have for centuries protected and nurtured the forests from destructive forces. The aim to develop the country has forced many governments to sell the natural resources of the patrimony to a few favored or multinational companies. The sad part is that some of these sites are found in the forested areas.

Sustainable Development

Sustainable development is to make available or usable resources that meet the needs of the present without compromising the ability of future generations to meet their own needs. This means everyone is entitled to receive all the basic and essential needs no matter what their status in life. This means that everyone is entitled to food, clothing, shelter, jobs and other legitimate aspirations for an improved quality of life. Sustainable development requires meeting all these needs without compromising the ecological well-being of the planet. (Conca, 230) however, as long as poverty, greed, and inequity among people and international institutions exist, there will always be people destroying the environment.

With so many people occupying this small planet, there is no room for lopsided standards of living between the have and the have-nots. It is a case of the gain of one is the loss of another. Greed will always reel its ugly head as the world's natural resources cannot afford to give everyone the same standard of living. History has shown that it is impossible to meet all the essential needs by achieving full growth potential without exploiting the poor or the environment. High levels of productivity and widespread poverty continue to coexist without improving the lives of the poor workers.

Most of the world's natural resources are nonrenewable and therefore there is no way sustainable development would be possible. The resources could only be prolonged as long as possible. Trees on the other hand are renewable and sustainable The problem is that we are cutting them down faster than we are growing them. Even if we can plant enough trees to replace the ones cut down, it will take a while before they grow big enough to replace the ecological functions they once played. The nature of the soil fertility can only sustain a few reforestation works after which the soil becomes infertile. Furthermore, whatever forests are reforested today are destined to cut down after a few years.

* * * * *

Sustainable development could mean different things to different people. Some government officials think that clear cutting the forests and converting the once forested area for monoculture plantations is part of sustainable development. Forests that have long been sustaining the indigenous people are removed to convert into other types of plantations and are considered development. Never mind if the action will evict the people from the land and drive the wildlife out of the plantations. Even before the plantations have been set in place, the impact on the soil fertility, biodiversity, water pollution, etc. have destroyed large sections forest.

* * * * *

As long as the population of the tropical countries with lush forests continues to grow, there is no way sustainable development of the tropical forests would be possible. The demand on forest products especially timber to sustain other sections of development will be needed at the expense of the forests. The density of most of the tropical countries is already so high that it can only be alleviated by encroachment on the forestlands. Even urbanization cannot cope with the huge population as essential services such as housing, schools, sanitations, transportation, health services cannot keep up with the influx of people.

There is a need to put an end to population growth. As it is there is not enough to go around for everyone. As the natural resources are being depleted, it would be difficult to develop them sustainably without sacrificing other basic needs.

Financial Institutions

Many financial institutions are bulging with petrodollars for loans. Much of these funds are allocated to the Third World because of its great potential for development and exploitation. These development projects have had the direct and indirect effects of destroying rainforests. Many cattle ranching, road projects, hydroelectric plants, and agricultural development projects have ceased, but they are now turning to lending loans for the exploitation of mineral resources. Stopping the flow of these capitals will slow down dramatically the rate of deforestation. Many of the destructive damages had been done and it will take centuries to restore these fragile ecosystems.

The World Bank, International Monetary' Fund (IMF), and other international financial institutions (IFIs) are behind many of the environmental degradations occurring throughout the tropical countries. Most of the Third World countries are too poor to develop their own natural resources and have to resort to borrowing from the IFIs for funding. As in all cases, the countries become beholden to their dictates. Examples of cases like these abound. The governments became too indebted that they are subjected to the dictates of these institutions which are in cahoots with the multinational companies in exploiting the natural resources of the countries requiring loans from them.

The five countries with the largest rainforests are also the most heavily indebted countries. It is their debt burden that made it easy for the IFIs to dictate on how to repay the loans. This is by opening up the natural resources for exploitation. This is how IMF and the World Bank were able to dictate the terms of additional loans that lead to the exploitation of the natural resources.

Madagascar is one of the most ecologically rich countries in the world with 80% of the species endemic to the country. In 19% it borrowed $118 million from the IMF purposely for development. As a result, it fell under the dictates of the IMF that required it to liberalize trade and open up the country for foreign investment. Among the measures adopted were to allow foreigners to own land and eliminate export taxes. One of the first projects entered into was the largest mining company called Rio Tino. This company was notorious for violating environmental laws and human rights violations. It was once caught dumping hundreds of drums of toxic cyanide into the Mahakam River in Kalimantan causing thousands of wild animals to be killed.[342]

Central African Republic used to borrow from IMF for development projects dating back to the 1980s. When a bigger amount of S66 million loan agreement was made in 1998, the government was encouraged to increase the exploitation of its forest and mineral resources. According to the agreement jointly made, the country's mineral resources should be fully developed As a result, its log production increased threefold from 1993 to 1999 and controlled by a few multinational corporations.[343]

In 2000, a new mining code was adopted at the behest of the IMF. The following year, a new finance law was also adopted lowering the duties on the export of minerals. These new laws are expected to cause further harm to the country's natural resources.[344]

* * * * *

During the economic crisis and the devaluation of the Rupiah in Indonesia in 1997, the government was forced to mm to IMF for aid. Whena second Letter of Intent (LOI) was negotiated and signed on January 15, 1998, a set of reforms affecting forests were forced on the country. Some of the major commitments to be implemented by the country included reduction in export taxes on logs, sawn timber, rattan, and imposition of appropriate resources, rent, taxes and removal of restrictions on foreign investment in oil palm plantations.[345]

There was no transparency during the negotiation of the terms of the agreements nor were those affected consulted. A further study by independent party found that conditions favor increased exploitation of natural resources by providing financial incentives for log export and reducing the export taxes. It claimed to be an incentive to conservation efforts when in fact it could only lead to more exploitation and deforestation. Because of the shortfall of domestic demand, the increased volume of export is expected to encourage illegal logging.[346]

The commitment to increase foreign investment in oil palm plantation can only lead to conversion of forests to plantations. This is contrary to the policy of the IMF and World Bank to save the forest and stop conversion to plantations. Part of the reasons is that the financial institutions are pressing Indonesia to keep up with the debt repayments. [347]

Sometimes the loans are extended by foreign governments. Unless they are grants with no strings attached, it is only a matter of time before they start to dictate on how we run our policies vis-A-vis their self interest, The only exportable goods that the lending countries do not own are the tropical timbers and other natural resources. They have their eyes on them too.

* * * * *

The Japanese government Official Development Assistance (ODA) focusing on large-scale technology and modernization through large-scale infrastructure development projects has negative impact on the recipient countries. The problem is that the development planners have not always taken recipient needs or the possible social or environmental impacts of aid interventions into account. Japanese ODA has frequently been used as a means of developing agriculture and forestry sectors in recipient countries in order to secure access to and control over natural resources. As a result it often leads to serious disruption of the ecological balance and threatens the livelihood of the local people.[348]

In the Limbang district in Sarawak, Malay sia, a logging road constructed in the early 1980s made it possible for extensive logging to take place. As a result, pollution of the rivers and the depletion of the main sources of food for the Kelabit and Penan tribes nearly destroyed their cultures. Other projects funded by ODA in India, Brazil, Thailand, etc. have led to deforestation and damage to the indigenous livelihoods. There were many protests and demonstrations from the local people most affected by the loans that the Japanese government was forced to change the emphasis of its loan toward environmental protection, social development democratization, and other soft issues.[349]

* * * * *

We are often convinced that the entry of the foreign lenders is good for the country because along with the aid and advice, they will help limit corruption and aid Ac recovery of the country. On the contrary, as in the IMF, its policies is to encourage import of manufactured good and technology from the West in exchange for the exploitation of natural resources including timber while the WB and ADB helped finance development projects such as hydroelectric dams, roads, and transmigration that contribute to deforestation. They are often assisted by the MNCs that devastate the forests to earn the foreign exchange to repay the loans extended by the lenders.[350]

The opposite can also be true. International financial institutions have a lot to say about how their money is going to be spent. It is time they flex their muscles to get their clients to adopt sustainable development of natural resources. This is what Citigroup, the largest US-based financial institution in the world did when it ordered its Asian timber client Rimbunan Hijau to obtain an independent third-party (Forest Stewardship Council) certification for its logging business.[351]

The Malaysian logging giant has a history of human rights abuses and illegal logging activities. Its employees were treated like slaves by the company's private paid police squad and forced to live in appalling conditions in company-controlled logging camps. Other allegations include harvesting of unlawful logs, destructive logging practices in defiance of national laws, local customs and the rights of resource owners and using the protection of political elites to impoverish the local people.[352]

The Citigroup acted on the recommendation of Rainforest Action Network on the investigation made by the London-based Environmental Investigation Agency, Greenpeace Australia Pacific and Dateline, Australia's longest-running internal current affairs television program, Another report released by the Papua New Guinea Department of Labor and Employment also found widespread corruption, bribery and human rights violations.[353]

Equator Principles

As if to mitigate its role in the past for the many destructive roles it has played in the destruction of the rainforests, the IFC, an arm of the World Bank, together with some NGOs have come up with the Equator Principles where investment for projects worth $50 million or more have to follow.[354] Banco do Brasil is the first state-owned bank and the 29th financial institutions to adopt the Equator Principles on March 3, 2005.[355]

The Equator Principles are a set of policies and procedures that address sustainability issues such as protection of natural habitats and indigenous populations, dam security, cultural ownership, international water projects, waterway projects and occupational health and safety.[356] This is the minimum criteria for extending loans to any project. The lenders are free to impose other stringent regulations for the release of the loans.

Hydroelectric Dams

Dam construction is very expensive not only in financial cost but also in terms of environmental degradation. The inundation of forests, wetlands, and wildlife are the hallmark of dams and the displacement of people are some of the ecological manmade disasters of unprecedented scale. The construction work entails the use of large amounts of lumber and timber.

As of 1996, at least 400,000 km² have been lost to dams worldwide. Many of them are the world's most ecologically diverse places on earth. Many of these places are the last refuges of the wildlife as they are being pressured to move away from human encroachment. (McCully, 32)

There are now more than 45,000 dams worldwide and construction are continuing in many countries Many of these dams failed to deliver what they promised. Cost-benefit assessment has revealed economic and ecological losses far outweighing the benefits of most of these dams. It is one cause of the fragmentation of the forests that isolated wildfire making inbreeding a cause of alarm. The displaced people have to seek new pastures that are only available in other forested areas and thereby caused more degradation of the forests. The most serious problem probably soil erosion that destroyed the topsoil needed by plants to feed the teeming population and shorten the life of the dams.

During the construction, new roads are constructed that soon served as pathways to new colonization of the forests. This attracted all sorts of people, from the landless who built new homes, to the illegal loggers who found it easier to transport their illegal cuts, and to the hunters who look for wildlife to hunt and kill.

* * * * *

Hydroelectric power plants are attractive to dam builders in forestlands due to the small local opposition and the high rainfall available but the usual flooding has destroyed large tracts of the ecosystem. The Kariba Dam flood caused the loss of about half a million hectares of some of the wildest natural setting for rhinos and elephants. The dam on the Volta in Ghana flooded one million hectares, displaced 78,000 people from 700 towns and villages. A dam in northern Quebec, Canada, flooded one million hectares of forestlands. The trees were not cleared first before flooding took place that made it doubly wasteful. The carbon contained in these flooded trees will be converted anaerobically into methane gas. But environment awareness is forcing indigenous people to take arms to protect their areas against intrusion from the government's plan for building dams.

In Asia where the population density is generally higher, the hydroelectric plant Pa Mong Project in Vietnam involved resettlement of half a million people. In Sri Lanka, the Victoria Dam displaced 45,000 people. Dam failure could be devastating to lives and properties.

Most of the dams are probably a necessity like the giant Tucuroi Dam on the Tocantins River. It can provide 8,000 megawatts of electric power for the city of Belem, the Carajas iron mine, aluminum refineries, and the new railroad to Sao Luis. Still the dam had displaced 20,000 people and flooded three Indian reservations covering an area of 240,000 hectares, What made it deplorable is no effort was undertaken during the early period of construction to remove the standing timber from land being flooded, despite contracts to remove the timber.

A comprehension environment impact assessment is often necessary to determine not only its effect on the local ecology but also on its feasibility. Problems like sedimentation and siltation. a major threat to all darns must be addressed carefully. The economic cost of the dam must also be determined. The construction of Balbina Dam in Brazil, partly financed by the World Bank (WB) was not done according to plan. The result was a 90% drop in energy output. It also flooded an Indian reservation located in a species-rich ecosystem. In some parts of the lake the depth is too shallow.

The WB spent half of its budget building large dams in the past. These large projects were designed to provide energy for industrialization but often led to massive displacement of people and loss of prime agricultural land. The Narmada River Valley Project of India envisions over 150 large and medium-size dams and 3,000 irrigation projects will make one million people landless. In two of the largest hydroelectric dams, an estimated 270,000 people will be displaced, most of them tribal tribes practicing traditional cultivation and have no legal title to the land and therefore will not get compensated when they are removed.[357]

* * * * *

Historical data on the hydrological variables such as rainfall, stream flow, sedimentation, etc. used in the designing of dams may no longer be applicable due to the disruption of the climate change primarily caused by gloobal warming The frequency and erratic behavior of the weather such as violent storms and unexpected occurrences of floods and droughts are changing the face of big dams. There are more possibilities of dam failure caused by deficient and defective designs of the dams.

One of the functions of dams is to mitigate the flooding of the low lying areas. This is pure fallacy. The degradation of the land such as deforestation, soil degradation, and increasing urbanization of people in and around the dams have been responsible for loss of lives and property damages in the fust place. Rainwater run off the mountains faster than when there are no disturbances to the areas. (McCully, 146)

In its war against flood damage, the US Corps of Engineers spent $25 billion from 1937 to 19% to control flooding along 500 dams and has erected 16,000 kilometers of embankments. As sedimentation continue to take its toll on the reservoirs, the embankments need to be raised until such time that it would be useless to hold the floodwater This is why flood damages since the passage of the Flood Control Act in 1937 has more than doubled while the number of people killed has remained the same. (Ibid)

It is common knowledge that dams need to be repaired as long as they exist. It is also common for dams to be filled up to overcapacity during thunderstorm. When water need to be released to prevent the collapse of dams, people downstream are greatly affected by flooding and destruction of their farmlands. If nothing is done to reduce the pressure, the dam may well collapse, a common occurrence. The Fushan Dam in China had one of the worst disasters four months after its completion. When water from the Huai overtopped the dam, it released 10 billion cubic meters of water and killed 10,000 people downstream. Of the 80,000 dams and reservoirs built, by 1980, 2,796 large dams and 2,263 small dams had collapsed. On the average 110 collapses per year with the worst year being 1973 when 554 dams collapsed. Two of the big dams that collapsed killed an estimated 230,000 people.[358]

Soil Degradation

Most dams are erected to generate electricity while most of the water are used for irrigation. In both instances, the greatest enemy of modem dams is the sihaQon of the reservoirs. Often the areas are the most fertile farmlands taken over by the reservoirs. Sometimes the amount of cropland consumed by the reservoirs is almost the same as the new land irrigated and in some cases even more. The Bakolori Dam was able to irrigate a maximum of 44,000 hectares but submerged 12,000 hectares of fields and wiped out cropping on 11,000 hectares further downstream when the water was diverted. Assad Reservoir behind Syria's Tabqua Dam on the Euphrates drowned 21,000 hectares of irrigated land, Seventeen years later, only 83,000 hectares can be irrigated but 60% were already irrigated by hand pump before the project was contemplated. Many of the irrigated soil were of poor quality that irrigation were not much help. (McCully, 166-167) The construction of canals leading to the irrigated sites and ending in the reservoirs serves as conduit for the siltation of the reservoirs and dams.

The Bargi Dam on the Narmada submerged 81,000 hectares of farmland and forest for a projected irrigation of 440,000 hectares. When it was finally completed in 1986, only 12,000 hectares were receiving irrigated water seven years late. The High Aswan Dam was supposed to irrigate an additional 690 hectares, according to government figures. This is disputed by the FAO when its statistics claimed that the area under irrigation, 2.6 million hectares remained the same as in 1989 when the project was started. Part of the discrepancy is due to the mining of over 100,000 hectares of topsoil taken over by brick makers and the urbanization of another 125,000 hectares. (Ibid, 167)

It is common for groundwater from rivers and canals to cany' dissolved salts from the rocks and soils. Once these waters are channeled to irrigation fields, the salts remain when the water evaporates. Before long, the soil becomes infertile due to the accumulation of the toxic salts. More water is spent to clean up the salt for the plants, but more of the salts accumulate. When these fields are abandoned to nature, it is difficult to grow anything even trees for reforestation. According to WB study in 1990, 2-3 million hectares of irrigated land became so badly affected by salinity that they have to be abandoned and it costs $ 11.4 billion annually the lost revenue. (Ibid, 169)

Destruction of Forests

Dams are usually located in rural areas where forests are an inevitable part of die landscape. Rural populations are displaced and needed to be settled. Resettlement is mostly available in the upland and forest areas, The resettled areas are unsuitable for farming or too small for the displaced households. Consequently, farmers are forced to look for alternative sources of income, which means illegally cutting wood for flitches, charcoal making, and selling firewood.

In India, die huge dams and power plants that the government has favored to foster industrial growth have displaced millions of peasants. It has been estimated that more than 11.5 million Hindus have been displaced in the last thirty years without being properly rehabilitated. In India, almost all primary rainforest are gone.

Two of the largest hydroelectric plants in the Narmada Valley project are expected to subject large areas for the reservoirs needed For the Sardar Sarovar Dam (SSD), up to 40.000 hectares are to be inundated of which 35% will be forestland. For the bigger Narmada Sagar Dam (NSD), 90,000 hectares are to be inundated of which 44% will be forestland.[359]

The Ministry of Environment and Forests (MEF) requires that for every hectare of forest destroyed, an equivalent hectare of trees must be planted m a non-forest area, or twice as much degraded forest lands can be replanted instead.[360]

* * * * *

Hydropower using large dams that floods huge areas of valuable land dmupt fish migration, assist in the spread of water-borne diseases, destroy forests and displace large communities, are no longer favoured by environmentalists and engineers. Many indigenous people have taken up arms to hght against encroachment on their livelihood and shelter.

A new approach to harness water power was invented by Alexander Gorlov, a former Soviet hydropower expert who is now a professor at the Northeastern University in Boston He was the designer of the Aswan Dam Instead of water being dropped into a turbine at great height to generate electricity, he patented a new hydropneumatic system that it designed so even slow moving water can be used to turn the turbine. It can be deployed in man-made canals, tidal straits, the open ocean, and imunpounded n versus idea has called the attention of many companies with their own free-flow turbines.[361]

Unlike other machines that use axial-flow turbines Gorlov's invention is a cross-flow turbine that can be mounted horizontally or vertically, stacked in rows like spools on a string and placed in water as shallow as three feet. The blades of an axial-flow turbine will turn only if they face the current, whereas Gorlov's tubine will function regardless of the direction of the flow and is ideal for tidal waters.[362]

In 2002, the Republic of Korea began tests on a Gorlov's Helical Turbine in the rapid tides of the Uldolmok Strait. If successful, they would advance to the next phase with a 15' tuibinc to produce 1,000 kilowatts of power for a nearby island. Again, if successful, the government plans to install a sufficient number of the turbines in the strait to produce 3,600 megawatts of electricity, the equivalent of four nuclear power plants.[363]

* * * * *

Water conservation minimizes the need for more reservoirs and tapping new sources of water which is usually located in far way places and must entail destruction of forest lands or inundation of large tract of land and displacement of settlers to bring the water to the populated areas. The cost of hydroelectric dams is enormous. Conserving water is cheap and profitable and has been known to delay a new project for years if not forever. In the meantime the money can be put to better use in the protection of the forests or uplifting the lives of the indigenous people who provide protection of the forests.

* * * * *

The accumulation of water in reservoirs behind the hydroelectric power plants is said to be responsible for earthquakes in Chile, Zimbabwe, and Greece.[364]

Golf Courses

Some countries equate the development of golf courses with the development of the countries. This wrong notion of development has been responsible for forest destruction for the benefit of the elites without any environmental benefits. Golf course is one land conversion scheme that is totally anathema to good land use. These golf courses incur various environmental problems, but the most serious is the conversion of prime agricultural and/or forested areas into a plaything for the rich and the famous. Food production has never been enough to support our own teeming populations, yet the governments in many tropical areas are willing to let this form of degradation go on. In the Philippines, there are already too many golf courses, more than 70 of them in existence and more are in the planning stages throughout the country to satisfy the fantasy of these aficionados. The US has more than 13,000 golf courses mostly located in the forest areas and another 300 are added annually.

Forested areas are particularly attractive to developers because of the cheap lands, with their rough terrain and existing trees that serve as obstacles. They are ideal sites for golf courses. In Indonesia and Japan their huge forests are cut down and cleared for golf courses. Even low-lying coastal areas and wetlands are not spared from development. Thousands of hectares of mangroves were destroyed even in the small island of Fiji to accommodate a golf course for the tourism industry.

The greening of the golf courses use alien grasses and need large amounts of fertilizers to maintain that are easily washed away during rainfall into the rivers destroying aquatic life. Another problem is the need for large amount of water for the greens. Together with the use of pesticides it is depleting the water supply and poisoning the underground aquifers.

Because of the congestion and high prices of urban lands, developers have opted to develop the lowland forested areas. The typical sizes of these courses range from 20 to 60 hectares. Access roads, clubhouses and parking areas add a few more hectares to the development. Most of the trees are cut down and replaced with grass.

Most of the golf courses today are being built in fragile ecosystems. In Thailand, golf courses are built by leveling entire ecosystems and displacing large communities. China is draining paddies and wetlands and Vietnam is building courses over rainforests. The use of force is not uncommon if the land cannot be bought. Communities often become laborers on golf courses and have to move to the cities to live in dirty and overcrowded urban areas. Most of the profits go to the pocket of the investors.

* * * * *

Japan's mounting environmental problem of deforestation come in the form of golf courses. All over Japan, forested slopes have been cleared to make room for golf courses, which caused landslides, while the chemical fertilizers applied on the greens are polluting waterways. Before World War II, there were only 23 golf courses. By 1956, the number had risen to 49 courses and today, the number of courses has rose to 1,700 with 330 more undergoing construction and an additional 1,000 more being planned.[365]

The demand for more golf courses is due to its high economic gain and living standard. Coupled with Japan's land terrain, the development of golf courses is made fairly simple. The same problems besieging other golf courses are also found in these terrains. Golf courses can retain only one fourth of the water a forest of the equivalent area can. They require three to four tons of germicides, herbicides, and pesticides each year which are harmful to humans and other wildlife.[366]

It was during the term of Prime Minster Nakasone that the Resort Law was passed supporting the construction of golf courses. The Resort Law granted tax privileges to developers of golf courses, hotels, tennis courts, ski resorts, and marina and reversed regulations which protected land and
forest preserves from land degradation through development. The Global Anti-Golf Movement even staged a World-No-Golf-Day on April 29, 1993 to try and spread awareness about the deforestation dilemma related to Japan's golf courses.[367]

The difficulties of constructing more golf courses in the country have fored the Japanese to look to Asia for investment in tourism abroad. The Japanese International Cooperation Agency (JICA) has been active in developing a master plan for tourism in the Philippines which include many more resorts with associated golf courses. To implement this plan in the Calabarzon area near Manila, the government evicted about 150,000 people from their homes and farms and converted 15,000 hectares of farmland into industrial sites.[368]

In Thailand, the existing golf courses routinely import machinery, grass, chemical, clothes and equipment to keep the golf courses to international standard. With more than 160 golf courses by the end of 1993, more are being planned in national parks by developers who want to privitize them and turn them into tourism zones with golf courses and luxurious hotels. NGOs and environmentalists have fought long battles again the plan As a result of so many golf courses catering to the rich, a water shortage has become a chronic problem in Thailand. Many reservoirs supply water to the golf courses have dried, yet golf courses operators continue to channel water away from public irrigation systems.[369]

The sixth Malaysian development plan (1990-1995) with its emphasis on tourism development was conceived by the JICA. Its plan has resulted in the development of 153 (1993) golf courses with more on the planning stage. There are also plans for a massive expansion of golf courses in Indonesia where golf courses are not so much a part of the tourist industry as a hobby of the new rich but as a status symbol for President Suharto and his military leadership. Confrontations between farmers and police and army have occurred as the government is forcing the farmers to sell off their land at Rp 30 ($0.03) per hectare to be converted to five-star resort.[370]

Chapter 11

AIR POLLUTION

Air pollution can be just as deadly as c utting down the trees. There are several sources of air pollutants but by far acid rain is a major cause of trees dying in the temperate regions caused by air pollution. Trees are good absorbent of air pollution to a certain extent that it does not compromise their ability to do so. Once the limit has been breached, it is only a matter of time before the trees wither and die.

There is now evidence that air pollution may be affecting the growth rate and health of some trees. Chronic injury to agriculture and forest by increased quantities and varieties of air pollutants now affect many parts of the world. Smog in the southern coastal basin of California contributed to the declinc in the production of citrus fruits and grapes and damaged trees in the San Bernardino National Forest, 80 kilometers south of Los Angeles. It is responsible for killing and damaging more than one million Ponderosa pines in the surrounding forests. Smog in the San Francisco Bay Area damaged commercial crops and vegetation in the Sacramento and San Joaquin Valleys and has injured forests in the Sierra foothills 160 kilometers away as well. Similar injuries are found elsewhere.

The main source of air pollution is the burning of fossil fuels such as oil, gas, and coal. Most of the burning has been done in coal-fired smelters and power plants with their high smoke stacks that allow the pollutants to disperse to larger areas. The trend is expected to continue until substitute energy sources can be found or expensive scrubbers are installed to reduce the sulfur from the coal.

Every year more vehicles and machineries are being added that require fossil fuels to drive them. As the population continues to grow, the demand for fossil fuels is expected to keep pace. In addition, the exploration of fossil fuels can be found in many forested areas and may entail their destruction.

Acid Rain

Acid rain is produced by the reaction of moisture and sulfur dioxide or nitrogen oxide and converted into sulfuric acid (SOx) and nitric acid (NOx) respectively. Each year, almost 160 million tons of SOx are pumped into the atmosphere, primarily from furnaces run by coal- and oil-burning utilities and nonferrous metal smelters. North America alone emits 50 million tons of this gas. A small quantity comes from natural sources, which include decaying vegetation and volcanic emissions. A variety of sulfur-containing gases such as hydrogen sulfide and dimethyl sulfide are produced by the action of soil bacteria on rotting vegetation and inorganic sulfate. Once in the air, these sulfur compounds are rapidly oxidized to SOx and further oxidized into acid sulfate.

The oxidation of SOx produces twice more acidity as the oxidation of NOx. Therefore, molecule for molecule, it makes more sense to reduce SOx emission. Acid sulfate appears to play a somewhat greater role than acid nitrate in acidifying lakes and streams because acid sulfate runs off more easily into lakes and streams while acid nitrate is retained more readily by the soil.

Emissions from volcanic eruptions are mostly sulfurous fumes, but they contribute an insignificant amount of acid sulfate. During major eruptions, much of the sulfur is injected into the stratosphere where it can travel several times around the globe before returning to earth. The sulfur is diluted as it travels and contributes little to acid deposition.

Nitrogen oxides, an acrid, reddish gas, formed when fuel is burned at high temperature, comes primarily from gasoline and diesel engine exhaust, electric utilities and industrial boilers that bum coal and oil NOx emissions promote the formation of ozone and other chemical oxidants in the air that speed up the formation of acid rain and are toxic to plants. One reason for the sharp increase in NOx emissions during the past few decades is that industrial boilers have been operating at ever higher temperatures in order to increase their efficiency. The higher the temperature of the furnace, the more nitrogen and oxygen in the air combine to produce more NOx. Motor vehicles account for nearly half of all NO_x emissions.

* * * * *

Acid rain is more destructive in the temperate zones because of the proliferation of power and smelter plants emitting the pollutants into the atmosphere. In 29 countries in Europe, 25% of all the trees and half of all the oak trees older than 60 years have suffered extensive damage due to pollution and bad weather. Czech Republic has the worst air pollution record in Europe had 72% of its trees significantly damaged, half of them irreversible.[371]

In terms of hard figures, in a survey in 1991, the total area of damaged forest is placcd at 475,000 km^2. The loss in revenue is pegged at S35 billion annually.[372] The cost of damages to buildings, monuments, metals, and building paints is around $20 billion a year. This does not include the cost of acidification of lakes and other water bodies. All these damages and the cost of cleanup up could run to tens of billions every year. The losses far exceed the $12 billion the European governments intend to spend cleaning up air pollution.

Defoilation is a common symptom of the effect of acid rain. An examination of 23% of forest trees in 35 European countries found that over 25% are defoliated.

* * * * *

Sulfur oxide is by far the main source of acid rain coming from coal-fired power plants. Technology is available to remove most of the pollutants. The flue gas desulphurization (FGD) is one solution. It can remove more than 90% of the sulfur dioxide from coal burning, Limestone is used to wash sulfur dioxide from the boiler gases in the FGD absorbent units. A by-product called gypsum is left from the chemical process. Dried by centrifuges, the gypsum can be used in the manufacture of wallboard, concrete and other building materials.

The world's largest FGD is located at the Drax Power Station in Yorkshire, northern England. It can treat 11 million tons of coal annually. It took more than six years to build. Because of its complexity and scale, the development has been compared with the building of the Channel Tunnel. The massive structure used 30,000 tons of steel, 200,000 tons of concrete, 85 kilometers of piping and 400 flue duct sections. No wonder, very few power plants have undertaken to clean up the pollutants at great initial investment.

Effects on Trees

Acid rain or acid precipitation is not a new phenomenon. Sulfur dioxide fumes from a large copper smelter set up after the Civil War in the US in Copper Basin, Tennessee devastated some 7,000 hectares of plants and damaged 12,000 hectares of surrounding timber land. Much of this originally forested mountain land are still barren. In the vicinity of a British Columbia smelter, which in 1929 emitted an average of 16,000 metric tons of sulfur pollutants per month, plant injury was observed as far as 83 kilometers from the smelter. Trees as far as 48 kms from the smelter sustained damages of 60% to 100%. Fluorides from aluminum smelters have caused similar injuries to native vegetation in Oregon and Washington. (Ang, Trees, 104)

Acid rain and other pollutants destroy the protective coating of plant tissues by promoting necrosis of leaf tissue, removing nutrients for foliage and forest soils, and causes scars and deformities in the leaves. Once the acid water reaches the ground it hastens the leaching of calcium, magnesium, potassium, and sodium needed by the plants. Acid moisture inhibits nitrogen fixing bacteria and increases root absorption of certain harmful metals. It attacks the trees from above and from below by starving the trees of nutrients or poisoning it at the roots. The cumulative effect of acidity and ozone leaves trees and vegetation more susceptible to natural stresses such as pest, diseases, cold, and drought. As with the pollution of lakes, acid rain raises the acidity of forest soils to a level at which toxic aluminum, usually bound chemical in them, is released and absorbed by the tree roots. This gradually poisons the trees.

Acid ram has been responsible for the widespread decline of evergreen forest in eastern US and Europe in the past few decades. Conifers seem especially vulnerable to acid rain, although hardwoods also suffer. Thousands of hectares of forests in central Europe are dead or dying from a combination of air pollution due to acid rain, ozone, and heavy metals from the exhausts of automobiles. On the other hand, in the American northwestern and mid-eastern areas, most threatened by acid rain and other pollutions, the trees are growing but in much slower pace. American forests that are suffering the most from acid rain are the less diverse conifer stands at higher elevation in the northeast. Several damages to forests in Germany have already prompted the country to undertake major reduction in SOx emissions.

As a result of acid rainfall, rivers and lakes are unable to support fish and other forms of aquatic life. Acid rain also encourages the leaching of toxic wastes from the soil, lessens soil fertility, and kills trees. In the UK, more than two-thirds of its forests and over half those in Germany and Switzerland have been badly damaged by acid rain. All in all more than 30 million hectares in western Europe are affected.

In some eastern European countries where pollution controls were never fully implemented, the soil has become so acidic that it will take decades before trees will grow again. The cost of cleanup is prohibitively high for these countries without the expertise, technology, resources and money to utilize.

Acid rain looms as a rising potential threat in many developing tropical coutries as well. Large portion of Brazil, Venezuela, Colombia, Nigeria, India and Southeast Asia have a growing problem with it. Many of these areas have underlain soils most susceptible to acidification. Once these soils are contaminated, trees will be unable to propagate and grow to full maturity. Even a small amount of acid intrusion can cause chronic stresses that the trees find difficult to resist.

Damage to existing trees is only part of the problem. The future of the forests is also at stake. Natural renegeration is no longer taking place in much of central Europe, and even the planting of nursery-raised stock provides no guarantee of success. Developments such as these raise the specter of wholesale and irreversible loss of forest lands. The importance of forests to the countries involved would lead to massive economic diruption and desperate actions are needed.

Methane

Methane is a colorless, odorless, lighter-than-air, flammable gas of abundant presence in nature. It is the chief constituent of natural gas. The gas is also called a marsh gas because it is produced during the decomposition of vegetable matter by anaerobic bacteria living under water in swamps, bogs, and marshes. Aerobic decomposition of animal and vegetable matter also produces methane. They are also produced in places like rice paddies and the intestines of plant eating creatures such as termites. The same is true as a byproduct of anaerobic metabolism of microbes in the gut of cud chewing herbivores such as cattle, sheep, buffalo, camel and goats. Methane are also released during coal mining, oil and gas drilling, and petroleum refining. Burning wood and garbage dumps also release methane to the atmosphere All these methane emitted annually amounts to 400 to 700 million tons annually. Methane is also 20 to 25 times more effective than carbon dioxide as a greenhouse gas. Therefore it pays to reduce the number of livestock and consumption of rice.

It has been estimated that cattle contributes about 100 million tons of methane to the atmosphere. A cow produces almost 700 times more methane than the human being. Methane is also suspected as contributing to the ozone hole.

The ever-increasing growth of populations can only lead to the formationi of more methane gas. The need for more food can be filled from more rice paddies cultivated and harvested and the limited consumption of beef that we need for protein.

As the global temperature increases due to global warming, the large quantity of methane stored in the frozen tundra of the North Pole is expected to be released. The methane hydrates trapped in the sea bed may also be affected with the increase in sea temperature. It is thought to be greater than all the hydrocarbon gases stored in reservoirs on land. The release of these global warming agents is expected to have synergetic effect in further increasing the global wanning and ushering even harsher warming in the coming years. With high temperature means more evaporation and therefore more formation of cloud that can also act as a mirror in reflecting sunlight back like the greenhouse effect.

The evaporation of the sea water to the atmosphere and the circulation of the rain clouds could be responsible for droughts in some areas and heavy downpour in others that have been causing massive flooding in many countries. The frequent occurrences of super storms and devastating hurricanes have visited the world in the 1990s up to the present.

Ozone

Ozone is a gaseous form of oxygen with three oxygen atoms per molecules. At high altitudes, it is a strong absorbent of short-wave ultraviolet radiation that is potentially harmful to living matter. Moreover, ozone at lower altitudes can cause severe environmental problems. It is a major component of smog. Ozone is formed in the air when exhaust gases from the car react in the presence of sunlight.

Ozone on the lower atmospheric and ground level is serious threat to all crops, vegetables and trees, particularly the conifers. Ozone damage to eastern white pine can occur after only four hours of exposure to 120 ug/cu.m. (0.06 ppm) while western ponderosa pine is damaged at about twice that level. The foliation change leads to the premature fall of needles that can add to fire hazard debris, increase in pine-beetle infestation, and decreases in seedling germination for future trees.

The first signs of widespread damage to trees far from power plants were identified in the San Bernardino forest eighty miles from Los Angeles. In the early 1960s excess ozone reduced growth rates of trees by 80%. Pine trees in the Great Smoky Mountains showed the same problem and virtually stopped growing. In Kentucky, three quarters of the white pine trees had been damaged by 1984 and mature red spruces were losing 90% of their foliage. On Mount Mitchell in North Carolina, where the hilltops are swathed in mist and fog containing very high levels of ozone and heavy metal particles, as well as acid rain a thousand times higher than normal rainfall, 73% of the trees were badly damaged by 1986 and over 60% had lost more than half their foliage.

Solutions

There are many solutions to acid rain problems being put up by industries as demanded by environmentalists and government regulations. As individuals we can do our share by reducing the use of fossil fuels by using bicycles or walking, using alternative source of energy. There are ubiquitous ways of helping the environment without affecting our lifestyle. The rich who can afford to spend should do more of their share by cutting down on energy use or use eco-friendly devices such as electric cars, cut down on use of private cars and other myriad ways. Imposing high taxes on the use of fossil fuels has a way of dampening demand on energy use.

Chapter 12

OTHER NATURAL FORCES

The rainforests are affected by many natural forces at work in nature. They include forest fires caused by lightning and drought that made them susceptible to forest fires. There are also other natural forces such as storms in the form of typhoons in the tropical countries and hurricanes in the temperate zones. These events occur in random and may involve large stretches of forests. Most of the destructions are not so serious that the forests cannot regenerate themselves. But there are few cases where destruction can be total. This would occur during volcanic activity.

Some natural forces are caused by human activities such as climate changes that bring droughts and thunderstorms. The droughts along with global warming and die effect of El Nifio have been responsible for some of the worst forest fires last seen in the decades of the last century.

Then there are the natural enemies of trees in the form of an enormous numbers of varieties of insects, fungi, bacteria, and viruses, each with its unique characteristics. Some of them are like the AIDS virus has been fatal to humans. Many of them are beneficial to the trees while some destructive ones are held in check by their natural enemies. Once the pest organisms takes over a tree, reduction in tree growth or total destruction can occur. These losses are tolerated as long as the destruction is localized and affect only a small number of trees.

All parts of a tree are potentially subject to attack by harmful insects, microbes, bacteria and fungi. Insects destroy more trees than any other agent. Bark beetles, including species of Ips and Dendroctonus and are among the most destructive insects. They bore into the tree just below the bark, where they create tiny channels that disrupt the flow of food to the roots, often killing the tree. Diseases frequently retard growth of trees. Another destructive disease caused by heartrot fungus gains entrance through any wound that damage the tree's protective tissue, Conifers and broad-leaved trees are particularly susceptible.

Destructive Pests and Diseases

Pest and disease of plants are not a monopoly of the temperate zone trees. Tropical forests are under attack by all kinds of pathogens albeit not as destructive. In the Philippines pests and diseases account for 17% of forest destruction in 1986. Tree plantations were not spared. In 1978, apitong trees in Cagayan Valley were reported dying of an unknown pathogen. Another varicose borer infested the native as well as PNG Species off Eucalyptus deglupta in the plantations of PICOP in Surigao del Sur. A cankcr disease also affected its Albizzia falcataria plantations. Benguet pines were attacked by a bark beetle while almaciga in Kaligao-Apayao mountains were reportedly attacked by a heartrot fungi. At one time psyllid infestation wiped out most of the giant ipil-ipil plantations throughout the country.

Insects and disease organisms have often been accidentally introduced to forests from other parts of the world. They develop serious epidemic conditions because of the lack of any natural control that are inherent in their origin. In this age of rapid global transportation, insects and fungal spores can be spread easily throughout the world.

Diseases are more deadly than destructions caused by insects. This is according to one survey that reported that insects deplete 1.4 million cubic meters of trees annually compared to 14.6 million cubic meters annually through diseases.[373]

Importing plants such as trees and flowers as well as logs can carry destructive pests and diseases into the country. The Dutch elm disease caused by the fungus Ceratocystis uinti was introduced into the US in the mid-1920s when a shipment of European logs was bought into the port of New York. It is estimated that 100 million American elm trees were killed so far and the disease can be found in every state.[374]

The prospect of importing Siberian timbers prompted the US Forest Service (FS) to make an inventory of the organisms associated with Siberian larch, a major timer species. One hundred seventy five arthropods, nematodes, and fungi were identified. (Ang, Trees, 97) For a long time Russia timber imports were closed to the US markets for fear of introducing of new pest into the country. However, new rules were enacted by the USDA in August 1995 lifting the ban on raw logs importation. Under the new regulations, raw logs must be sterilized to kill pests prior to reaching US shores.[375]

It is not uncommon for countries to import tree plants in the hope of propagating new species. In the 1800s, the US imported plants that carry the gypsy moth from Europe. It has since been defoliating trees from Maine to Michigan and Virginia. In the early parts of the 20th century, the US imported chestnut trees that carry the chestnut blight fungus *Endothia parasitica*. The fungus has now spread over 200 million acres and killed billions of mature trees. The white pine blister rust was introduced into the US from Europe. In a span of less than 20 years it has killed 80-95% of the white pine trees in infested stands from California to Montana.[376]

Large-scale monoculture plantations are susceptible to disease and pest outbreaks. They require heavy applications of insecticides, fungicides and herbicides to prevent the invasion of other plants. Most of these pesticides are highly toxic to humans and the environment.

The seriousness of the situation should prompt us to improve and enforce plant and animal quarantine laws. The growing legal and illegal trade of wildlife animals could inadvertently bring pests and diseases to the recipient countries. Many tropical countries do not have the technology and trained personnel to deal with the problem once it strikes. Disasters strike where quarantine has failed or been imposed too late. The USDA is very strict about imported fruits and plants.

Pesticides

The fight against pest is a losing war. Pests often become immune to pesticides after as few seasons of applications, while mammals including humans are contaminated with their residue long after they are taken out of the market. DDT, long banned in many countries is still present in the environment.

Applications of pesticides sprayed from the ground or from low-flying aircraft offer a short-term measure to check sudden plagues of insects or outbreaks of fungi disease. This should be the only time that the use of pesticides is recommended. Actions are often taken against exceptional outbreaks of defoliating caterpillars. However, large-scale chemical treatments of forests are rare and are restricted to a small proportion of the areas at risk.

One disadvantage of blanket treatments by potent, broad-spectrum chemicals is that both parasitic and predatory insects are affected. Pesticides have also adversely affected bird life.

Volcanic Activity

Volcanic eruption can be devastating to a locality even if there are no forests standing. The 1991 eruption of Mount Pinatubo in the Philippines destroyed more than 80,000 hectares of mostly agricultural land around its cone. The loss of agricultural land and unemployment problems forced some people to trek to the forest to survive by practicing swidden agriculture and even carabao logging. The lahar killed 700 people, displaced 250,000 from their homes and rendered 650,000 jobless. The effects of that eruption are still being felt fifteen years later everytime typhoons hit. Not only that billions of pesos were lost due to corruption as government tried to mitigate the effect of the lahar.

The 1988 eruption of Mount St. Helen in Washington State destroyed 30,000 hectares of forest in just a minute. The lava flow burned large tracts of forest while the released gases killed wildlife.

Storms

Storms can cause extensive damage when strong winds slash through the canopy of the forests. A falling tall tree can bring down other trees that are connected through the lianas and other vines or hit by another fallen tree. It can cause a chain reaction affecting other trees. However, a healthy forest can recover from moderate storm damages in a few months or years. The old-growth forests have a better chance of weathering a typhoon than secondary forests where the trees are much younger and not as deeply rooted.

Strong typhoons can cause substantial damage that may take decades to centuries to recover. The 1880 unusually strong winds damaged large areas of Kelantm forest in the northwestern part of peninsular Malaysia A study in the 1950s found the most common tree species, still characteristic secondary forest and dipterocarps - typical of southeast

Asian rainforest - remained sparse. Similarly, recovery from Hurricane Hugo (1989) for the Luquillo montane forest in Puerto Rico is expected to take at least 250 years.[377]

When trees are fallen, loggers are often called in to salvage them instead of letting them rot in the field. Unscrupulous loggers have been known to cut down good standing timber to augment their income.

Chapter 13

WOOD PRODUCTS

Types are a universal source of useful materials. From prehistoric times when they provided firewood, shelter and canoes, they have grown to more than 10,000 uses today. Many of them are essentially in the original form with a little processing. Housing and construction industries are the two major beneficiaries of the wood industry.

The housing industry is one of the major users of lumber produced by the timber industry. It is hard to imagine building a house without using wood in one form or another. It has some advantages over other building materials. The price of wood is often cheaper than other construction materials such as steel, concrete, aluminum, etc. It uses less energy in manufacturing. A house wall built of wood requires about 20% less energy for heating during winter and 30% less for cooling than a house made of other materials. In many parts of the world where wood is abundant like the US, 80% of the homes are chiefly built of wood.

Another use for wood and greatly in demand is in the furniture industry, Different woods have different characteristics that make them excellent materials for furniture. This in turn has made it a liability for the forests where they can be found. The insatiable greed of the rich for furniture and construction needs has taken its toll on the forest. Other useful but nevertheless wasteful wood products include disposable chopsticks.

The chief reason fuelling the demand for forest products is the runaway population. People need to be sheltered and schoolrooms are needed for the education of the schoolchildren. Along with these homes and schoolrooms are the needed furniture, school desks, cabinets, blackboards, etc. that are often made from forest trees. There is presently a wide gap that needs to be filled up and the demand for wood is not expected to slacken anytime in the future. It is therefore imperative that something be done to stem the runaway population explosion. Until the day we can achieve equilibrium between demand and supply of forest products, the pressure to destroy the forests is always there.

Housing Industry

Construction of houses and public works are by far the biggest consumers of timbers turned into plywood and finished products for the homes. It is in this industry that fuels the demand by the Japanese of timbers around the world. The post-war economic recovery of Japan and its export oriented industrial development pattern caused serious trade disputes among its neighboring countries. The US forced the country to spend more money for construction that would lead to more importation from its trading partners of their forest resources.

Since 1983 when Prime Minister Nakasone took over the rein of government, he introduced several amendments to existing laws for urban renewal and construction of new homes. As a result, the construction of projects skyrocketed throughout the 1980s and 1990s. In terms of dollars, its increase was from tens of billions to some hundred of billions annually. Since the 1960s and for the next 30 years, it built about 30 million houses but only less than half that number of housing stock increased. This is because 16 million houses were lost or destroyed due to urban development and decay. The average lifespan of Japanese homes is about 26 years. Today, an average of more than half a million houses is destroyed every year for the same reasons. This massive destruction is the main reason for the large importation of timber. Even while its population may have stabilized, it will continue to construct new homes as old ones are tom down.

Plywood

Plywood is the main product produced from hardwood. A lot of these plywood are used for finished walling and ceiling and other furniture such as cabinets and drawers. But by far most of them go into the formwork during construction. According to statistics, 84% of the logs imported by Japan from Southeast Asia were used to produce plywood, accounting for 48% of the total logs consumed for this purpose. Some of these species have been so endangered that it has been placed in the IUCN Red List.[378]

* * * * *

Plywood used as fotmwork during construction of slabs, walls, beams and columns is often destroyed after a few applications. In order to minimize this deterioration, use waterproof compound on the surface of the plywood before concrete is applied. It can then be reused and is more economical in the long run and saves trees.

The sizes of these slabs, beams, and columns should be designed in a few uniform sizes so that the plywood forms and wooden braces can be cut into sections with minimum wastage and can be reused repeatedly.
Likewise the length of the slabs can be designed so that lumber and plywood which come in fixed length could be accommodated without too much trimming.

* * * * *

Plastic material is one of the most difficult to recycle. Due to this, plastic lumber was conceived in the 1970s. The recipe for making plastic lumber is different for every manufacturer, but the basic idea is the same. The semi-melted plastic wastes are crammed into a mold of a two-by-four or some other standard-size wood product. The molded plastic is then cooled in a water bath and ready for use.

Although plastic lumber is a bit of a fire hazard and weighs twice as much as wood with only a fraction of wood's stiffness it can be used for the outdoor. Plastic lumber never needs paint. Unlike treated wood, it won't leach or leach very minimal toxic wastes. Plastic wood's resistance to sunlight, termites and borers is high and will probably outlast treated wood. It can be cut, nailed and bolted just like wood. When using plastic lumber for its load-carrying capacity, one-third more support than normally used for wood is necessary.

Non-wood Substitutes

Hardwoods are distinguished from softwoods by the cell structure of the timbers. Because of the difference, its use can be different too. Hardwoods are usually used for structural and external building applications due to their durability and load carrying capacity. It is not ideal and economical for interior use. In view of the diminishing forest products especially lumber for use in the construction, many are using concrete and steel for the structural part of the building. They are stronger, more durable and last longer. Walls around the house can make use of hollow blocks, plastered over, and painted instead of using decorative panellings Posts can be substituted with concrete and steel.

Because of the diminishing forest products, inferior products are being used in the construction industry. George Dcffet, a former contractor, frustrated over the inferior studs from immature trees decided to do something about it. He patented a new stud that is stronger, straighter, and cheaper than wood. It is made entirely from recycle old cars and appliances. With more than 1.4 million houses build every year in the US, more than 10 million trees can be spared. At least 5% of these studs can be found in new homes across America.

There are many substitutes for wood coming into the market and it would be great for the forests if we can take the time out and look for them. New inventions or substitutes can also take the heat off the trees. It could even be profitable for the inventor. Ceramic and marble tiles for the floorings are being substituted for parquet and other hardwood. Even vinyl tiles are being used with grain designs that look like wood.

* * * * *

Household utensil such as bowls, knife handles, bread boxes, cutting boards, etc. are often made of wood. Avoid buying these products to reduce the demand on forest products. Before buying, make sure no substitute materials are available. Other products such as toilet seats, towel racks, picture frames can be substituted with either metallic plastic, fiberglass and other synthetic products that can be more durable. It is another way of relieving pressure on the forests.

It is difficult to imagine a small piece of toothpick could be responsible for injuries and deaths. It is under attack by physicians and dentists. According to a report by the Atlanta-based Center for Disease Control in 1987, more than 8,000 toothpick-related accidents occurred the preceding year with three fatalities. The swallowed toothpick punctured the stomach or intestines causing the death. Children five years old and below are frequently injured in the eyes and cars. It is also partly responsible for the early decay in the teeth of the children. (Taintor, 28-29) The two best substitutes are the dental floss or even water pick which uses pressurized w ater to dislodge any debris.

The use of wooden toothpick is small, but its effect on the leftover food can be fatal. Toothpicks were banned at all eateries across South Korea in an effort to reduce waste and increase food leftover as animal feed. Animals have been injured and sometimes killed by inadvertently swallowing toothpicks mixed in with the food. Not only is the toothpick a waste of wood products, sometimes they even come scaled in paper or plastic packaging that is used only once. As a substitute, toothpicks are now made of wheat that are hardened like uncooked noodle and are edible even for humans.

* * * * *

Faber-Castel introduced a new pencil made from old newspapers and cardboards called American EcoWriter, a nontoxic pencil that is almost indistinguishable from the familiar wooden pencil.

In a response to a boycott organized by RAN, Empire Berol USA has decided to stop using the tropical hardwood jelutong in the pencils it manufactures. The company succumbed to pressure that the jelutong is now being harvested on a sustained-yield basis. The company's pencils are now made with incense ccdar that is harvested in the US. Thus, the company joins two other major US pencil manufacturers, Faber-Castel and Dixon-Ticonderoga in reducing the destruction of tropical rainforests.

Avoid buying toys made of wood. They are not as durable as those made from steel, plastic, fiberglass or other synthetic materials. It is also a matter of time before they will be discarded. Paints from the wood products are often contaminated with toxic chemicals such as lead that can be taken into the mouth by the children. Children often outlive the toys in a few years. Give them to the orphanage, the poor and the disadvantaged.

Only if no substitutes can be found should we use wood products, However, we must avoid buying these products unless the raw materials come from forests classified as sustainable. We can go one step further by choosing the relatively fast-growing softwoods that mature in less than ten years and not the tropical hardwoods that take a lifetime to mature.

Composite Woods

India has been in the forefront of using composite wood because its high deforestation rate has forced the government to impose a ban on the use of wood or timber in the building construction since April 1993. The Indians are now producing boards, panels from waste products such as sawdust, jute sticks, jute fibre, glass reinforced gypsum, fly-ash polymer composites as substitutes. They use sisal fibre corrugated sheets for roofing in place of asbestos.

We have been consuming more wood than we have to and it is time to cut down. A typical 185 m² wood-frame house uses lumber coming from about 40 to 50 trees. This can be reduced by using other substitutes. Walls can be constructed with "rammed earth," the materials used in building the Great Wall of China. It is an ancient technique where moisture mineral soil is placed in a mold and compressed to harden it. Pierce Parker, an agricultural waste innovator is using straws, heating and compressing in into two-and-a-quarter-inch panels and then covering them with paper. Since the straw has its own adhesive properties, no glue or resin is needed. He called his product Easiboard, and it is designed to replace walls of two-by-fours and plasterboard.

Another innovation is a wood substitute called Environ-biocomposite. It is made from a combination of wastepaper and soybeans glued together to form lumber and panellings. Every 25 kilos of wastepaper and bushel of soybeans and glue resin are enough to produce 22 boardfeet of this composite wood. The result is a product that looks life granite that is more than twice as hard as oak but much lighter and performs like wood. It can be drilled, sawn and sanded. It has been used for furniture, tabletops, and other household and construction uses.

Woods are being engineered for specific purposes in the construction industry. They are made with definable properties for use in certain parts of the home. Using glue, the woods are being bonded together to form i-joists, glu-lam beams and oriented stand board, all of them can be made stronger and less costly for the consumer.[379] Many of the characteristics of ordinary solid sawn lumber such as sturdiness have been overcome.

Glu-lam is a contraction of the words glue and lamination. By using glue short woods can be glued together into longer and large pieces of wood such as beams and boards. Small pieces of wood and slats can also be put together in layers and glue together under pressure and then laminated for aesthetic reasons. Glu-lam beams can be made into different shapes and sizes with varying sections to fit one's need. They are ideal for roofing and floor slabs.

Particleboard, sometimes called chipboard or flake board is produced by mixing a resin-bonding agent with wood particles and bonding them together by means of heat and pressure. These low-strength finished products are for non-structural use such as furniture, flooring, cabinets, drawers, paneling, etc. They are sometimes laminated to produce different colors and designs of melamine sheets for beauty. A hardier product is the solid hardboard which made use of compressed wood fibers.[380]

There are several grades depending on where they are going to be used. The low density particleboards are prepared using agro-wastes like rice straw, paddy husk, jute sticks, jute fibre, marble dust, etc. Medium density boards are made from chips of wood which are bonded together with organic binder or glue depending upon the end use. The high density are made of jute stick boards and are suitable for partition walls, false ceiling, paneling, doors and windows, furniture, etc. The jute fibro-boards have been found suitable for acoustic treatment of auditoriums, cinema halls and offices, etc.[381]

There are also fibreboards that are made of wood and compressed to form sheets or boards. They are often used as temporary wall partitions, They are lightweight and can be laminated to extend their usage. There are several grades that could be used for more durable finishing. There are the gypsum wallboards using materials coming from power plants and glued together with two layers of heavy paper.

* * * * *

Engineers and scientists are always moving to improve wood with other materials such as plastics to make them more durable and useful. They can be produced for structural and non-structural use. One of these is the wood-plastic composites. Thermoplastic polymers are added to the wood using the extrusion and injection molding process to come up with the composites that could be used in exterior environment that are water resistant and without using preservative. The wood can be anything from fibers, wood flour, particles, strands, veneers or lumber.[382]

Most of these composites today are aimed at mimicking and replacing solid wood materials. The composites can be tailored to any shape and size while maximizing performance and minimizing material usage to reduce cost. The composite can be also designed with hollow cross-sections to remove ineffective regions of the composite and also improve strength. There will be less wastage.[383]

Plastics are nonrenewable materials, but they are being discarded as refuse in landfills in large quantities. They are seldom recycled for reuse as there is little market for them. Government agencies and the plastic industry have invested millions of dollars researching on how to use discarded plastics. One of them is the plastic lumber. By 1995, about one million tons of plastics were recycled in the US out of the 19 million tons being discarded, according to die EPA figures.[384]

There are three products that can be made out of recycled plastics. The high-density polyethylene (HDPE) commonly used in milk jugs and grocery bags can be 100% recycled into plastic lumber. There are however, many shortcomings. They are heavy, slippery, subject to warping, contraction and expansion by the sun's heat and lack the strength of wood.[385]

A 50-50% composition of HDPE and wood has been produced by Mobil Chemical called Rivenite. The improved composite product is lighter, stronger and sdffer and less affected by thermal expansion and contraction. It is now produced by a spin-off company called Trex and sold under the same name. These lumbers are produced with dimensions that match those of conventional lumber.[386]

AERT, Inc. of Junction, Texas uses a combination of HDPE, low-density polyethylene (LPDE) and wood fiber to produce plastic wood under the name of ChoiceDek. They are used for decks and handrails. The wood fiber came from oak or red cedar chips left over after extracting the aromatic oils. All ChoiceDek are of uniform silvery gray becausc of the consistent type of wood used instead of wood waste.[387]

The U.S. Plastic Lumber uses several composite products to produce SmartDeck. It is a complete system with planks, posts, railings, stair treads, trim and fascia boards. Railings are hollow for easy installations of wires. The company also produce fiberglass-plastic composite by incorporating fiberglass into the recycled HDPE to increase its strength, Another company with products similar to SmarkDeck called Nexwood uses rice hulls - the veiy strong fiber left over after threshing rice. It is produced by Composite Technology Resources Ltd. of Quebec.[388]

Furniture

Furniture is part of modem life. The demand for furniture is growing faster than the demand for houses because of the numerous appliances coming into die market. Most of the furniture in the market are cheaper today because they are made of reconstituted wood or particleboard. However, there are still those rich people who insist on having furniture made of tropical hardwood because of its beauty and durability. The near exhaustion of these woods in many tropics and their environmental impact during harvesting should dampen and leads to less deforestation, It is time to change our attitude toward the trees as the world cannot afford to accommodate our wasteful lifestyles.

Most furniture can last a lifetime. When broken it can be repaired and if not, can be converted to other uses. When the old furniture are replaced, instead of storing the old ones, it can be given away or sold in the open market. There are second hand furniture shops where buyers can find them. Shopping for second furniture can be a bargain. Avoid buying furniture made of hardwood. Each piece of furniture left in the market is one less piece of hardwood saved.

* * * * *

Christmas is celebrated in Christendom, but many countries of different faiths are cashing in on the Christmas spirit. One of the products heavily traded is the Christmas tree. These trees are often stripped from immature plants and "killed" by being painted over. Plantations have been setup precisely for growing trees for the Christmas season. Even then these trees are often de-rooted and practically useless for replanting. This is a wasteful practice and should be outlawed. Small frees should be sold with their roots intact so it could be replanted. The tree can be grown in one's own backyard or in a friend's and even in schools or wherever it is needed. Millions of trees could be spared. Artificial trees made of metal trunks and plastic stems are in vogue in place of trees. They are good substitutes and can be reused for years.

Disposable Chopsticks

Chopstick is a known Chinese invention and has been in use for three thousand years. It is also the main producer, consumer and exporter of wooden chopsticks in the world. People there have become accustomed to the Japanese way of using disposable chopsticks and it does not bode well for the trees because of its huge population.

China produces about 50 billion pairs of chopsticks every year. The chopsticks are made of birch and poplar trees while the high-quality ones use Korean pine. In the year 2000 there were over 22 billion pairs exported to Japan and South Korea.[389]

Like the Japanese, the Chinese eat a lot of noodles and they can only be eaten with chopsticks. They often use durable chopsticks made of plastic and other more permanent materials such as bamboo. It was only in the mid-1980s that disposable chopsticks were mass produced and used in the country, long after Japan, South Korea and Hong Kong have been using them. It was promoted by the government to fight communicable disease and at one point even required restaurants in various cities to the cities them. The economic upturn and the movement of peasants to the cities with their hectic lifestyle and take-out mentally only encouraged their use.[390]

According to government statistics, China produces and discards more than 45 billion pairs of disposable chopsticks every year and exports another 15 billion pairs abroad, mainly to Japan and South Korea. In the process, as many as 25 million trees are cut down annually. As the problem of disposing of these chopsticks and other throwaway wastes litter the environment followed by the destructive floods of 1998, concern to reduce the harmful wastes ignited the environmental movement.[391]

This is not as difficult as it seems. The government can ban the use of disposal chopstick once and for all. South Korea has largely switched to metal chopsticks after a ban of disposable ones in all restaurants was enforced in 1995. In China, some restaurants have unilaterally banned the use of disposal chopsticks and the Finance Ministry is preparing a new tax on throwaway chopsticks to discourage their use.[392] Using fork and spoon is another way, although a little awkward for those who prefer eating long string of noodle. For those who insist on using chopsticks, they can always carry their own metallic or bamboo chopsticks that can be washed after each meal. Educating the people to the need of protecting the trees will discourage their use. Production of disposable chopsticks could also increase die cost and discourage their use. Sanitizing the disposables is another way and can be enforced by law. For those take-out meals the best way is probably the use of disposable plastic utensils that can be easily washed and reused.

* * * * *

The disposable chopsticks are the common implement used by Japanese in restaurants and takeaway lunches. They are generally made of white birch or bamboo and imported from China. According to the Japanese Forestry Agency, in the year 2000 the per capita use is 200 pairs and account for 25.155 billion pairs for which 24.23 billion were imported.[393] There is no end in sight for this culture of destruction even in the face of the diminishing forest cover around the world. Plantations have been deliberately set up just to supply this profitable market. The sources of wood used to be taken from the tropical forest until so many of them cannot keep up with the demand. Chopsticks are now being imported as far as Canada. According to Entity Mission, a chopstick manufacturer in British Columbia produced 7.5 million pairs of chopsticks a day.

There are some risks although very minimal in using disposable chopsticks. This is due to the fungicides in treating the trees and the bleaching agents used in making the chopsticks white. The prices of chopsticks have also fallen and therefore did not affect the demand. The tion and recycling of disposable chopsticks to make paper is also ing the demand high.

* * * * *

Two Japanese conglomerates, Mitsubishi and Daishowa Keiretsu are currently clear cutting the boreal forest of northwestern Canada to harvest frees and to turn them into chopsticks and plywood for concrete forms. A total 100,000 sq. miles of land mass have been given away under forest management agreements at a giveaway price of $1.1 billion. In return the Japanese companies expect to gross $8.2 billion or more in the process. The Canadian government has historically undervalued its timber for fear that it could lead to the loss of livelihood for its more than one million loggers.[394]

Most of the trees are one hundred year old Aspen trees in Alberta and British Columbia. Much of the lumber are turned into chopsticks known in Japan as *waribashi*. They are used not only in Japan but through the world where Japanese restaurants can be found. Mitsubishi and Daishowa produce about 20 billion pairs annually and they are used only once by the Japanese as they do not wish to reuse one utilized earlier by another. They believe that the chopstick was given to them by the gods, and are therefore sacred and held in high regard.[395]

One unreasonable demand about chopsticks is that they must be unblemished by any know or even a small scar. This strange behaviour has been a concern for many environmentalists. They believe this attitude should change in the face of deforestation to supply an already bad eating habit. Many foreigners dining in Japanese restaurants have already picked up the bad habit.[396] Just because they can afford to pay for their bad habit is no justification for destroying the forests of another country. The Japanese are also fearful of getting infected of communicable diseases. Wooden chopsticks are difficult to sanitize whether by dry heat or wet heat. Dry heat will turn the wood into charcoal while wet heat will turn the wood into pulp. Irradiation is too costly. The only solution is disposable chopsticks but the cost to the environment is even more costly. The only other solution is to use alternative products for chopsticks. The chances of getting contaminated is very nil with well-washed plastic or metallic chopsticks.

The San Francisco-based Rainforest Action Network (RAN) has called on the world to boycott Mitsubishi Corporation in the hope of stopping its destructive way of extracting forest products around the world. Everyday, the company manufactures 8 million pairs of chopsticks in Canada using only the finest-grain Aspen trees with its high-tech chopstick mill. As a result three-quarters of the trees are left to rot in the field and had outraged Canadian foresters and activists. The chopsticks are then shipped to Taiwan for finishing before being exported to Japan. To add insult to injury, the packaging even contains a motto saying "chopsticks that protect nature," and is discarded after one use.[397]

* * * * *

The nature of the chopstick is a wasteful use of lumber. Only 40% of the lumber can be utilized into making the chopstick. This is because of the trimming waste, the rounding of the chopstick from the initial square lumber and the polishing. Then there is the quality control. Even with the best Aspen tree only two or three make the grade for export. The rest of the lumber is wood waste or sawdust and good only for burning in biomass power plant instead of more productive use. Another problem is that Aspen trees suitable for chopstick making are difficult to ascertain until it is cut down. By then it is too late unless there is another different mill that can make use of it. Otherwise, left alone it can easily rot.

The wastage can be reduced dramatically with a more comprehensive use of the wood. The core can be produced as brush handles, ice cream sticks and the skin of the wood can be used as fuel. With this kind of utilization, the utilization rate goes up to 75% to 85%.[391]

Bamboo

There is no other non-tree product that has more uses than the simple bamboo. Since ancient times, it has been used by the Chinese and the Japanese in more ways than Westerners could ever conceived. It has been used as framework for the house, thatches for die roof, paper supplies, awnings for his sheds, blinds for his veranda, thousand of articles for thc home furniture, shaving and shreds for his pillows and mattress, as a carpenter's ruler, fanner's waterwheel, irrigation pipes, cages for birds, crickets and other pets, etc. It has been used as a weapon such as spears, shooting blowguns and bows and arrows. It has been used as several forms of musical instruments, baskets, waterproof coats from its dried leaves, smoking pipes, etc. (Farrelly, 16)

The uses of bamboo read like the ABC of many practical things we use today. It has been used as the main cables for bridges, as writing implements in the form of brushes, candlesticks, carrying poles and dancing poles such as tinikling, carts, fences, defense shields, chairs and tables, and toys, In time of famine, it seeds serves a food for the hungry. In 1864 the flowering of the bamboo in the Soopa jungles in western India provided food for 50,000 Indians. In 1921, during the famine in Hunan, the bamboo flowered and saved the people. (Ibid, 44)

Believe it or not, one variety of bamboo was used as filament for the light bulb. In 1880, Thomas Edison learned that finely shredded bamboo serves as a firm support for round hemp palm leaf fans. Taking his clue from this hint, he collected all available varieties of bamboo from all over the world, including Japan. After repeated tests, he ascertained that a variety from Kyoto would best serve his purpose. In 1882, he set up a company to produce incandescent lamps from the filaments of Japanese bamboo and illuminated the nights of New York. The world's first light bulb made over a century ago still burns with bamboo in the Smithsonian Institution in Washington, D. C. (Ibid, 51)

* * * * *

Bamboo, a grass has played an important role in the economies and cultures of Asian and many tropical nations for centuries. It has traditionally been a key source of lightweight rot-resistant "wood" for homes and public buildings in the rural areas. This grass is also a dietary staple for livestock, lemurs, gorillas and the pandas. It has a special property different from wood. Its flexibility also makes it ideal for furniture of different shapes, giving the room an attractive and natural look. It is fast-growing, light and cheap. It has been used for scaffolding by painters and glass installers.

There are 1,200 species of the bamboo and half of them are in danger of extinction, according to the joint report of the UN Environment Programme (UNEP) and the International Network for Bamboo and Rattan (INBAR) study. Their loss could make some species of animals such as the red panda, mountain tapir, birds, the Himalayan black bear, etc. that depend on them for food and shelter vulnerable.[399]

The bamboo has been traditionally used for packaging and paper pulp in many areas. The Japanese use bamboo more widely than any other material. It is used to wrap countless pastries, candies, fish and soybean lunches. Miniature bamboo objects became the trademark package of different areas. In China, before the discovery of paper, records were first kept in thin strip of bamboo They were proven to be durable to survive two thousand years in fresh and legible condition. (Ibid, 55, 272)

The original form of true paper as we know it today is made from the cooking of several materials including rags, straw, bark, bamboo wood and other fiber materials. Additionally, bamboo is used as the sieve on which the wet fibers of pulp were lifted from the vat. Thin strips of bamboo, as many as twenty to forty to the inch, provide a surface from which the wet sheets cold be removed rapidly. This invention made it possible to make papers in commercial quantities. (Ibid, 272-273)

Like trees it has been subjected to overharvest. A new technique could allow botanist to breed a better version faster than heretofore possible, Bamboo in the field can take more than a century to flower and produce seeds. This new development could be a quantum breakthrough for reforestion in many depleted tropical countries.

Coffins

The fabrication of coffins has been partly responsible for millions of trees being chopped down. Cheap species are not spared because the poor cannot afford the hardwood. Other substitutes are more expensive and out of reach for the majority of the people. It has been implicated as one of the sources of deforestation in China due to its huge population. The same can be said of many developing countries with diminishing forest stands.

The US imports half of its mahogany from South America. Because of increasing demand, loggers are pushing into wildlife protection and indigenous areas. A large portion of the import is used in making coffins which can fetch as much as $10,000 for hand-made ones.

In Spain, there is a company engaged in harvesting almond for consumption. The shell is used for heating the fumace but with so much excess, the company decided to do something about it. They ground the shell into powder and with resin and glue they were able to mold it into coffins that has the same texture as one made from wood. They called the new coffin Metalon. They are light and combustible and therefore can be used in cremation. The old wooden coffin uses 50 kilos of wood which they hope to save. In 1995, they produced 10,000 coffins and saved

2,000 trees a year. With 5.3 million deaths annually in the original EU countries, they hope to increase the coffin production to save one million trees a year. Since the compound of almond, resin and glue can be molded into different shapes, other products such as baggage and hard casings have been made from the compound.

A news report datelined Webster, New Hampshire has an interesting story. A coffin maker named Bill Hale is making coffins that can serve as furniture. His coffins can serve as coffee tables, book shelves, liquor cabinet, blanket chests and also as gun cabinets. Other uses were also found. The price ranges from $700 for a simple pine coffin to $2,200 for a black walnut coffin with molded stiles and rails. The cost is well below those sold through the funeral homes which range from $2,000 to $8,000 for hand-carved caskets. Not only is the price much lower, the wood used in making them serves another purpose while the owners are still alive.[400]

Chapter 14

PAPER PRODUCTS

Wood from the forests is the source of the bulk of the world's paper, accounting for 90% of all papermaking fibers. Every year some four billion trees are cut down to make paper products and the demand is growing.[401] Other sources include, cotton, cloth rag, bagasse, bamboo, manila rope, straw from rice and wheat, hemp, kenaf, etc. The current world pulp requirement is more than 225 million tons. It is increasing tremendously as more people from the Third World are getting more education accompanied by the ever increasing population growth. Most of the papers are used by people in the developed countries, but those in the developing countries are catching up. This massive volume requires millions of hectares of forest plantations solely for the production of high-fiber softwood trees used for papermaking.

Paper is a versatile product with a guaranteed market. It has many uses as printed matters for books and newspapers that made the people of the world well informed of what is happening elsewhere. Books have been printed that made it possible for others to learn and improve on their knowledge. Although the original use of paper is for writing, its low cost and lightweight has been adopted in other industries. It can be found in packaging and other industrial uses. Specially treated papers have been manufactured for a wide variety of applications such as filter, battery use, diaper, wallpaper, wallboard, acoustics, and countless others. New applications for paper are being discovered.

The demand for paper is expected to grow as the population grows. Technological advances along with paper and paperboard recycling have substantially reduced the need to produce pulp for making paper. In 1970 paper and paperboard consisted of 80% wood pulp. By 1997, due to efficient production processes the figure has been reduced to 56%. There is even a secondary market for recycled paper. New uses are also being found for specialized paper that it is expected to keep the demand continuing.

Wood Pulp

Tropical hardwoods are not desirable in making wood-pulp that can be used in making paper and other related products. Instead some paper makers and their producers are turning to a technique called "whole-tree utilization" where magnificent giant trees are turned into wood chips. This was pioneered by the Japanese when it invaded the forest of Papua New Guinea.[402] In Madang, PNG, a chip mill using a giant 8-foot chipper blade could clear cut all the trees in an 8,000 square kilometers of the rainforest within a year. (Ang, Trees, 165)

As soon as these trees are clear cut, monoculture plants are planted for future harvest Non-indigenous trees such as eucalyptus are used for paper-pulp production. Brazil has become of the world's largest paper-pulp producers in the world, all at the expense of the once pristine rainforests.[403] Other places with huge pulpwood plantations include Chile, Indonesia, Thailand and Portugal. They are intensively managed, set in blocks of a single species of either eucalypts, poplars, pines and acacias. They produce industrial round wood at high growth rates and competitive prices, harvested in less than 20 years instead of 50 years for normal forests.[404]

There are so much denuded lands that can be used for softwood plantations for the paper industry. The problem is that more often than not, instead of reforesting the denuded forests for the setup of pulpwood plantations for the future, the loggers prefer to continue with the onslaught of the ancient forests.

J

The largest tract of essentially undisturbed temperate forest in the world remains mostly in southern Chile and partly in Argentina. It is dominated by southern beeches such as ulmo and laurel. This did not escape the piying eyes of the Japanese pulp and paper industries that import more than 99% of half of Chile's wood chip production. Between 1984 and 1994, 700,000 hectares of ancient forests have been cleared just for making wood chips. Big and small loggers and landowners have been implicated in destroying the native forests.[405]

In the Philippines, farm tree production of pulpwood is used by the PICOP. To augment their sources of pulpwood, there is a program to contract tree farmers to plant Albizzia falcataris (falcata) on plots of about 10 hectares to supply pulpwood to PICOP. The farmers are given seeds and were paid on a staggered basis based on the survival rate of the trees until they are four years old. It takes only eight years before the trees can be harvested. While waiting for the trees to mature, they are allowed to grow crops and livestock for their subsistence needs. What started out with one farm in 1968 had reached more than 22,000 hectares by 1981 with 4,500 farmers involved. The monetary rate of return is about 30%. Aside from getting a source of raw material for the paper mill, PICOP was able to reduce the number of insurgents operating in the provinces by getting them involved in tree plantations.

Currently, there are an estimated 10 million hectares devoted to fast wood plantations worldwide. An additional one million hectares are being added annually. This is a response to the growth of world consumption of paper. Most of these projects are subsidized by the government. The World Bank estimates that they are subsidized in the amount of around $14 billion annually worldwide. The subsidy has a way of reducing the clearing of forestlands.

It is not all bad for the environment. These fast wood plantations as they are sometimes called have produced some hardwood for the building industry, charcoal for the steel industry and as raw material for the paper industry. They also reduced pressure on some natural forests by providing jobs and income and contribute in a small way to preserving biodiversity.

Substitutes for Making Papers

Presently, there is a disproportionate number of people using paper. North America, Europe and Japan contain 16% of the world's population but they consume two-thirds of the world's paper and paperboard and half of its industrial wood.[406] This huge demand is expected to increase and there is a need to find substitutes. There are other agricultural products that can be used as substitutes in making papers. They include such waste as straw and bagasse (sugarcane residues), espardo grass, reed, bamboo, fibrous hibiscus species, cotton, denim scraps, kenaf, com stover, hemp and agricultural wastes. In fact hemp can supply four times as much pulp as those coming from pulpwood plantations. Many of these alternative pulps produce less pollution from manufacturing paper than those coming from the tree fibers. (Huxley, 105)

With the world's paper demand projected to double by the year 2010 from the 1994 consumption, there is good reason to shift production toward "treeless papers" - those that are made from non-wood pulp. In China, more than 80% of all paper fiber is made from non-wood sources. Treeless papers were manufactured in 45 countries in 1992, and accounted for 9% of the world's paper supply.[407] With proper economic incentives and support for technology and market development, the use of treeless paper could expand greatly.

There are also several advantages in using treeless paper. The fibers can be gathered from fast-growing plants. Most of them have more fibers than trees. These papers are usually grown from weeds without pesticides and chlorine- and acid-free and therefore free from such pollutants as dioxins and furans inherent in tree-based papermaking.

* * * * *

Research undertaken by the Forest Products Research and Development Institute, an agency under the Department of Science and Technology (DOS O of the Philippines has found that many parts of the coconut tree possesses promising fibers that can be used for the pulp and paper industry. The coconut trunk, petiole and midribs, both parts of the leaves can also be used for paper making. The coconut trunk is high in cellulose, low in silica and lignin which are desirable attributes for pulps.

Pure coco trunk pulp has been found feasible for the manufacture of onion skin paper and heavy duty bags for packaging. Both papers exceed the specified standard strength. Pulp from a mixture of 60% coconut coir and 40% abaca have been found to meet the US federal specifications for strength and optical requirement.

Even the stalk of the banana tree is a good source of paper pulp. The stalks are usually thrown away, creating a large pile of trash. A company in Costa Rica is using it in making paper. No chemicals are used to make and colored banana paper. The different colors can be done by adding dirt to pulp. Note pads, posters, and stationery made from the banana plants are now available from the AE-natural-New Orleans Paper Company.

There are other substitutes that can be used. They include coffee wastes after brewing. Used denims can also be sources of fibre because they are made of cotton, one of the strongest fibers. Even the old dollar bills have been blended with cotton to add more strength to the recycled paper.

Recycling Paper

Papermaking from the virgin fiber is one of the highest users of energy in the industries. Not only that wood contains only 30% cellulose and requires strong chemicals to remove the cellulose from the wood pulp, On the other hand, recycling paper uses half the amount of energy- and water and therefore reduces air and water pollution. As the recycled papers have been bleached, there is no need to bleach again. Any bleaching can be done safely with hydrogen peroxide. It is often said that each ton of paper uses 17 trees to make them and recycling them should save the same amount.[408] Recycling one ton paper saves 2.5 m³ of landfill space.

In one study, the resources and energy requirements for a ton of first class paper are 2,385 kilos of wood, 440,000 liters of water and 7,600 Kwh of energy; for ordinary paper the wood required is 1,710 kilos, 280,000 liters of water, and 4,750 Kwh of energy. For 100% recycled paper the resources needed are wastepaper, 1,800 liters of water and the energy requirement is 2,759 Kwh. Big companies can make great savings. In one AT&T office in New Jersey, recycling paper earned enough to save about 62,000 medium sized trees and energy saving of about 9,000 barrels of oil. Multiply this by the millions of offices around the world and the saving could be enormous.

The Warmer Campaign puts the figure at 58% saving in industrial water compared to using virgin paper, 40% for energy saving, reduction of air pollution by 74% and water pollution by 35%. (Dudley, 104)

Currently the rate of recycling is going up as a result of the shortage of wood pulp and a mushrooming demand for papers and packaging for the export markets especially in China. Americans are now recycling half of the papers they normally use - 300 pounds per person per year. The price of papers for recycling are also going up as the demand of several Asian countries led by China are bidding for American scrap papers. The export of scrap papers accounts for $8.4 billion last year (2004), making it the number export by volume.[409]

The demand for wastepaper for recycling is due to the shortage of virgin paper. Recycling paper is more expensive and the quality is not as good. That is why in 1990, the US recycled only a third of its paper. That has changed as timber for papermaking has become expensive. It is hope that by 2012, the Americans will increase the amount of recycling to 55%, still far below that of Germany and Finland with recycled paper to 75%.[410]

In Portland, Oregon, the recovery of used paper reached as much as 550 pounds per person last year as a result of the city's policy of charging garbage pickups. Homeowners who maximize recycling can save $73 to $170 a year on their garbage collection bill.[411]

The price of scrap paper used for recycling is in the vicinity of $80 to $120 a ton. Most of the US scrap papers end up in China's massive new Nine Dragons paper recycling mill in Dongguan, China It is the world's largest and is unique in its ability to turn low-quality mixed papers into respectable paperboard for boxes and packaging.[412] In 2004, Chinese mills purchased about 6 million tons of the 50 million tons of waste paper recovered in the US. They even bought at higher prices than some of their neighboring countries. They can afford to because the workers there are paid only $3.40 a day to sort mixed papers by hand compared to $5.15 per hour in the US.[413]

The Mareal Paper Mills, one of the largest paper mills in the US uses wastepaper in all its paper products. It does not even own any forest or logging firms. It processes 150,000 tons of wastepaper annually and hopes to boost that figure. Much of the wastepaper came from the municipal collection program. Currently it accepts recyclables from over six hundred municipalities, representing more than a thousand communities in four states. It is expanding its collection efforts to include undelivered third-class mails from the postal system.

Bergstrom Paper Company of Neenah, Wisconsin, converts more than 160 tons of wastepaper daily into paper for all kinds of uses but never own a forest. In fact as many as 200 paper mills in the US rely exclusively on wastepaper to produce their products.

Recycling paper can be done at home. Gather some used papers, tear them into pieces and place them inside a blender. Add some water and switch on the blender until the paper turns into pulp. Prepare a pan half the size of the used paper and pour one-inch depth of water into it Place a very fine screen into the pan and pour a measured cup of pulp over the screen. Spread the pulp entirely into the water with your fingers. Lift the screen and let the water drain. Place the whole thing between two pages of a newspaper and close it. Carefully turn over the newspaper so that screen is on top of the pulp. Place a board on top of the newspaper and press down to squeeze out the water. Open the newspaper and remove the screen. Leave the newspaper open to let the pulp dry for at least a day. Once it is dry, carefully remove off the newspaper and you have a finished recycled paper. Although this is a crude way of recycling, the basic procedure is the same for large recycling plants.

* * * * *

In many poor Third World countries, recycling paper is not a priority even though they have to use hard-earned dollars to import them. Except for newspaper, which can easily be recycled, there is almost no demand for the other type of glossy papers. Even then, there is little incentive to collect and sell the newspaper to a secondary market partly due to the fluctuations in prices of used paper and low rate of return. In The Netherlands, the government maintains stockpiles of wastepaper and acts as a middleman to stabilize the market. Newspaper consumes a lot of paper, and many publishers use a lot of recycled wastepaper. A law requiring a minimum content of recycled fiber will encourage more recycling and sets up paper recycling enterprises.

In the US, the demand for recycled paper is increasing as a result of the government's requirement that all official government documents need to increase the use of recycled fiber. This has led to a new crime: stealing wastepaper from recycling bins or raiding boxes of free news sheets. Nationwide, as much as $100 million in theft of wastepaper was reported in the US, according to the magazine Resource Recycling. The boom in theft of wastepaper, mostly newspaper has led to tighter legislation in the in the US. In New York, stealing old newspaper can result in a year's imprisonment.

Hemp

Hemp is a versatile weed that has many uses. It can supply fiber for the paper industry better than wood because it contains 70% cellulose compared to 30% for wood. In fact it was used by the Chinese for thousands of years as sources of paper making. Thomas Jefferson drafted the US Declaration of Independence on hemp-based paper in 1776.[414] In Canada where hemp has been legalized under a restricted atmosphere, it is being used and cultivated for hemp seed production and made into staple plant sources of protein and fat in the form of nutritious food. Other products include hemp cereals, hemp baked goods, nutrition bars, butter and even hemp beer.[415]

Hemp trees have been planted for centuries before they were banned in many countries. In Britain the seed was once traded on the stock exchange like oranges and spices today. The hemp can grow fuel for the oil lamps. The flowering tops was kept and used as medicine for the body, the seed for food, the stem for wood, pulp and fiber and the roots to bind and invigorate the soil. In twenty weeks it could grow up to 20 feet.

Hemp cultivation in die US ended after the Marijuana Tax Act of 1937 placed a prohibitive tax on those who want to deal with hemp. The new association with drug abuse and the availability of other substitutes forced people to shift to chemical-based products. Today it is illegal to grow hemp without a government permit which is very difficult to obtain.[416]

It was briefly allowed to be grown during the Second World War as 1937 US Army and USDA sponsored the "Hemp for Victory" program where patriotic farmers were asked to grow hemp to offset war shortages of fibers needed for rope, uniforms, and other products. After the war, it was banned again [417]

The confusion between hemp and marijuana stems from the fact that both are by-products of the plant cannabis sativa, and both contain a psychoactive chemical called THC. Marijuana contain THC of 4% to 20%, but seed varieties of the hemp plant have been developed through genetic engineering that cany THC of less than 1% and are incapable of producing a "high" effect no matter how much is smoked.[418]

Several countries such as England, Germany, Holland, Hungary, China, Chile and Switzerland have limited planting programs and are using hemp in many of their products. China is die largest exporter of hemp paper and textiles. Presently American companies cannot grow hemp, but they can buy sterile seeds and stalks from abroad and use them as raw materials. It has created 10,000 jobs in the last five years and did an estimated $50 million in worldwide sale in 1995 Hemp is also strong and can be recycled eight times as opposed to an average of three times for wood based paper. They have a shelf life of 1,000 years and never turn yellow. It is ideal for paper money bills as it lasts a long time and does not disintegrate.[420]

Kenaf

Kenaf (Hibiscus canabinus) is a non-wood plant that is native to Africa but can be grown elsewhere. It can grow to heights of 12 to 18 feet in just five months, 2 to 4 times faster than trees. It requires few or no pesticides, depending on where it is grown, less herbicides, fertilizers, and low water need. It can grow on marginal land or salty soil without much irrigation. Once matured, it can produce 5 to 10 tons of dry fiber per acre. The plant itself contains two types of fiber - the outer bast fibers and the inner core fibers[421]

Kenaf once an obscure weed is making news in the paper industry. It can be processed into paper without many of the attendant problems, There is no need to use chlorine and other chemicals during pulping processes. At present it has been processed into rope, textiles, food, and feeds for animals in the tropics.

Kenaf is widespread and can be found in about 50 countries worldwide, The fast-growing kenaf plant produces five times more pulp per hectare than other plants used for paper pulps. For every hectare planted with kenaf, four hectares can be devoted to reforestation. And the pulp has all the main qualities needed for making most grades of paper.

It has several other advantages as tests by the USDA show. Kenaf newsprint is as strong as tree newsprint. The paper made from kenaf is brighter, slower to yellow, and less susceptible to ink run-off and smudging. The cost of paper is comparable to high-quality printing paper.

Although it is well known that kenaf can be a good substitute for other trees, the demand has not caught on making it difficult for farmers and paper mills to risk investing in mills using kenaf without established markets. Farmers are also wary of growing kenaf without long-term contract with paper mills to buy their crops. It could be devastating to the farmers should they lose thc market. Another drawback is that unlike trees that can be harv ested when needed, kenaf is harvested once a year only and must be stored which presents a challenge to both farmers and millers.

Dung Paper

Amazingly, animal dung can be transformed into the paper we use daily. This is because the cellulose in the grass eaten by the animals is not digested and comes out with the dung. The Chinese have been using scarab dung for over a thousand years in making paper. More recently, the Thais have been producing paper out of elephant dung. Each elephant can drop more than 100 pounds of dung a day, enough to make 115 sheets of paper. Tbe dung is first washed and later boiled for five hours. The wet mass is then spun dry for up to three hours to allow workers to cut the fiber into smaller pieces. Finally, the fiber is pressed into paper products. In one of its advertisements, it is marketed as 100% odor free, 100% bacteria-free, 100% recycled, and 100% handmade – with the exception of some help from the elephants. The pioneer of this project is the Thai Elephant Conservation Center in Lampang, Thailand.[422]

In Scandinavia the elk poop is made into paper and is one of the stationeries of choice in most offices. The Australians are also planning to use kangaroo poop to make stationery and other paper products. The problem is getting enough poop while in Thailand the problem is marketing the paper. This is one way of recycling animal wastes.[423] The dung from the American bison have been turned into paper for artworks[424]

Paper Use

Paper is probably the single most important product coming from the trees. While papers can be manufactured through other sources, trees are still the predominant source that can supply the worldwide demand.

Paper has so many uses it is difficult to comprehend a world without them. Yet, it is one of the most neglected pieces of merchandise.

Paper products can be found everywhere. In restaurants, food arcades, shopping centers, and even in airplanes. Napkins are used for wrapping utensil, cleaning glasses and a host of mundane uses. Try saving the paper by not using them in the first place. Also return them unused so that they won't be thrown away as wastepaper.

The conveniences demanded by people have resulted in the creation of a lot of unwanted wastes. Some of these wastes are the throwaway paper cups and plates. To avoid disposable paper products is to reduce wastes and save trees. Every year we use billions of these disposables as we move from glasses to throwaway paper products. After use, they are usually too dirty to clean and recycle and thus end up in our garbage cans adding to the garbage disposal and landfill problems. The paper plates and cups came from paper bleached with chlorine which produces dioxin that poses health problems and water pollution. We should return to the old practice of using glasses for our drinks and ceramics or china for our plates. They usually last for years.

Most of the filters we use for coffee or water filtration are made from chlorine-bleach whitened paper. This makes it possible for dioxin to leach into our drinks. Dioxin causes cancer, cell mutations, and many other harmful effects even at extraordinary low concentrations in the human body. Use cloth filters and save those papers.

Shopping bags made of paper are not considered to be an intelligent choice because they are not durable and easily torn unless they are made of considerable thickness and strength. Avoid them whenever possible, When shopping, bring along your durable plastic or straw bags. Some supermarkets charge customer for the shopping bag, so bring your own durable bags.

In a typical office, as much as 85% of all office waste is discarded paper. Millions of trees can be spared from destruction even if only a small portion is reused or recycled. Office paper is prized by recyclers because high quality bond and computer papers can be reprocessed into other quality products. The lower grade wastepaper can be reprocessed into lower-grade products like toilet paper and paper towels.

The computer is supposed to usher in paperless communication. But the negative seems to be true. We need to be computer-smart to make computer what it was supposed to do. Use the computer to make rough drafts. The programs available have many versatile features that can help us check errors, set up margins, use different fonts before printing. Messages can even be sent to other computers without putting them on printed paper Other programs for other purposes are also available. The information can be sent to other companies or offices simply by accessing the internet or the local networking.

Corporation annual reports are usually voluminous and each subscriber is entitled to a copy of the report. Most subscribers do not even bother to read the fine prints. A summary report should cut down the paper use. If full report is necessary, some companies have resorted to printing the report on computers and subscribers are encouraged to access these reports.

There are over a billion telephones worldwide. If each phone will have one directory, there will be more than a billion copies of the telephone directories distributed to every subscriber. Many households and offices with multiple telephones need only a copy of the directory while the excess are discarded or stored away. Pick up only the number of directories needed and leave the rest for reuse or recycling by the telephone company. The US uses more than 650,000 tons of paper for its telephone directories annually.

Reuse the envelopes as often as possible. Paste a patch of paper over the old address and reuse the envelopes for mailing purposes. Try to open the envelopes without destroying them. Do not seal the length of the envelopes unless necessary to preserve it for future use. Collect the stamps. Used postage stamps are worth money especially those less common foreign ones. It could be a worthwhile hobby. Charitable organizations often collect and sell these stamps for their charity work. Donate them for charity.

Refrain from using envelopes with windows. They are more expensive and difficult to recycle. If windows are required, use the new envelopes with recyclable gl as sine windows that can be recycled with the other paper products.

Telephone companies can dispense with so many telephone directories by giving discounts to those who do not need the directories. This will greatly reduce die need for directories which are seldom used in the first place.

* * * * *

Our judiciary system uses a lot of paper. It is second to the government in paper use. Communications between the courts and the litigants usually come in several copies. Court hearings in criminal cases are especially voluminous, sometimes running into hundreds or thousands of pages. Complaints, manifestations, memoranda, pleadings, etc. need a lot of paper and they come in several copies. It has long been a standard practice for records to be typed in double or even triple spacing. This wasteful practice is largely to be blamed for the voluminous paper. The wastage is especially glaring in the transcription because the stenographers get paid based on the number of sheets. The margins and line spacings are large and wasteful. As much as 50% or more are lost as a result. There must be a standard form that would reduce the usage of paper.

Typing in single space will reduce the amount of paper used by half, Another page can be saved by using both sides of the paper Use of small prints will further reduce the number of papers. Reducing the margins on all sides will even save more paper space. All in all, court papers can be reduced by at least 75%. With millions of cases worldwide it would mean millions of trees saved.

Typewritten pages are often not fully used up. The use of standard size instead of legal size paper whenever possible would save 15% in paper. All these practical savings could be adopted for all government agencies and even private institutions. Use proper size of paper to minimize waste.

In California, a law regulating contracts by the state for printing jobs requires the use of recycled paper products to the maximum limit. Any company bidding on a printing project must specify thc percentage of recycled material for paper used. State agencies are expected to achieve the 35% of high grade recycled papers after January 1, 1997 and 40% after January 1, 2004. This is not difficult to attain since there are already in existence paper mills that produce 100% recyclable papers.

Governments around the world, whether local or national, can mandate the use of recycled papers in all their offices for most of their documents. Exceptions to important documents can be made.

* * * * *

Every minute of every day, more than two million photocopies are made. Multiply this number by 60 minutes per hour and 24 hours per day and you can just imagine how many trees are needed to supply us with 5.76 million reams of paper we use every day just for photocopying. Each pulp tree can produce about 12.5 reams of paper. Millions of trees can be saved every year by cutting down on unnecessary photocopies.

A news report in 1996 claimed that photocopier dust can cause serious lung disease. Christine Armbruster and colleagues at the University of Vienna described the case of a man who developed two conditions from the tiny metal particles in the photocopier toner. Toners are made of a fine particulate powder called carbon black. The powder is suspended in a solvent for the wet type or mixed with polymers in the dry toner. Some of the chemicals used are hazardous to health. The man was diagnosed with grandulomatous pnuemonitis caused by breathing in tiny particles of metal and lymphadenopathy.

Spanish doctors also wrote about a 44-year-old woman who suffered another lung disease called siderosilicosis, from working in a photocopying shop. Fetuses in pregnant women are particularly susceptible to DNA alternation.

Another problem associated with photocopiers is the formation of ozone when oxygen is energized by high voltage. Ozone makes breathing difficult and decreases one's resistance to infection. It may be mutagenic. The solution for ozone is simply good ventilation, but many offices today are located in high-rise building with totally sealed windows.

Ricoh of Japan had invented a reverse photocopier than can undo what a photocopier had done. It can erase what was printed on paper which uses toner in copying. At present the machine can undo three pages per minute and each paper can be erased up to ten times Improvements are being done to increase its capacity. Government bureaucracies and large companies are the greatest users of paper and probably can afford to buy the machine.

* * * * *

Avoid using disposable diapers. They contain chlorinc-blcachcd paper containing the dangerous dioxin. An average size tree can produce between 500-1000 diapers. With more than 500 billion disposable diapers used worldwide annually, at least half a billion trees are destroyed every year. Not only that, disposables add to the disposal problem because it takes 500 years to decompose, create seven times more post-consumer solid waste and over three times more solid waste during processing and manufacturing than reusable diapers. Without first rinsing the feces in the toilet bowl, which the correct practice before disposal, the raw fecal matter can be a public health hazard and a contamination to our groundwater.

Disposable diapers contain plastics coming from fossil fuels which are dwindling nonrenewable resources. A typical child uses 8,000 to 10,000 diapers before becoming fully toilet trained. Use of cloth or cotton diapers will save precious natural resources. Each diaper can be reused 150 times. Four dozens of them will be enough for each child and the torn cloth can be used as rag and finally when thrown into the landfill takes only six moths to decompose. The cost of cleaning the diaper is also cheaper, about 58% of the cost of landfilling the disposable diaper.

The so-called "biodegradable disposables" are made with starch filler. These plastics need either sunlight or soil contact to break down. In a garbage dump, few diapers will get cither. Even if the starches in them do break down, the many pieces of plastic still last for centuries.

* * * * *

Worldwide, more than 100 million trees are cut down to be used for producing junk mail. Many of the mails are not made use of recycled paper and are difficult to recycle because they contain silver papers with designs and cellophane envelopes. In the US junk mail alone is responsible for the felling of 10 million trees every year. In 1987, more than ten billion catalogs were sent out to Americans. Forty-five percent of these mails were never opened and were immediately thrown away.

Many of us at one time or another had received mail from magazine publishers and credit card companies soliciting for subscription or gift items. They are mostly made from high quality paper Do not throw the brochures away. Try to reuse whatever portion is available for notes or keep them for recycling. Adopt a policy of returning unwanted, unsolicited mail to the senders. They will soon get the message that your working place is not receptive to such practice. As a protest gesture, use the paper for notes and return them after it has lost its usefulness.

Often times the junk mail is mailed to one person several times. By careful checking by the sender its mailing list, the unnecessary mailing will be minimized. Smith & Haw ken took a step further in 1990 aimed at reducing the amount of unwanted and undelivered mail it sends. The catalogs urge customers to contact Direct Marketing Association to remove their names from the mailing list, and a $5 gift certificate is awarded to customers who send back duplicate labels.

There are other services available in the US. These are the Mailing Preference Services that are run by the marketing industry to stop unwanted junk mail being mail to people. However, it does not prevent "scam mail" such as lotteries and bingo games that prey on senior citizens who have no relatives. The private messenger office could possibly help in removing junk mail. The Center for a New American Dream offer similar services. More information can be found in its website in www.newdream.org/junkmail.

Some environmentalists are calling for a stop the use of postal offices to deliver these junk mails as third or fourth class mails. They should be charged at rates as all regular mails to reduce their widespread use.

* * * * *

Document transmission using the fax machines reduces the need for envelopes and mailing cost. Activities such as delivery to and from the post office, manpower sorting, and stamps manufacturing are eliminated. But before using the fax machine, a telephone call may do the trick faster and more economical.

Fax paper (thermographic) is not difficult to recycle. Most of the prints disappear after some time and it has been customary to photocopy the message and discard the fax copy. Use the fax paper for taking notes and message before discarding it. Another way of saving this non-recyclable paper is to use a half-page cover sheet instead of a full page FAX machine. It will save paper for short messages. In the US alone, it will save about three million kilometers of non-recyclable fax paper in one year.

A fax machine using plain paper is now available. Less pollution can be expected because plain paper uses less chemicals in manufacturing than the fax paper and more savings are expected by recycling the paper for another use.

Computer printers use different sizes of font for printing purposes. By using the smaller size than we normally utilize, we can reduce the amount of paper needed. Reducing the margins can also save papers. Saving papers can be easy by reducing the size of paper we normally use. Using black ink alone makes recycling much easier. Bank statements nowadays use smaller sheets of paper with small print. Letters too can use small print on small size paper. Try to squeeze as much information in as a little space as possible. Brochures that usually take several pages may be reduced to a single page to save paper. Using both sides of the paper saves 50% of the paper.

Cashless Society

Paper money has a lifespan of about 18 months before they are replaced. Coins have been good substitutes except that they are minted only as small denominations. Imagine how much savings can be made from the printing cost and pollution from the chemicals used in making paper money. In the US alone, it is estimated that $400 million is saved every year using coins for small denominations instead of paper money. The use of coins in the Philippines saves about P300 million annually and in the lifespan of 30 years of the coins, it could mean P9 billion. Throughout the world, small denominated currencies are being replaced with coins.

There are more than 50 billion pieces of banknotes in circulation worldwide. The US accounts for about 12 billion pieces worth $380 billion in paper currency circulating worldwide. Keeping all these paper currencies is a costly chore for the government. Most $1 bills wear out in about 17 months. The bigger denominations last a little longer. To retire, destroy, and replace all these aging currencies will cost the government an estimated $200 million a year. Old currencies are dirty and cumbersome as well for businessmen. People have to count them, transport them by armored cars and store them in bank vaults under security guards before they are destroyed. There is also the wave of bank robberies and armor car hijacking to contend with. New currencies likewise have to undergo the same procedure every 18 months or so.

Modem trend in business circles are using less cash and checks. Paper money is dirty and checks are expensive to handle. In the US about 55 billion checks are written every year and the processing cost the nation's financial institutions about $1.30 each or $71.5 billion annually. Some banks end up losing money on about half of all checking accounts due to the small amount involved. Making cash payment or the easy or electronic payment scheme (EPS) will save on paper used to make the checks and reduce handling costs that often exceed the interest earned by banks.

When the European Union shifted to the common euro as the currency effective January 2002, 16 billion euro notes were initially slated to be distributed. Due to the technical specifications of the currency, the bills will be made of cotton fiber and not wood fiber. In other countries, they are shifting to the use of predominantly plastic money that can even be washed with water.

Companies and government payrolls are being paid through banks electronically. All the recipients need is an automatic teller machine (ATM) to access the account. The US government saved $133 million by paying 47% of its 815 million bills by computer rather than by mail in 1995. In 1993, General Electric, which received 40% of its $60 billion in revenues electronically expects to save $2.5 million in stamps and envelopes annually to pay 1,000 of its suppliers. It saves time, paper, stamps, while reducing transport pollution from going to the post office. It is also the safest form of transferring money. The benefits have probably increased several folds since then.

For wire transfer, an electronic transfer costs only $0.15 per blip or less. The big users of electronic transfers have reaped substantial benefits beside the safety of not carrying the amount. The other weapon against bringing cash and checks is the credits cards. Credit cards are proliferating faster because of the many promotional benefits being given away by credit card companies. Users should be wary of using the cards as they have a tendency to overspend.

Newspapers

There are more than 50,000 newspapers worldwide, 8,000 of which are dailies with a total circulation of more than 395 million copies (2004). In the US alone, there are 59 million dailies in 1994 but has decline to 55.6 million for the daily issues and 59 million for the Sunday issues as more people are turning to the Internet for their daily news. In fact in most western countries dailies have slightly dropped in circulation although the worldwide newspaper circulation has increased mostly in Asia. If all these newspapers were from virgin paper, imagine the number of trees being cut daily just so we can read the news on print. Just a single issue of the New York Times Sunday edition uses 75,000 trees weekly not counting the newspapers published from Monday to Saturday.

Most of the income generated by newspapers comes from advertisements. A typical Sunday newspaper usually consists of over a hundred pages of newsprint. By reducing the size of the advertisements, we can correspondingly reduce the number of pages of newsprint while saving advertisement cost. In the US, about 500,000 trees are cut down weekly for the printing of the nation's Sunday edition alone. Some newspapers have reduced the broadsheet paper by one-inch on both sides. Even this small reduction could mean big for newspapers with high volume of publication.

Advertiscment can be done through the Internet. Most of the big companies have their profiles and products advertised in the Internet with minimal cost and are accessible throughout the world.

The *Los Angeles Times* prints and distributes 1.24 million newspapers daily. Eighty percent of the newsprints came from 320,000 tons of at least 50% recycled fiber. It is the largest consumer of recycled newsprint in the world, with a far higher recycled fiber content than California mandated for the year 2000.

The US uses 85 million tons of paper a year that is the equivalent of more than one billion trees. About 25% of the paper is recycled or is equivalent to 250 million trees saved by recycling. Doubling the paper recycled will save another 250 million trees while reducing air and water pollution and energy consumption.

Many stores in the US allow their customers to recycle their old newspaper in bins set up outside the grocery stores. To encourage recycling, these recycling centers can promote giveaway gifts or coupons that can be redeemed for other items.

In office buildings, a common recycling center can be set up to collect old newspapers and arrange for pickup and delivery to a local recycling center on a weekly or monthly basis. Separate bins for different materials can be strategically located where all these recyclable materials can be placed. Buy a few copies of the morning newspapers and place them in strategic places throughout the building. People can read them throughout the day. The system works in libraries and it should work equally well at the office.

At home, we can recycle newspapers and other paper products by collecting and bundling them together. Contact the local buyers when there are enough old newspapers to be hauled away to economize the hauling trip. We can save on subscription of newspapers by sharing the papers. Avoid buying newspapers that we do not read. Set up communal daily newspaper-buying.

* * * * *

Newspaper and book publishers and other businesses engaged in paper products use a lot of virgin fibers for their paper needs. Therefore they have some clout in mitigating the destruction of the forests as to how their suppliers operate their logging firms especially if the papers were directly imported from the paper mills. The *New York Times* once terminated a contract with MacMillan Bloedel for its newsprint supply. Canada's largest forest products company has been clear cutting in Clayquot Sound, North America's largest remaining lowland temperate rainforest. The Times uses 300,000 tons of newsprint annually. It was joining a growing number of companies including Scott Paper and Kimberly Clark that have terminated these contracts with the Canadian company The Sierra Club, which publishes the Sierra magazine had stopped using the Canadian supplier too. The San Francisco Chronicles canceled its contract with MacMillan Bloedel despite a personal visit from the British Columbian Premier Michael Harcourt. There are others that have switched suppliers of newsprints.

* * * * *

The demand for papers for newspapers, books, documents, etc. have urged industries to try to find substitutes to get the news across. All day and night news channels have been setup. Others give periodic updates on news of the hour. Most of them even come to our living room live. People with access to the Internet can read all the news and more to their heart's delight. Many of the largest newspapers in the world have made e-news available free of charge in most cases. Online newspapers and their numbers that are soaring also offer faster access to information than printed newspapers can. More readers are actually canceling their newspaper subscriptions and getting their news from the Internet instead, Internet traffic grew 32% in 2004 and 350% over the five years for the newspaper web sites. Internet advertising revenues also increased by 21% in 2004 compared to the year before[426] Even archives can be accessed to those interested in history. In some cases, even the live news can be heard through the sound system.

* * * * *

Bottle deposit for beverages has been in practice for decades. In environmentally conscious places, bottle recycling is particular high in areas with mandatory laws. This practice can also be applied to newspapers and other paper products. Newspaper, which is usually a one-time use generally gets a higher recycling rate. However, there is still room for improvement. By requiring buyers of newspaper to turn in their old newspaper before they can buy a new one, the amount of wastepaper would increase dramatically. There is always a market because it has been a standard practice of newspaper companies to take back unsold newspaper for recycling. In the US, the more than 50 million newspapers are printed daily used more than 20,000 tons of newsprint. This is equivalent to an average of one tree per person of newsprint annually.

Paperless Communications

Businesses before used a great deal of papers in transaction. All these have changed with the coining of age of the computer. In the more sophisticated offices around the world, communications between offices at different locations are being done digitally with the use of modern attached to the computers. They can be set up to communicate with one another through the Internet. This paperless communication can be scent instantaneously half way around the world by pressing a few keys on the keyboard. The messages can be stored on the computer indefinitely.

The computer monitor has become a sort of "digital paper" for people to read news and even books. The e-Books or electronic books are machines connected to the Internet and downloaded to the computer monitor. The book can be saved and read anytime. Some companies are even giving the e-books away for free.

They can also be downloaded to a machine such as that offer by Nuovomedia Rocket eBook. It is a small electronic book about the size of a paperback with a port and cable to link it to a personal computer and a backlit display screen. The books can be downloaded and aid for via Bamesandnoble.com. Another digital book is the Softbook from SoftBook Press.[427]

Beside all the billions of books and articles that are printed for the general public, technical literatures are increasing too. It is estimated that 2.5 billion copies of journal articles are published in the US each year. Only 10% or roughly 250 million articles are ever read. There is now a demand for selected sets of articles reflecting individual interests rather than the entire journal. It is cheaper and uses less paper. This is made possible by electronic publishing on demand. Those engaged in this business will publish any article that is in the computer upon request of the customers. Publishing books on demand will also cut down excessive printing of books that cannot be sold out.

Advances in computer discs have also allowed huge quantities of information to be carried within the small computer disc (CD). Wholo sets of encyclopedia and other tomes that usually use massive quantities of paper can be digitally reduced to a few pieces of CD. As more and more people are getting hold of smaller electronic gadgets, they can be conveniently earned around for easy reference. This will undoubtedly reduce the consumption of papers but is not expected to end the paper crisis as publishers will continue to print books, especially new ones coming out into the market.

Education has great potentials for teaching students electronically. Students have become accustomed to reading online on the computer. They are being assigned homework using the Internet for research materials. Most of the books are no longer in printed form as many books have been reduced to CDs. In fact the contents of 180 textbooks and references used in all grades from primary through high school could fit onto two CD-ROMS.[428]

There are some drawbacks with the use of computers. In many instances the coming of the paperless era that was touted with the coming of the computer has actually the opposite effects. This is especially tnie in the education department when students are required to work on research and term papers and dissertations in word-processed file format They often write long documents that have to be drafted and edited in printed from many times before the final document is completed.

Government agencies are moving from paper to electronic media to get their message across. The Philippines government has advanced rapidly on this field with the passage of some laws regarding procurement for government offices. Government forms are made available on the Internet without the need of traveling to the offices to get the forms and thereby cutting down on unnecessary trips and waste of precious gasoline.

The Chinese government is currently pushing a national project to broadcast official information via the Internet. Although only a handful of government-related Web sites are open so far, the goal is to have 80% of all government offices using the Internet within two years. It will eliminate the need to print all official documents and they can easily be accessed anywhere in the countiy.[429]

Withdrawals from the banking system need not be laborious and time-consuming. With the availability of automatic teller machines, withdrawals can be done almost anywhere in the world. Most banks even allow transfer of funds between accounts.

* * * * *

Packaging

Packaging is important. While it keeps the goods clean and free from damage, it can serve as an advertisement. But many products use too many layers in packaging material in promoting their products. Being environmentally conscious, we should refrain from buying over-packed items to show the manufacturers that we cannot be intimidated by their practice. The cost of many products we buy from the market includes the cost of packaging which may run as high as 30% for some items. As long as there are enough of us to make a dent in their sales, it will make them think twice about their practice. Another way is to tax the raw materials used in packaging until manufacturers are forced to minimize their use. Avoid buying small items in single packaging. They use more packaging and are cosdier. Buy in bulk.

We should buy goods without packaging whenever possible or package with materials of high recycled content. The biggest problem faced by recycling center is not the lack of technology but the demand for recycled products. The demand for many recyclables is often soft and we can increase the demand by buying wisely.

* * * * *

Some papers used in packaging contain strips of aluminum and plastic. Together with Styrofoam containers, they are costly and difficult to recycle. Simple packaging with a single layer of paper, metal or aluminum is easier to recycle. Avoid products in the market with more than two layers of packing. Most of the money we pay for the product goes into the extra packaging.

Everyday we consume millions of packets of potato chips, biscuits, fruits drinks and snacks. These minipacks take far more energy and money to produce than standard packs which can be reused. Buying foods that are not heavily wTapped will cut cost, pollution and save trees.

* * * * *

Corrugate cardboard is a paper product made by sandwiching a fluted corrugated layer of paper between two layers of flat paper. They are made of Kraft paper, the common brown paper grocery sack. Many of the things we buy are packed in corrugated or plain cartons. Forests are deliberately cut down to serve the needs of the Japanese and other industries. The Japanese are known for packing their export goods with high quality cardboard boxes coming from virgin forests.

At the Honshu Container Company in Tatsuka, Japan, corrugated boxes made for such firms as Sony and Hitachi come from chip mills located in the rainforests. There are thousands of these firms and hundreds of these rainforests being cut down to serve them. It is a good idea to store these boxes for future use. Whenever we need to send gifts, we can make use of them without buying new ones and pack them ourselves at great savings.

Like all paper materials, cardboard boxes can be recycled. Ben & Jerry's, an ice cream manufacturer founded in 1978 at one time generated more than 8 tons of cardboard every week. By equipping their manufacturing plants with cardboard balers to collect the cardboards and have them recycled, die company saved $17,400 annually in hauling costs alone. Veryfine Products, a manufacturer of vinegar and fruit drinks recycled 350 tons of corrugated cardboard in 1992, saving more than 7,500 trees, 1,800 megaw atts of energy, about three million gallons of water, clearing 10,000 kilos of air pollutants, sparing landfill of 1,000 m' and waste disposal costs.

In 1996, the US generated 29 million tons of corrugated cardboard resenting 13.8 % of the municipal waste. Approximately 90% of them come from the commercial sector with the supermarkets and department stores supplying the bulks. To minimize the landfilling of cardboard, the Orange County Landfill banned commercial corrugated cardboard in 1996 because it is easy to recycle and takes up a lot of landfill space, Some commercial dumpster refused to allow the dumping until the cardboard is removed. Others are penalized double the normal tipping fees. The penalty could increase dramatically if thc landfill inspector found corrugated cardboard contains more than half the load. As a result, the corrugated cardboard being landfilled dropped from 10% to 4% in a of four years[430]

Chapter 15

CONSERVATION AND REFORESTATION

Tree planting and reforestation programs have been going for some time, but forest continue to be depleted. One reason is that the demand for wood is not matched by our efforts at reforestation and afforestation. More efforts should be undertaken to reverse the trend. Another reason is the indifference of the government to the destruction. It often falls on the NGOs and individuals to take the initiatives before the government will act. Sometimes actions are taken only after calamities have befallen.

Demand by the runaway population has swallowed the moderate tree-planting efforts of many countries. Wood-producing programs have to be undertaken on a far greater scale not only to offset the present consumption, but to ensure enough wood for the future generations. It is one of the renewable and important natural resources that have been neglected to the detriment of the environment as well as the well-being of many rural communities.

Experts estimate that some 20 million hectares of new trees must be planted annually if developing countries are to meet thc peoples' needs for tree products. The cost is enormous, about S8 to $10 billion a year, Almost all of the countries in dire need of reforestation cannot afford to finance this huge outlay, but everyone in his capacity can help reduce the demand for trees and even plant trees for the benefit of mankind.

Very few tropical countries are able to reforest more than they are destroyed. Even if the reforested areas are larger than the denuded forests, it cannot compensate for the volume of carbon emitted to the atmosphere because of the bigger trees destroyed compare to the new saplings. Also, most of the reforestation efforts are done on a monoculture species that do not reflect the original old-growth ecosystem. This will lead to a loss of biodiversity. Many of the flora and fauna that used to reside in the intact forests may no longer survive under a different environment. There is a loss of symbiosis among the natural inhabitants that would affect biodiversity for centuries.

Conservation

Since man first began to convert forestlands into other uses, the world's forests have been reduced by half in the 20th century alone. In the tropics the reduction is not being replenished rapidly enough to compensate for the losses due to agriculture, logging, burning, cattle ranching, public works, transmigration, etc. all in the name of progress. The process is still going despite the knowledge that it is bad for the environment and the world in general.

Unlike mineral resources where only conservation can guarantee the availability of these resources in the future, forest products can be conserved and developed sustainably for perpetuity. Today in the developing countries ten trees are cut down for each one that is replanted. In Africa the ratio is thirty to one. While timber harvesters are required to plant ten trees for each one harvested, only a small portion, less than 1% mature to become full grown. One way of alleviating pressures on the forests is to obtain a yield of resources from the forest that exceeds the economic return of forest removal. In many regions aquatic and terrestrial animals, fruits, and nuts from the forests provide food sources that highland farmers can harvest and sell to the public. Forest reserves can be a good example of increasing use of forests in their natural state for management of selected species. Patronizing products obtained from the forest without harvesting the trees will prove effective in the long run.

It has taken the primary forests thousands of years to develop, but only a few years to chop them down. If we lose the primary forests, the other forest inhabitants invariably go too. The forests richness in the species cannot be underestimated. In Brunei there are 2,000 plant species, but we know only a tiny percentage to regenerate them as seedlings and even then they may not regenerate in certain conditions. Besides, any replacement forest would be poor, both in volume and diversity because the soil is degraded when the original forest is cut down.

Forest conservation consists largely of forest management practices of existing trees that improve the quality and quantity of forest crops. It consists of reducing losses in growing timber; improving forest stands and reducing losses in utilization. Both the reduction of loss and timber growth and the improvement of forest stands have the effect of increasing the sustained yield which is the basis of conservation. In essence it is an annual harvest of wood that does not exceed the forest s net annual growth and hence can be sustained. Besides all these conservation measures that indirectly affect the trees are to be taken into account.

Losses in growing trees are reduced chiefly by protecting forests from destruction by insects, disease, fire, and certain weather phenomena. Foresters are devoting a major effort toward achieving control of insect pests that damage or destroy desirable species. One method of controlling disease is sanitation cutting which removes diseased trees to prevent the disease from spreading. Use of pesticides should be limited, Biological control and integrated pest management should be adopted whenever it is possible to reduce air and water pollution. Fires can also cause spectacular losses and require preventive measures. The tragedy of forest fires are caused mostly by man and could have been prevented.

Forest stands are often improved by regular harvesting and thinning. Care should be undertaken that only mature and over-mature trees are removed to make room for young trees. Their removals are balanced off by the growing trees as more sunlight and nutrients can be absorbed by these young and vigorous trees to increase their rate of growth. They are also able to sequester more carbon from the atmosphere as they grow whereas the over-mature trees have a tendency to be stunted.

Sustainable development of forests in the tropical countries is very different from those of the temperate forests. The tropical forests are under tremendous pressures from the inhabitants and lowlanders because of the high population density encroaching on them. Even without timber harvesting in the locality, thc sheer volume of firewood gathering is making a big dent on the regenerative power of the forest to sustain itself. The rate of growth is inversely proportional to the rate of firewood gathering. This serious implication must be studied carefully to reduce firewood gathering. Local participation is necessary if we are to succeed at all stages of plantation development.

Investment in forestry can be a self-satisfying experience. Instead of cutting down the forests, we can help the environment by sequestering carbon against global warming, maintaining biodiversity for possible medicine and food, and safeguarding or maintaining the ecological balance that can only exist under the forest system. Any harvesting must be based on a sustainable level. Whether it is tree plantations, timber harvesting of old growth or second secondary growth, careful control of harvest methods must be enforced to reduce damage to residual stock. By careful monitoring and feedback of the state of the forests or forest plantations it will ensure better management. It is important that continuous forest cover is maintained. In harvesting, soil compaction should be avoided by using light machineries and animals.

Reforestation

The forest may look lush and rich, but this is deceptive. The underlying soils are really very poor in nutrients and it is easily washed away by rain when the soil has been disturbed by human activities. At the same time, about 80% of the soils in the humid tropics are acidic and infertile. Reforestation should be done immediately at the sites of the forest degradation to minimize the loss of soil fertility. This is the ideal place due to the presence of some forest cover to protect the seedlings from intense heat and the presence of nutrients before erosion takes them away.

Reforestation is not an easy task. It requires patience, experience, hard work, technical knowledge, maintenance, monitoring, etc. China with the best reforestation record is a good example of the difficulties involved in reforestation^. From 1948 to 1978, the Chinese established trees on 330,000 km and its forest cover increased from 8.6% to 12.7%. From 1979 to 1983, the forest cover actually declined by 50,000 km² despite annual planting of 40,000 km². The reason is that peasants hungry for fuelwood are forced to chop down the trees at night.[431]

Since 1963, China has planted 700,000 kms² of trees around the Gobi Desert, but the survival rate was as low as 10% due to inexperienced planting, poor maintenance inhospitable growing conditions and theft of fuelwood.

According to the FAO Global Forest Resources Assessment 2000, the net loss of forest area at the global level during the 1990s was an estimated 95 million hectares, an area larger than Venezuela and equivalent to 2.4% of the world's total forests. This is equivalent to an annual loss of 12.5 million hectares of natural forests and an annual gain of 3.1 million hectares in the form of forest plantations.[433] The highest loss of forest cover between 1990 and 2000 came from Brazil, Indonesia, Sudan, Zambia, Mexico and the Democratic Republic of Congo, all of which are tropical rainforests. Those with the highest gain during the same period include China, US, Belarus, Kazakhstan, and the Russian Federation, all from the temperate zone countries.[434]

* * * * *

People are the main cause of deforestation and they are the ones who should solve the problem. However, no amount of reforestation will succeed as long as the problems of poverty, rapid population growth, and environmental and natural resource degradation are not resolved. The European Commission (EC) and the United Nations Development Programme (UNDP) have joined hands to set up the Small Grants Programme to Promote Tropical Forests (SGP PTF) to address the problem. The program is funded by the EC and administered by the UNDP and is based upon and works closely with the existing and highly successful SGP that was funded by the Global Environment Facility (GEF). Nine countries in Southeast Asia have been included in the program including Viet Nam.[435]

Viet Nam, once covered with 43.7% foresdands have rapidly been denuded to 23.6% by the year 1983 due to the combined effects of agricultural encroachment, fuel wood consumption, logging, shifting cultivation, overgrazing, war and fire. With the help of EC/UNDP through the National Reforestation Programmes, its forest coverage has increased by 32.2% in 2001. The creation of livelihoods that goes hand-in-hand with the protection of the environment and ensuring the communities' rights to use and participation in forest management is part of the agenda.[436]

* * * * *

Not all logged or useless abandoned pasture can be successfully reforested. The next best thing is to turn them into productive farmland where the forest dwellers can grow plants and trees that they can subsist on. This will reduce the chances of taking resources from die nearby primary forests or the practice of slash-and-bum cultivation by burning down new forest.

In the Peruvian Amazon near Pucalpa, indigenous people were able to transform 7.5 hectares of useless abandoned cattle pasture into productive farmland. By using organic matter and a variety of crop species and trees, the inhabitants were able to achieve production rates higher than those accomplished by nearby farms with their modern methods of agriculture. This success story is expected to encourage others to adopt the practice.[417]

* * * * *

Some wood species are more valuable than others in the world's market. It is therefore more profitable to plant these trees instead for the money and the demand. There is always a demand for hardwood because of their beauty and durability. Some of these species are mahogany, narra, yakal. lauan, etc. that are available in the Philippines. While they may not grow as fast as desired, they play an important role in the ecology of the country, sequestering more carbon because of their size and long term growth. They are considered long-term investment that the government can take the initiative since all forests are considered patrimonial. These important species can be planted interspatial to give a semblance of diversity.

Teak is one of the highly prized woods in the world. It is sought after for use as furniture, shipbuilding and decoration that in 2001, the Indonesian furniture industry exported $800 million. It is a well established source of employment and income for the people in Java that employed about 6 million workers. Because of the demand, many private individuals and communities have dedicated themselves to planting teaks in their private properties and community woodlots. Some private individuals planted the teak on their backyard as a 'saving account' for their children.[438]

Teak, like other hardwoods is a long-term investment but its initial capital cost and labor is minimal. A fully matured teak with a diameter of 80 cm log is worth $830 a cubic meter in 2001. The smaller diameters are less expensive. It is therefore more worthwhile to harvest the tree when they are fully matured.[439]

There is no better place to plant the big trees than in the denuded forests. Most of the rural people are poor and have no opportunity for employment. Most of the women are tasked to do household works, fetch water and gather firewood. This is where they can be harnessed for reforestation work. Their enormous number can provide a great force to tree planting like the Greenbelt Movement of Kenya. Payments may be partly in cash and partly in free supply of LPG or electricity to minimize wood gathering which for the Philippines accounted for more than 26 m^3 in 1980 and may have increased to 40 m^3 in 1995.

In Kenya, the Greenbelt Movement sponsored by the National Council of Women has mobilized more than fifteen thousand farmers and half a million children to plant more than two million trees. Even in the industrial nations people are planting. The American Forestry Association has proposed an urban reforestation program to plant one hundred million trees in cities and suburbs around the US. The pool of labor required for large scale reforestation is enormous but available. It has been proven time and again that if we have the will, it can be accomplished.

In Uttar Pradesh, India, a forestry project was started with a five-year goal of planting 30,000 hectares of woodlots and plantations. The goal was exceeded within three years with another 13,000 hectares of degraded forests rehabilitated and 17 million working days of employment were generated in the process. Four million working days were done by women. Employment in the rural areas is hard to come by and it would be a productive undertaking to employ women in forestry projects.

SODEVA, a farm products company in Senegal, started an interesting experiment by paying immediately the farmers who planted *Acacia albida* seedlings. In the first year, the loss was over 70%. The nest year, under a new innovation, the farmers were paid 100 francs for each living tree after six months, and in 50 francs and 25 francs per living tree each of the following two years. The cost of planting and maintaining each tree until it was three years old came to 175 francs or about $0.88 (1995). SOVEDA agents found that the yield was 100% living trees.

Skill, incentives, and willingness are important factors in growing and caring for trees. The fanners or new hands must be willing to learn newer method of planting and caring for trees. In Costa Rica, in an effort to recreate the dry forest of the Quanacaste National Park, farmers were paid to plant trees over part of their own land to reduce soil erosion while providing windbreaks, fuelwood, and timber for the future.

* * * * *

During a National Conference on Integrating Forest Conservation with Local Governance, DENR Secretary Defensor decried the failure of the reforestation program on corrupt government officials for sabotaging he program by their accepting financial favors, most probably pocketing the money with those who are supposed to be helping in the reforestation works or logging companies who are doing their share of reforestation. He also blamed flawed government policies and the inability of the public to understand the benefit of a healthy forested environment. So far, the success rate is only 30%. He went on to cite several solutions such as regular monitoring and the participation of the community to ensure successful reforestation.[440]

The government reforestation program has been generous. In the early 1990s, the DENR pays contractors P20.000 for each hectare planted. Each family is given one to ten hectares for a period of three years while communities were granted six to 100 hectares. They are initially given 15% of the contract price for the mobilization fee. The full balance will be paid if the survival rate at the end of the three year period is at least 80%. From the start, the contractors and the DENR is already besieged with problems. They include lack of funds, ineffective monitoring, illegal cutting, forest fires, pest and diseases, and corruption. (Vitug, 62) All these problems combined to make reforestation works possible only in cyber space. Instead we should work toward more stringent monitoring of our existing forest from illegal logging.

Monitoring

There are two aspects to the monitoring system. Not only do the reforestation work need to be monitored, the system of fund utilization is even more prioritized because of the many dirty hands trying to get the funds before it is disbursed to its intended objectives. When the Philippine borrowed from the ADB $325 million for a national reforestation plan, the project failed miserably that it refused to extend any more loans for reforestation. According to Ford Foundation and the NGOs, there is widespread corruption in the reforestation sector. According to Frances Korten, a representative of the Ford Foundation, most of the funds end up in the pocket of local politicians in their election bids. Even forestry officials profited from the funds. They made use of trees of cheap and therefore short-term value which can be harvested instead of long-term value reforestation. Even "fly-by-night" NGOs without any technical knowledge of reforestation sprouted to get hold of some of the funds.[441]

Planting trees is one thing, making sure they survive to maturity is mother thing. Experiences have shown that even in the best reforestation projects the survival rate for seedlings is less than 50%. The trees need to be taken care of for years before they can stand alone in the face of nibbling animals, firewood gathering, fires, encroachment of people, etc.

On-site monitoring and surveillance are the key elements to a successful implementation of logging operation and reforestation works. Modern technology and community participation may lead to identifying problems before they arise. Loggers mandated bylaw to cut only certain marked trees will not deviate if they are being monitored. Periodic assessment of reforestation work will ensure compliance of the regulations of the timber permit. Loggers especially in the tropical countries are often not interested in reforestation or cutting within the boundaries granted. They would rather earn the money at the expense of others. Cutting outside their concession is a common violation.

Reforestation can easily be faked if monitoring is going to be done through photography. There is no substitute for on site monitoring. In one reforestation project I witnessed in the Visayas, the fast-growing softwood, *falcata* was planted to replace the native hardwoods that were cut down. A careful inspection revealed that the replanted trees were done only near the vicinity of the road for window dressing. A few feet behind the trees, an expanse of clear cut forests can be seen. The reforested strip was designed to give an impression that reforestation was being done. This same practice has been going on in many temperate forests where clear cutting is practiced to avoid outcry from the citizenry.

Billions of pesos have been spent on reforestation works throughout the country. But several anomalies have been discovered. Instead of spending the money on reforestation and caring for the young trees, corruption has made it possible for unscrupulous planter and corrupt officials to pocket the money. What is needed is strict monitoring of reforestation and to see to it that the young plants are cared for until they mature enough to survive alone. Money should be released on an accomplishment basis. Video shots should be taken to monitor the progress of the reforestation works.

* * * * *

With some incentives, monitoring can be done by the very people who did the reforestation jobs. This is what happened in Armenia when most of its forest has been depleted. It is important to reforest before the topsoil erodes because rejuvenation would be unfeasible without the topsoil. The Armenia Tree Project works by having community-based tree-planting programs and with Armenia forest NGO to replant Tsitsemakaberd Park. The community was coaxed into planting 1,000-3,000 seedlings during a period of 18 months. With each seedling becoming a sapling, the family is paid fifty cents. The community would be forced to see that they are taken care of. As a result, this enabled each participating family to supplement their incomes by $500 which is three times more than what the average family makes. A method known as coppicing has resulted in a 100% survival rate and extensive re-growth.

Supertrees

Scientists search for other plant species that can help in developing fast-growing trees that could be more productive for a given region. The trees are selected for their drought-resistance, rapid growth, and capability of growing on poor soil. They can be planted in semi-arid areas to arrest the growing desertification or in coastal areas to protect coastal lands and serve as habitats for marine life.

Most of these plants are legumes such as cowpea, bean, lentil and leucaena. They have the ability to fix nitrogen, produce wood at greater rate and in extremely poor soil. These trees are mostly found in South America and Southeast Asia. Other researchers are breeding trees that grow faster and straighter than nature's own. Foresters are sent out to find mature trees with superior characteristics to serve as progenitors. Tall, straight, with few limbs are the ideal characteristics. Marksmen use special bullets to shoot off high limbs, and the branch tips called scions are collected and grafted onto young nursery stock and planted in seed orchards. Within a few years, the scions retain the maturity of their source and the trees begin to yield seed. The seeds are collected and cultivated for a year and later planted in the field.

There are hundred of varieties of leucaena, ranging from sixty-five-foot trees suitable for timber to fifteen-foot hedge trees. They are drought resistant and fast growing with great carbon dioxide intake, and many can grow up to 6 meters in height in a year. A favorite is the largest of them all, *leucaena leucocephala*. Its leaves can be used as nitrogen-rich fertilizer, cattlefeed, or sweet protein-rich food for humans. The seed pods can be eaten raw or cooked. The gum can be used as a thickener for food and cosmetics, and even the white flower is very poplar with the honey-producing bees. (Day, 266)

Another tree used to combat the creeping desertification is the hardy acacia species. Once established they can bind the sand and gradually accumulate soil underneath. The falling leaves around the trees produce organic matter in which soil organisms can multiply and humus created, retaining the limited moisture of continuing growth.

* * * * *

Advances in genetic engineering have made it possible to create genetically modified (GM) trees. Scientists can now develop trees for various uses. It could be fast-growing trees and resistant to insects, trees that produce more biomass that can be converted to fuel, to sequester more carbon than normal trees and even clean up waste sites.[442]

However, there are fears that the traditional varieties of trees and crops could be contaminated with low levels of DNA from GM crops. The outcome is unknown and that is what made scientists fearful about the GM trees. It could lead to infertile private timber, possibly lacking enough lignin content making it useless as sawn timber but easier to use for papermaking. Combined with internal pesticide production, pine and poplars trees in the wild could lead to forests unable to reproduce, produce food for animals or create marketable timber.[443]

One of the first species to be planted on a large scale is the hybrid poplar. The fast-growing tree has been planted on a 30,000 acres land in Minnesota in 1995 to replace the expected shortage of aspen trees that used to supply the paper, pulp and other wood products. The hybrid poplars can grow 6-10 times faster and can be harvested in 10-15 years compared to 40-60 years for the aspen trees. The only drawbacks are that the super poplars are highly water intensive, and rotation times could be so short that they will use up most of the soil nutrients. This is the experienced at pine farms in the south. Short rotations and intense growth cycles caused increased reliance on chemical fertilizers with their attendant problems for human and environmental health and water quality and quantity.[444]

In 2002, the State Forestry Administration of China approved the use of insect-resistant GM poplar trees for commercial planting. Immediately, it launched the world's largest tree planting project with the hope of covering an area of 44 million hectares by 2012. The reason for using the GM trees is insect infestation which is a serious problem.[445] The leaves of GM trees have been genetically inserted into the tree's DNA a natural toxin. *Bacillus thuringtensis* or Bt that contain pesticides that kill the insects immediately after nibbling the leaves.[446]

The area chosen for its project is near the Beijing area where the sandstorms from the Gobi desert frequently turn the air in the city yellowish brown that reduces visibility to a few meters. The desert is creeping relentlessly towards China's capital city. By 2003, a million insect resistant GM Populus nigra trees and 400,000 GM hybrid popular trees have been planted.[447]

Scientists at Japan's Toyota Motor Corp. have reported that through genetic engineering they were able to enhance the ability of trees to absorb nitrous oxides by doubling the number of chromosomes by widening air inlets on stems and leaves. It usually takes 20 regular trees to absorb the annual emission of one tree, but this improved tree can absorb 30% more.[448]

* * * * *

It could take a long time to manually handle created supertree clones with millions of its seedling with identical characteristics. Each group of cultured cells generates a cluster of shoots which must be individually plucked and placed in a growth medium where they turn into seedlings. To automate the process, robots have been designed to cut the cost of this once labor-intensive technique. The robots will be able to produce 750 embryonic trees with a single attendant and three robot assembly lines.[449]

The robot technology is coupled with a program to develop better trees. Researchers seek out wild trees with superior features such as fast growth, denser wood or resistance to disease and map their genomes. They then locate the genes for key traits and find markers that go with them. The markers allow the forestry researchers to identify which seedling carries the required traits early on instead of waiting decades for the tree to mature. The best seedlings form the basis of tissue cultures.[450]

Goldman Prize

Like the well-known Nobel Prize, the environmental movements have their own award for individual efforts to protect the Earth. This is the Goldman Prize. It was established by an American couple, Richard and Rhoda Goldman, in 1990 with head office in San Francisco. Some of the winners have gone to win the Nobel Peace Prize, be elected to public office in their home countries or simply continued their environmental works. The Prize is given each year to six environmental heroes – one from each of six continental regions: Africa, Asia, Europe, Island Nations, North America and South/Central America. Initially each recipient receives a $60,000 award from Goldman Environmental Foundation. The award stipend has been raised three times since and currently stands at $125,000. [451]

Some of these winners were Wangari Muta Maathai of Kenya who launched a women's tree-planting movement in Kenya; Tokyo activist-writer Yoichi Kuroda who tried to reform his nation's role in tropical deforestation; and Peru's Evaristo Nugkuag, an Aguaruna Indian of South America who helped preserve the Indians' rainforest homes. Individual efforts can and do help in changing the attitudes of government and industries to protect the environment.

In 2005, there were six recipients of the Goldman Environmental Prizes. One of them is a Catholic priest, Rev. Jose Andres Tamayo Cortez, from Tegucigalpa, Honduras who won an award of $125,000. He heads the

Environmental Movement of Olancho, a coalition of farmers and residents dedicated to stopping the logging spree. He has led thousands of people on two weeklong marches to the nation's capital, drawing national and international attention to the problems caused by unregulated logging, associated crime such as murder, and alleged corruption in the Honduran forestry agency. The second march, in June 2004, led to a government investigation of the forestry agency and the resignation of its general manager. Tamayo was also the recipient of the 2003 Honduras National Human Rights Award.[452]

Parks and Reserves

The world's first national park was established in 1872 when President Ulysses S. Grant signed an act of Congress designating more than 800,000 hectares, mostly in Wyoming and Oregon as the Yellowstone National Park. Since then the park has expanded in size to about 2.3 million hectares, the second largest in the US. Since then, many more parks and reserves have been set up throughout the world.

Parks and reserves are areas in the natural environment that are specially set aside for human enjoyment or serve as habitats for indigenous people, wildlife, and biodiversity. It is the world's most important form of nature preservation especially because of the growing pressures of population growth. There are more than 1,200 national parks and reserves in more than one hundred countries and more are added every year.

According to the UN and 1UCN definition, a reserve must exist in a relatively natural condition with very few roads and may be a hotel to accommodate overnight tourists. They must be large enough to accommodate humans and animals as a sanctuary' without causing much stress. Most national parks contain 2,000 hectares or more in areas.

National parks and reserves are usually protected by law. They are mostly untouched by men and human exploitation of their natural resources is prohibited. Exceptions are few but with so many legal and illegal intrusions, many degraded forestlands have been put under the system to protect them from further destruction. These parks are owned by the government for the benefits of all the citizens.

* * * * *

The push for new tropical forests to be declared as parks or reserves will serve to place more lands under proper protection. Their significance will be apparent when one realizes that 93% of our parks and nature reserves have an area of less than 500,000 hectares and 78% less than 100,000 hectares. Not only do they serve as recreation for mankind and sanctuary for biodiversity, the vital roles they play for the future of humanity such as watershed protection, sequestration of carbon, protection of biodiversity, etc. can never be quantified.

These realties are prompting conservationists to redouble their efforts to create more national parks and reserves. They have learned that only areas protected by law can likely survive intact in the future. To bring more areas under park protection, it is important to relax the rule defining parks and reserves even if they have been exploited by men. This is what many NGOs are doing in the hope that they can restore old glory to the devastated ecosystems.

* * * * *

Setting aside forested lands to protect against human intrusion is recognized as an important solution to deforestation. But in many countries it has failed miserably for many reasons. Contradictory laws and policies and lack of coordination among the different government agencies in charge of implementing them hamper a coherent national conservation strategy. Often, there are not enough funds to protect the areas and the cooperation of the rural communities is not harnessed.

Sometimes reserves are allowed to be exploited as long as they are not degraded by human intervention. These extractive reserves are especially set aside for indigent people such as the Amazon Indians who practice extractive gathering of forest products without harming the forest itself. They extract rubber from the rubber trees and gather fruits from the trees. This is one of the best hopes of saving the Amazon from outside interference. Due to the work of Chito Mendes, who was murdered by cattle ranchers, extractive reserves are now one of the main thrusts of Amazonian conservation movements. Since January 1990 four big reserves have been established and ten more are in the offing covering a total of 5 million hectares. One of the reserves was named in honor of Chico Mendes who made it possible. Aids and grants are coming from

UNEP, WB, ITTO, British Oversea Development Agency, International Development Agency, Kiwanis Club International and the Japanese.

Samar is one of the poorest provinces in the Philippines but it harbors one of the most diversified biological ecosystems. Within the province can be found the 333,300-hectares Samar Island Nature Park. A survey by experts in 2001 showed the park was worth $43.5 billion over 25 years with a net projected value of $12 billion.[453]

The park also contains one logging concession, San Jose Timber Corp., a company partly owned by a senator. It is also the site of a huge deposit of bauxite whose deposits is worth about $21 billion. The logging concession, dormant for over sixteen years has been granted the right to operate again when Environment Secretary Michael T. Defensor signed the order to that effect on August 16, 2005.[454] Howls of protests lead by some priests and plans for rallies finally forced DENR Secretary Defensor to back down and revoke the license he had earlier approved.

His act has earlier triggered some environmentalists to take the initiative in carrying out the battle against mining and logging firms. The Haribon Foundation and the Rainforest Restoration Initiative (RFRI) have launched the "Rainforest Restoration Organizations and Advocates" (ROAD) to 2020 in the hope of restoring one million hectare of rainforest in 15 years.[455]

* * * * *

Many of the parks are nothing but "paper" parks because they are not protected and exist on maps only. They continue to be intruder by people due to population pressures and greedy businessmen. Commercial exploitation, firewood gathering, and other activities continue to take their tolls inside the parks. Most loggers cannot be trusted to be honest. The Temenggor Forest Reserve in Perak, Malaysia is a 148,900 hectares rich and valuable ecosystem and the abode of the hombills. When the Tenaga National Berhad (TNB) engaged two contractors to extract logs that were inundated dunng the construction of a hydroelectric dam at Tasik Temenggor, other logs above ground were illegally felled. Instead of carrying out logging on the lake only, they also carried out logging on land as well. The trees felled had earlier been by tagged. [456]

Trees along the banks have been cut down in many places leaving behind a trail of destruction. The logs would be dragged to the lake and left there for days so that it would appear to be taken from the underwater lake before they are taken to a collection center. Some foreigners were suspected of illegally harvesting Aquilaria trees for agarwood, the resinous heartwood used in perfume and incense that can fetch several thousand dollars per kg.[457]

* * * * *

Sometimes it would take the death of an environmentalist for government to act. This is case of Sister Dorothy Stang, an American nun who was murdered for her active role and outspoken efforts on behalf of landless peasants and wildlife in the Amazon. Brazilian President Luis Inacio Lula da Silva finally signed the decree creating two new parks under the Amazon Region Protected Areas (APRA). The two parks contained 9.4 million acres of rainforest right in the heart of die Brazilian Amazon. They include the 8.3 million acre Terra do Meio Ecological Station and the 1.1 million acre Serra do Pardo National Park.[458]

Social and environmental organizations have been pressing for the creation of these protected areas for several years as a way of easing conflicts over logging and land use, protecting the rights of local residents and conserving the irreplaceable biodiversity of die Xingu River basin. Several threatened species such as jaguars, macaws and harpy eagles are expected to be given a new lease on life. WWF assisted the parks' creation by providing scientific and technical advice in their design and by supporting stakeholder consultations to ensure that the rights and needs of local inhabitants were incorporated into die conservation planning.

The key to effective implementation of this vast network of parks will be a $240 million conservation trust fund set up by the World Bank, thc Brazilian government, the Global Environment Facility, the German Development Bank and WWF among others. The goal of ARPA is the establishment of 25 million acres of protected areas and 23 million acres of sustainable use reserves by the end of 2006. With the latest additions, ARPA now has nearly 22 million acres of protected area and more than 13 million acres of sustainable use reserves.[459]

Ecotourism

Ecotounsm essentially means ecological tourism. It is one way of saving the rainforests while earning hard currency for the country. It is an educational and responsible travel that conserves the natural environments without jeopardizing thc livelihood of the local people and even improving on them. Tourism is a growing $3 trillion business. In many tropical countries, nature preserves are the main attraction of tourism. Ecotourism started in the 1980s and its importance was recognized by the UN when it declared 2002 as the "International Year of Ecotourism. "

There is a great potential of ecotourism to national economy for many tropica] countries and is the source of important foreign revenues. It was an important consideration in the development of Costa Rica's system of protected forest areas. In 1986, Costa Rica earned $138 from ecotourism while its neighbor Ecuador earned $180 million from tourists visiting the Galapajos Island. Other important tourist destinations are the Tijuca Forest near Rio de Janeiro, Brazil, several nature reserves in Java, Indonesia, and the Caribbean National Forest near San Juan, Puerto Rico.

Although the income is small initially in comparison with the one time revenues from logging, the income derived form ecotourism can save the forests from exploitation and is worth all the efforts.

A park and tourist area is a good place to learn about tropical forests. One of the best examples is the Tambopata Reserve in Madre de Dios, Peru. It began in 1986 to preserve traditional knowledge of medicinal plants. The money collected from tourism was used for collecting medicinal plants, reforestation, and research into biological pest control and help the local people set up a butterfly farm.

Another way to earn dollars was to set up safaris to attract animal lovers and photography bufTs Long a moneymaker in Africa, and the Galapagos Islands, this form of ecotourism is spreading to other countries. It is Kenya's biggest foreign exchange earner, making $350 million annually. Visiting these countries will give us a first-hand understanding of the forces bearing down on the rainforests and the role some of the governments around the world are doing. Share your adventures with friends and encourage them to visit these places.

One of the latest parks opened to ecotourism is the Manu National Park located in Peru. It is a 1.8 million hectares of jungle choked with plant and animal life as it was before the Europeans landed in the New World 500 years ago.

In the US less than 100,000 people visited their national parks in 1905. By 1990, as more parks were established, they were visited by more than 350 million people and this is increasing annually. The problems these national parks are suffering from at present are very limited accommodation to house too many people that visit to enjoy these parks.

* * * * *

There are roughly 1,000 national parks and 7,000 protected reserves in the world. Most of them are protected only on paper because of lack of funds and local support. In developing countries, the entry fees charged the visitors are often low although most are willing to pay a higher fee for die sake of the environment. Even when there is large income coming from ecotourism as in Kenya, less than 3% is returned to the park for improvement. The same is true in Costa Rica where the budget remained the same for years.

It is one thing to set aside forests as parks and reserves and another thing to see that they are well protected from undesirable intrusions. The best guarantee of success is the development of local political support in conjunction with long term funding. Parks and reserves require considerable financial support that most ccotourism cannot generate. Lack of funds is the usual culprit for most of the failures to protect the reserves. Those assigned to protect the forests must be well paid and equipped for effective monitoring. Many tropical countries are too poor to allocate financial supports to protect the forests because it is not considered a priority. Priorities have to change if we want to secure the continued benefits we have enjoyed from the forests.

It is important that continuous funding be maintained. International aids should be directed at conservation measures instead of building infrastructures that can only destroy ecosystems. Much of the financial supports have been directed at producing commodities for the West while paying lip service to the need for protecting thc foreit. An international fund should be created to carry out the main objective of saving the trees.

Urban Forests

Air pollution continues to plague the cities even with the many laws requiring enforcement for clean air. There are just too many sources of air pollution. To solve the problem, we can plant trees. Planting trees in the urban areas can provide valuable functions for the surrounding areas, especially with so many automobiles contaminating the atmosphere. They offer a recreation park w'hile removing carbon dioxide and other toxic gases from the atmosphere. They also provide cool shade for people while reducing the ambient temperature, produce oxygen through photosynthesis, deflect and absorb noise pollution and serve as research center for students.

Government should provide the land from which urban forests with wild habitat can be created throughout the metropolitan areas around the country. In the US where statistics are available, there are 27 million hectares of urban forests specially created for Americans who have limited access to the rural areas. They include the old, disabled, disadvantaged, low income people, minorities, and people too busy with their work. One advantage of these urban forests is that they can be well-maintained and there won't be problems finding volunteers to do it.

Many colleges and universities in the urban areas occupy large campuses that can be utilized for urban forests. At present most of these places are planted for greening with a few trees lining the streets. However, Miriam College campus in Loyola Heights, Quezon City has allocated about one hectare of land to a mini-forest teeming with trees. It was started about fifteen years ago and was Sister Marissa's pet project whose devotion made it successful.

* * * * *

India, a highly congested country even found areas devoted to forests that are so close to cities that it can be classified as urban forests. One of them is the Sanjay Gandhi National Park that serves as the lungs of Mumbai. Another park located within the city is the Guindy National Park. It was originally a game reserve with an area of 400 hectares in

1958. Today, the park has only 270.57 hectares. Inside the park are 350 species of plants. Animals that graze in the open grassland include toddy cats, civets, jungle cats, pangolins, hedgehogs, birds, turtles and tortoises, lizards, geckos, chameleons and monitor lizards.[460] Zoological and botanical gardens can also serve as urban forests.

NGOs and Foundations

Private foundations and NGOs are needed to administer these national parks and reserves if it is going to be effective. Direct land acquisition for the formation of private reserves is one way. Still, rural community cooperation is needed as they may continue to depend on the forests for their livelihood. At least, the owners can convince the community not to engage in invasive and extractive livelihood that are likely to destroy the forest.

After decades of trying to get the local community to act to protect their forest that is to their benefit, still there are few success stories. Money donated by these groups often go down the drain. It is important to get the local people involved. The locals should be hired to maintain the forest while being overseen by a well-trained field staff. A system of reward may be necessary to induce the whole community to cooperate in the preservation of the forests. It is difficult to get government forestry personnel as watchdog because they are often underpaid and easily corrupted. The reward system can extend as additional incentive for them.

The need of the community must be sustainable through other activities that will bring income to the people. Sustainable agriculture, appropriate forest management and ecotourism should be encouraged in the buffer zones and even within the protected areas. If their daily needs are addressed, coupled with strict monitoring, the chances of destruction will be minimized as these people do not need much beyond their daily existence.

* * * * *

There are many international and national organizations in the forefront fighting for the protection of the forests. It is only fitting that they should be mentioned and given credit for their efforts. Among the first to take up the cudgels for protecting against wanton destruction of the environment is the Friends of the Earth (FoE). It was established in 1984 in UK when it first questioned the UK and European timber companies that caused tropical deforestation. It organized boycotts against tropical hardwoods and lobbied hard for trade and aid issues. It also earned out work on illegal use of aid funding, the potential for sustainable management of tropical forests and the misuse of plantation as carbon stores. (Dudley, 111)

Greenpeace has been working against the pulp and paper industry for years and has been campaigning against their operations in Siberia and British Columbia, Canada. They are also known for taking drastic and high profile actions against other environmental issues such as whaling and illegal disposal of toxic wastes to Third World countries.

The Tiaga Rescue Network is more concerned with the boreal regions and is active in the northern hemisphere from North America to Siberia. They are linking up with other NGOs in these areas and come out periodically with reports of the ongoing activities. The World Rainforest Movement (WRM) is more active in the tropical areas with emphasis on local and indigenous peoples* rights and sustainable use of the rainforest. Other organizations such as WWF and IYCN have been mentioned elsewhere in the book.

Most of the local organizations are created spontaneously as their forests are being destroyed by loggers. Most of them are villagers and tribesmen that are not well-funded. They resorted to setting up roadblocks against logging trucks and like the Chipko Movement, tried to embrace the trees against the chainsaws. The more unorthodox methods used are driving spikes on the trees to make them difficult to process. Some rebels in the mountains that try to win the favors of the villagers would even use arms to prevent logging operations.

Still others would use the law to prevent logging by tying up their operations through lawsuits. More often, this does not work but gives the forest some breathing spell.

There are also organizations set up by the UN or under its auspices. The original one is the FAO. There is also the UN Conference on Environment and Development (UNCED) or more commonly known as the Earth Summit that meet in June 1992 at Rio de Janeiro. Some Forest Principles were agreed upon but failed to establish a global forest convention. Another is the Commission on Sustainable Development (CSD) which sets up new meetings on the Convention on Biological Diversity and the Climate Change Treaty. (Dudley, 115)

Debt-for-Nature Swap

According to the Friends of the Earth, 27 developing countries with staggering debts possess 97% of the world's rainforests. The international financial institutions are willing to extend out loans knowing they have the resources to repay. Most countries rely on the export of timber and other natural resources to pay for their debts. The problem arises when many corrupt officials pocket the money without developing the country. This is exacerbated by the inefficient conservation and ineffective measures needed to protect the environment. The huge loans made it difficult for them to repay the loan. Financial help to reduce these debts is essential if they are to reduce the destruction of the rainforests and the debt-for-nature scheme was initiated.

In this scheme, a foreign government or an NGO purchases a portion of a country's debt from foreign banks or government-to-government loans in return for a piece of ecologically important land to be preserved or conserved. The debtor country or lending bank sells the debt for a fraction of its value to a debt buyer such as NGOs who gets the satisfaction of preserving a large parcel of land for posterity at a fraction of the original debt. Debt for nature swaps is seen as a good alternative to defaulting on loans or continuing to pay the burdensome debts. Debt for nature swap was first suggested by Thomas Lovejoy of WWF in 1984.

The total debt of the developing countries now totals more than $1.3 trillion with interest payment of about $70 billion. With so much debt, a large portion of the rainforests can be preserv ed by swapping. Many of these debts were developed to transform commercial debts into financial aid for the protection of the tropical forests. The first debt for nature swap was implemented in Bolivia in 1987. Conservation International, a private conservation group bought $650,000 debts for $100,000 from Citicorp Investment Bank in return for 1.5 million hectares of rainforest to be put under preservation. The NGO die swapped the face value of the debt with the government for implementation with the help of the local NGOs.

Five years after the agreement was signed, the Bolivian government had not provided legal protection for the reserve. It had contributed only a measly $100,000 to the reserve management fund in 1989. Timber companies were allowed to cut thousands of mahogany trees from the area, with most of the lumber exported to the US. Important lessons can be gathered from this swap. Legislative and monetary requirement should first be established before the swap is completed. The proposals for sustainable development must be monitored carefully by NGOs to make sure that true protection are undertaken.

So far, $38 billion worth of debt for nature swap have been undertaken, but less than 2% have been implemented. This is due to the lack of incentives on the part of the debtor or the creditor and the lack of well-developed supporting institutional infrastructure to undertake the conservation efforts to make it succeed. The cost of environmental protection programs can be substantial if the developing country does not have the appropriate institutional infrastructure in place. The program will require the input of professional public administrators and environmental experts.[461]

In Madagascar where only a relatively small amount of debt was retired by the debt-for-nature scheme, it has nevertheless succeeded in helping die ecological ecosystems. The money was used in recruiting and training hundreds of government agents to patrol the huge island, persuading villagers to halt the bush-clearing that each year destroys 200,000 hectares of forest. Some of the funds were to fund projects such as schools or bridges in exchange for the local people to plant a forest or maintain woodland forest that would beneficial to the community.[462]

* * * * *

One form of debt-for-nature swaps involving debts to a government is the $16 million swap between the US and Jamaica governments and The Nature Conservancy. In return for writing off the debt, Jamaica committed itself to devoting an equivalent amount over the next 20 years to fund projects to conserve and restore important tropical forest resources in Jamaica The agreement was made possible through a grant of $6.5 million from the US government and a contribution of $1.3 million from The Nature Conservancy.[463]

The agreement was made possible through an act of Congress when it passed the Tropical Forest Conservation Act of 1998. It was first funded in 2000 to provide eligible developing countries opportunity to reduce concessional debts owed the US while generating funds to conserve their forest. Other recipients of this Act so far are Bangladesh, Belize, Colombia, El Salvador, Panama, the Philippines and Peru. Together, these agreements generated over $95 million to protect tropical forest over the next 10 to 25 years.[464] It costs the NGOs roughly $16 million in contributions. The Pulog and Isarog National Parks in the Philippine was placed under this scheme. Although a small fraction of the commercial debt is retired, it paid for significant conservation efforts.

Another creditor, American Express Bank, in January 1989 sold $5.6 million of Costa Rica's IOUs to the Nature Conservancy for $784,000. The Conservancy then traded back the paper to the Costa Rican central bank for $1.7 million in local currency bonds, with the interest to be paid to a local conservation group to manage nine projects. In Ecuador, the WWF and The Nature Conservancy acquired debts of $9 million for a little more than one million dollar.

During the early 1970s, the US banks vastly overexposed their loan portfolio with variable interest rates on loans that made it unlikely that the loans would be repaid. The secondary debt market, where debts are discounted down was seen by banks as a way to recoup some of the exposure. This was further enhanced by a US Department of Treasury ruling that allows lenders a face-value tax write-off as long as the debt is offered to private voluntary organizations involved in environmental welfare. The NGOs would buy the debt in hard currency, with the commitment from the indebted countries that they will invest an equivalent sum of their local currency and use it for environmental programs. The country has reduced its debt by settling accounts internally in its own currency and not hard-earned export dollars to alleviate environmental degradation. (Hecht, 225-226)

As an alternative, swapping debts for indigenous stewardship would permit the return of large areas to native care with restriction as to forest clearing may be more effective in protecting the forests. Thousands of natives protecting their own forests will be much more effective than a few forest rangers roaming the forest looking for timber robbers. Giving the local people control over die rainforests will instill within them a sense of security and land tenure. As long as outsiders continue to intrude into these sanctuaries, there is no end in sight to environmental degradation.

* * * * *

There are some misgivings about the schemes. It is unfortunate that most of these debt-for-nature swaps are restricted to South America. The tropical forests in Asia and Africa are just as important. Another unfortunate thing is that the WB/IMF which holds a lot of the Third World's debts is not willing to negotiate under this scheme.

There is also the lack of funds of the NGOs. It will take an organization created precisely for funding this scheme with universal contributions to retire most of these debts before more forests are destroyed permanently. Aside from the NGOs, governments in the industrialized countries should be willing to act because it could mean the loss of a vital source of cheap and useful industrial products. It will take more horrific events as a result of deforestation to prod governments to act with dispatch.

Endnotes

[1] "Forest Lands Coverage," www homedepot.com/HDUS/EN_US/corporate......

[2] "Forests: the earth's lungs," www peopleandplanet net/doc php?id=1480&section=l, December 16, 2004

[3] "Rates of Rainforest Loss," "Money in the Rainforest," www.ran.org/Info_center/factsheets/04b.html

[4] "Deforestation Continues at a High Rate in Tropical Areas," www feo.org/WAICENT/01S/PRESSNE/PRESSENG/2001.........

[5] www dhushara com/book/diversit/cathed.htm

[6] Ibid

[7] "Rates of Rainforest Loss," "Money in the Rainforest," www.ran.org/info_center/factsheets/04b.html

[8] Nick Paton Walsh, "It's Europe lungs and home to many rare species..." www.guardian.co.uk/international/story/0,3604,1045062,00.html, Sept19, 2003

[9] Ibid

[10] Ibid

[11] "Problems: Illegal logging and forest crime," www panda.org/about_wwf/what we do/forests/problems/illegal......November 13,2005

[12] Ibid

[13] "About Rainforests," www.ran.org/info_center/about_rainforest.html

[14] Ibid

[15] www.dhushara.eom/book/diversit/extra/deforest.htm#anchor........(New Scientist. May 16, 1998)

[16] "Species Extinction," www ran org/info_center/factsheets/03b. html

[17] "Forests: the earth's lungs," www pcopleandplanet.net/doc.php?id=1480&section=l, December 16, 2004

[18] "Species Extinction," www.ran.org/info_center/factsheeets/03b.html

[19] "Forests-the Earth's Lungs," www.infoforhealth.org/pr/ml5/ml5chap6/shtml

[10] "Species Extinction," www.ran.org/info_center/factsheeets/03b.html

[21] "Forests-the Earth's Lungs." www.infoforhealth.org/pr/ml5/ml5chap6/shtml

[22] "The Harvest of Sustainable Forest Products," www mongabay com/1003.htm

[23] Ibid

[24] Ibid

[25] www.dhushara.com/book/diversit/cathed.htm

[26] "Medicinal Treasures of the Rainforest." www.ran.org/info_center/factsheets/05f.html

[27] "About Rainforests," www.ran.org/info_center/about_rainforest.html

[28] "Species Extinction," www.ran.org/info_center/factsheeets/03b.html

[29] "Medicinal Treasures of the Rainforest," www.ran.org/info_center/factsheets/05f.html

[30] www dhushara.com/book/diversit/cathed.htm

31 http://home.alltel.net/bsundquist 1 df2.html#F

32 Ibid

33 www.rcfia-cfan.org/english/issues/12-6.html

34 "Rainforests and Global Warming," www.ran.org/info_center/factsheets/04a.html

35 Vanessa Baird, "The big switch," www.newint.org/issue357/keynote.htm

36 Ibid

37 Vanessa Baird, "The big switch," www.newint.org/issue357/keynote.htm

38 www rcfa-cfan.org/english/issues/12-6.html

39 Vanessa Baird, "The big switch," www.newint.org/issue357/facts.htm

40 Chris Sudzina, "Final: Methods and Effects of Tropical Rainforest Deforestation," http://jrscience.wcp.muohio.edu/FieldCourseOO/PapersCosta

41 "Climate Justice: The Facts," www newint.org/issue357/facts.htm

41 David Shukman, "Greenland ice-melt 'speeding up,'" http //newsvote bbc.co uk/mpapps/pagetools/print/news.bbc.co uk/2/......

43 "Q&A The Kyoto Protocol," http://newsvote.bbc.co.uk/mpapps/pagetools/print/news bbc.co.uk/2/......

44 Vanessa Baird, "The big switch," www.newint.org/issue357/keynote.htm

45 Miguel Bustillo, "Rain Forest Nations Seek Incentive to Conserve," LA Times, November 27, 2005

46 "Kyoto pact stronger after meet," Philippine Daily Inquirer, Dec. 12, 2005

47 *The New York Times*, "US eases stance on climate talks," The Philippine Star, December 12, 2005

48 "Carbon trading Benefits Industry and Communities," www.ciforcgiar.org/docs/-ptf 1 /ref/publ i cat ions/newsonl ine/31 /ca........

49 Miguel Bustillo, "Rain Forest Nations Seek Incentive to Conserve," LA Times, November 27, 2005

50 "Carbon trading Benefits Industry and Communities," www.cifor.cgiar.org/docs/-pf71 /retfpubl ications/newsonl i ne/31/ca.......

51 Supertrees, CO_2 Eating Algae," www.globalwarming.org/article.php?uid=222

52 Global Witness, "A Choice for China," October 2005 p. 39

53 http //home.alltel.net/bsundquist1.df2.html#F

54 Ibid

55 http //home.alltel.net/bsundquistl.df2.html#F

56 "Deforestation Continues at a High Rate in Tropical Areas," www.fao.org/WAICENT/OIS/PRESS_NE/PRESSENG/2001..........

57 MC Rodriquez, "Deforestation imperils Ambuklao," www.ncbi.nlm.gov/entrez/query.fcgi?cmd"'Retrieve&db.......

58 Jefferson Mecham, "Causes and consequences of deforestation in Ecuador," www rainforestinfo.org.au/projectv3efferson.htm, May 2001

59 http://home.alltel.net/bsundquist1.df2.html#F

60 Ibid

61 Ibid

[62] Ibid

[63] www.dhushara.com/book/diversit/cathed.htm

[64] Ibid

[65] Clinton C. Shock, "An Introduction to Drip Irrigation," www.cropinfo.net/drip.htm

[66] www.dhushara.com/book/diversit/bomb.htm#anchor255699

[67] Ibid

[68] John Bongaarts, "Can the Growing Human Population Feed Itself?" wwwdhushara.com/book/diversit/extra/feed/fced.htm#ancho.....

[69] www dhushara com/book/diversit/bomb.htm#anchor255699

[70] Charles Hanley, "Earth's 'Lung,' the Amazon Forest, Breathes Uneasily in a Time of Climate Change," www.cnn.com/today_PF.html?id=7126

[71] The Causes of Rainforest Destruction," www.rainforestinfo.org.au/background/causes.htm

[72] Tarko Sudiamo, "Sumatra highway project to tear apart world's lungs," Jakarta Post, November 5, 2002

[73] Ibid

[74] Ibid

[75] "Forests-the Earth's Lungs," www.infoforhealth.org/pr/ml5/ml5chap6/shtml

[77] "Conflict, transition and deforestation," Institute for Natural Resources Management

[78] Ibid

[79] Roads of Deforestation in Brazil: How soya and cattle are destroying the Amazon with the help of the IF," www.wrm.org uy/bulletin/93/Brazil. html

[80] www fpe.ph/PCIJ%20Report%20on20%20Iilegal%20Logging.htm

[81] Daniel K. Benjamin, "Light Truck Lessons," www.perc.org/publications/percreports/dec.1997/tangents.php

[82] "Corruption, lawlessness, fuel epidemic of illegal logging in Indonesia," httpp://newsroom.wri.org/newsrelese_text.cfm7NewsReleasseID-20

[83] www dhushara.com/book/diversit/cathed.htm

[84] Ibid

[85] Paul Salstrom, "New Book Details West Virginia's Deforestation," www.wvhighlands.org/VoiceAug98/Salst BkRev.Aug98.htm

[86] www dhushara.com/book/diversit/extra/deforest htm#anchor........(New Scientist, August 22, 1998)

[87] Ibid

[88] Ibid

[89] Chris Sudzina, "Final: Methods and Effects of Tropical Rainforest Deforestation," http://jrscience.wcp.muohio.edu/FieldCourseOO/PapersCosta.....

[90] "Mitsubishi and Daishowa's Involvement in Canadian Deforestation," www.american.edu/TED/canchop.htm

[91] Ibid

[92] Ibid

[93] Robert Bryce, "Are We Running Out of Wood?' www.austinchronicle.com /issues/spec/greenbuild/timber.html

[94] "Forests-the Earth's Lungs," www infoforheahh.org/pr/mI5/ml5chap6/shtml

[95] "Supporting responsible forest management in Panama," www panda.org/ about wwf/what we do/forests/index.cfm?........November 18, 2005

[96] "#1 for timber traceability," www tracelite com/'>kw=sustainablc_forestry

[97] "UK government's buying responsible timber - Glorious Good Wood," www.forestrycenter.org/News/news.cfm?News_lD=928

[98] Global Witness, "A Choice for China," October 2005 p 26

[99] Ibid

[100] UK government's buying responsible timber - Glorious Good Wood," www.forestrycenter.org/News/news.cfm?News_ID=928

[101] "Germany moves to ban illegal timber marketing," wwwillegal-logging.info/textonly/newsSingleltem.php?news..........April 20, 2005

[102] Ibid

[103] Laura Snook, "Saving Mahogany, saving forests, saving lives," www.cifor.cgiar.org/docsZ-pf/l/jeffpublications/newsonline/....

[104] Ibid

[105] Ibid

[106] Barbara Coyner, "Waste Wood finds a Place of Honor," www.forestrycenter.org/News/news.cfm?News_ID=897

[107] Norman Bordadora, "Mike D scraps 8,000 forest management agreements," *Philippine Daily Inquirer*, January 10, 2006

[108] Ibid

[109] "Upland Philippine Communities: Guardians of the Final Forest Frontiers," www.asiaforestnetwork.org/pub/pub07.htm, p. 6/32

[110] Ibid

[111] "Deforestation in Asia by country," www.tqnyc.org/NYC052139/Asia.htm

[112] Indy Bay Indy media, "Pacific Lumber Begins Logging Old-Growth Redwood Grove, environmental Groups Seek Long-Term protections," http ://forests.org/aiticles/print asp?linkid-48369

[113] "Paying people to protect their environment in Bolivia," www.cifbr.cgiar.org/ docs/-pf/1/_ref/publications/newsonline/37pa.......

[114] "Logging," www.mongabay.com/0807.htm

[115] Ibid

[116] Sheikh Alkinky Sanyang. "Illegal chain-saw logging in Berending forest,' ww.observer.gm/enews/index php?option=com_content.......

[117] "Argentina: Forest conserved by the Wichi destroyed by agricultural companies," www.wrm.org.uy/bulletin/49/Argentina.html, August 2001

[118] Ibid

[119] Ibid

[120] "Sustainable Forest Management in Asia-Pacific," www.ciforcgiar.org/docs/-pfi/1/_ref/publications/newsonline/.........,May 2005

[121] "Synopsis of Policy Developments on Indigenous Peoples Rights Recognition in the Philippines," www.firstpeople.org/land_rights/Philippines/what_new.htm

[122] "Mitsubishi and Daishowa s Involvement in Canadian Deforestation," www.american.edu/TED/canchop.htm

[123] www.culturalsurvival org/publications/csq/print/artide_print........

[124] Ibid

[125] Mark Shepard, "Hug the Trees!" www.markshep com/nonviolence/GT_chipko html

[126] Ibid

[127] Ibid

[128] Ibid

[129] www.culturalsurvival.org/publications/csq/print/article _print......

[130] Ibid

[131] Ibid

[132] Ibid

[133] www.mima.gov.my/mima/ntmls/papers/pdf/zmz/zmz- palawan.pdf

[134] http //groups msm com/WELCOMETOAWORLDWEDON'TSEE/en.....,November 12, 2005

[135] Ibid

[136] www.american.edu/TED/PHILWOOD.HTM

[137] Philippines: Shrimp Farming and Mangrove decline," www.wrm.org.uy/bulletin/51/Philippines. html

[138] "Malaysia: Converting mangrove forest into shrimp farms," www.wrm.org.uy/bulletin/96/Malaysia.html

[139] "An introduction to the biology of Eastern North American and Caribbean mangroves," http://216.156.75.137/mangrovewa.html

[140] "Forest Loss in Papua New Guinea, "www wrm.org.uy/deforestation/Oceania/Papua.html

[141] Greenpeace," Partners in Ancient Forest Crimes." www greenpeace org, April 2002

[142] Ibid

[143] "Forest Loss in Papua New Guinea, "www.wrm.org.uy/deforestation/Oceania/Papua.html

[144] "Deforestation in Indonesia and the Orangutan Population," www.American edu/projects/mandala/TED/orang.htm

[145] Ibid

[146] Heather Sarantis, "Defending the Forest: The Mitsubishi Boycott Campaign,' wwwburmalibrary.org/reg.burma/archives/199606/msag00058........

[147] Ibid

[148] Ibid

[149] Ibid

[150] Ibid

[151] Ibid

[152] "Illegal logging in Indonesia," www cifor cgiar.org/docs/-pf71/jef7 publications/newsonline/

www mongabay com/20philippines. htm

[154] Ibid

[155] Michael Astor, "Brazil Police Arrest 78 Officials and Businessmen in Crackdown on Illegal Logging," www enn com/biz.html'·id=660

[156] Ibid

[157] Ibid

[158] "Problems Illegal logging and forest crime," www panda.org/about_wwf7 what_we_do/forests/problems/illegal November 13, 2005

[159] Katherine Adraneda, "1 year after, logging back in Aurora," The Philippine Star, November 29, 2005

[160] Ibid

[161] "Southern Leyte Disaster Relief Fund,"www.coralcay org/archives/ 2003/12/29/10.55.40 php

[162] "A strategy for Indonesian forest management." www.cifor.cgiar.org/docs/- pf71/ retfpublications/ne.vsonline/

[163] Ibid

[164] "Indonesia's chainsaw massacre," www enn com/afTPF html?id=434, February 24, 2005

[165] Yenin Kwok, "Chainsaw massacre," Asiaweek, November 26, 1999

[166] "Illegal logging ruining Leuser National Park," www.illegal-logging.info/ News.php?printerFriendly=ªl&news, November, 15, 2005

[167] Yenin Kwok, "Chainsaw massacre," Asiaweek, November 26, 1999

[168] Ibid

[169] "East Kalimantan loses US$100 million annually in timber revenue," www.cifor.cgiar org/docs/_pf7l /publications/newsonline/........

[170] Ibid

[171] Ibid

[172] "Problems: Illegal logging and forest crime," www panda org/about wwf? what _ we_do/forests/problems/illegal........Novermber 13, 2005

[173] Henry Chu. "Deforestation, burning turn Amazon rain forest into major pollution source, " www post-gazette com/pg/05171/524318.stm, June 20, 2005

[174] "Problems: Illegal logging and forest crime," www panda org/about wwfl what_we_do/forests/problems/illegal November 13. 2005

[175] Mauel Baliao, "Philippine Government starts antitimbcr poaching drive anew," www forestrycenter org/News/news cfm?News ID=760

[176] "Philippines to file illegal logging complaints against financiers, officials." www.forestrycenter org/News/news cfm'·News_ID-765

[177] Inquirer News Service, "Probe ordered of illegal logging in C. Mindanao," http://news.inq7.net/common/print.php?index=l&story_id"35532&

[178] Jeffrey M Tupas, "Environmentalists alarmed by illegal logging activities," www.sunstar clm.ph/static/dav/2005/04/28/news/environment

[179] "Free-for-all Illegal Logging of Mahogany in Peruvian Parks, says Duke-based Monitoring Group," www.ascribe org/cgj-bin/behold pl?ascribedid

[180] Roger Harrabin, "US blocks forest protection plan." www forestrycenter org/News/news cfm?News_II>ᶦ887

[181] Greenpeace." Partners in Ancient Forest Crimes," www.greenpeace org. April 2002

[182] Ibid

[183] Ibid

[184] Peter Denton, "New Tool to Help Cameroon Combat Illegal Logging." http://allafrica.com/storesies/printable/200504010813.html, April 1,2005

[185] Ibid

[186] Global Witness. "A Choice for China," October 2005 p 35

[187] Ibid

[188] "Supporting responsible forest management in Panama," www panda org/about_wwf7what_we_do/forests/index.cfm?........November 18, 2005

[189] www. american edu/TED/PHILWOOD HTM

[190] Ibid

[191] www dhushara com/book/diversit/extra/tim htm#anchor307958

[192] Ibid

[193] Greenpeace," Partners in Ancient Forest Crimes." www greenpeace.org, April 2002

[194] "War" www mongabay com/0810 htm

[195] "The Devastating Ecological Effects of the Vietnam War." www.teenink.com/Past/2003/Februarv/Environment/TheDevastating

[196] Ibid

[197] "UN Study: Many Forest Areas Breeding Grounds for Conflict," www.ciforcgiar.org/docs/-pf7l/_ref7publications/newsonline/.......

[198] Ibid

[199] www csdp.org/edcs/page47.htm

[200] WRM Bulletin, Issue Number 71, June 2003. www wrm org.uy/bulletin/71 /Asia html

[201] Ibid

[202] "Philippine Archipelagos Losing Last Remaining Rainforest," http://forests.org/archicve/asia/agtaland htm

[203] Global Witness, "A Choice for China," October 2005 p. 10

[204] Ibid, p. 11

[205] Ibid, p. 12

[206] Ibid, p. 20

[207] Ibid, p. 23

[208] Alan Sipress, "Illegal logging in Cambodia," www.ecologyasia.com/ncws-archives/2003/mar-03/thestar_2........., March 18, 2003

[209] Ibid

[210] Ibid

[211] "Accountability. It's tough to find in the U.S. Forest," www forestry center org/News/news.cfm'>News_ID='893

[212] WRM Bulletin, Issue Number 85, August 2004, www.wrm.org.uy/bulletin/85/general html

[213] TED Case Studies: Philippine Sugar and Environment

[214] Ibid

[215] Ibid

[216] Amy Bracken, "Deadly Floods in Haiti Blamed on Deforestation, Poverty," http //forest org/print. asp?l inkid*35207

[217] Ibid

[218] WRM Bulletin, Issue Number 85, August 2004, www.wrm.org.uy/bulletin/85/general.html

[219] Ibid

[220] "Roads of Deforestation in Brazil: How soya and cattle are destroying the Amazon with the help of the IF," www.wrm.org.uy/bulIetin/93/Brazil.htral

[221] Axel Bugge, "Amazon Destruction Accelerating in Brazil," www.enn com/today_PF.html?id-7773, May 19. 2005

[222] "Roads of Deforestation in Brazil: How soya and cattle are destroying the Amazon with the help of the IF," www.wTm.org.uy/bulletin/93/Brazil .html

[223] Ibid

[224] Ibid

[225] www. dhushara com/book/diversit/extra/deforest. ht m#anchor........

[226] WRM Bulletin, Issue Number 85, August 2004, www.wrm.org.uy/bulletin/85/L A html

[227] Ibid

[228] WRM Bulletin, Issue Number 85, August 2004, www.wrm.org.uy/bulletin/85/Asia.html

[229] Amy Alesch, "Banana Cultivation in Costa Rica," http.//jrscience. wcp.muohio.edu/fieldcourses05/PapersCostaRicaArt   5/19/05

[230] Ibid

[231] Chris Wille, "News from the Front: Banana Ecolabeling Program is World's Largest," www rainforest-alliance.org/news/canppy/can2-00.html

[232] Ibid

[233] Leif Bronem, "The Limits of Cotton: White Gold Shows its Dark side in Benin," www fpif.org/fjpiftxt/160, July 14, 2005

[234] Chris Wille, "News from the Front: Banana Ecolabeling Program is World's Largest." www rainforest-alliance org/news/canppy/can2-00 html

[235] WRM Bulletin, Issue Number 85, August 2004, www.wrm.org.uy/bulletin/85/Asia html

236 Ibid

237 "Asia-Pacific's Forests Vital to Australia," www.cifor.cgiar.org/docs/-pf/l/ref/publications/newsonline/.

238 Ibid

239 Ibid

240 WRM Bulletin, Issue Number 85, August 2004. www wrm.ore.uv/bulletin/85/general. html

241 Lorien Holland, "Whose Forest?" *Newsweek*, December 26, 2005

242 Ibid

243 WRM Bulletin, Issue Number 85, August 2004, www.wrm ore uv/bulletin/8 5/AF. html

244 Ibid

245 Ibid

246 Ibid

247 Blanche S. Rivera, "P45-M grants for forest conservation," Philippine Daily *Inquirer*, January 5, 2006

248 "Honey Production in Zambia," www.cifor.cgiar.org/docs/-pf/1/ ref7 publications/newsonline/.......

249 "Wood fires that fit," http://joumeytoforcverorg/atwoodfirehtml

250 Humberto Marquez, "Haiti Petroleum Greases the Deforestation Process," http://forests.org/articles/print.asp7linkid-48349

251 "Deforestation Backgrounder," www.lehigh.edu/~kaf3/books/reportins/deforest/html

252 Rainer Hennig, "Forests and deforestation in Africa - the wasting of an immense resource," www.afrol.com/printable feature/10278

253 "Wood fires that fit," httpy/joumeytoforever org/at woodfire html

254 James A Duke. "Euphorbia lathyris L.," www.hortpurdue.edu/newcrop/duke_energy/Euphorbia_lathyris.......

255 James A. Duke, "Pittosporum resiniferum Hemsl," www hort purdue edu/newcrop/dukeenergy/Pittosporumresin

256 John Fennucio, "Hemp seen as fuel substitute" www globalhemp.com/News/2005/September/hemp-seen-as-f

257 Ibid

258 Marcy Nicholson, "Revenue, potential high but so are the cost," www.globalhemp.com/News/2005/September/revenue-potenti........

259 Jeff Caldwell. "Switchgrass could be the Midwest's next big energy source " www.newfarm.org/news/2005/0805/082305/switchgrass_prin.. ..

260 Patricia Reaney. Gras Hailed as Potential Source of Clean Energy " http://enn.com/today PF html?id=8725

261 "Wood fires that fit," http//joumeytoforever org/at_woodfire html

262 "Solar Box Cooker," http://joumeytoforever.org/sc.html

263 Daniel Kammen, 'Cookstoves for thee Developing world," http://ist-socrates berkeley edu' -kammcn/cookstoves html

[265] "Improved Cookstove," www crtnepal.org/new/
technologies php'>mode=detail&techno
[266] Ibid
[267] "Solar Box Cookers," http://joumcytoforever org/sc html
[268] Daniel Kammen. "Cookstoves for thee Developing world," http://ist-
socrates berkeley edu/'-kammen/cookstoves.html
[269] "Roads of Deforestation in Brazil: How soya and cattle are destroying the
Amazon with the help of the IF," www.wrm org uy/bulletirV'93/Brazil html
[270] "Role of Cattle Raising in Conversion of Tropical Moist Forests"
www.ciesin org/docs/002-106/002-106c html
[271] WRM Bulletin, Issue Number 85, August 2004, www.wrm.org.uy/
bulletin/85/L A html
[272] "Money in the Rainforest," www ran.org/info_center/factsheets/04f.html
[273] "7 things you can do to save the rainforest," www.ran org/info_center/
factsheets/Olc html
[274] "Livestock, Development & Deforestation Brazil's Amazon,"
www.cifor.cgiar org/docs/-pf7l/_ref7publication&/newsonline/........
[275] "Role of Cattle Raising in Conversion of Tropical Moist Forests"
www.ciesi n.org/docs/002-106/002-106c.html
[276] "Beef exports fuel loss of Amazonian Forest," www cifor cgiar org/docs/-
pf71/_retf publications/newsonline/........
[277] "Roads of Deforestation in Brazil How soya and cattle are destroying the
Amazon with the help of thc IF," w·ww. wrm org.uy/bulletin/93/Brazil.html
"Beef exports fuel loss of Amazonian Forest," www cifor cgiar org/docs/-
pf71 /retfpubl icat ions/newsonl i ne/........
[579] Ibid
[280] David Kaimowitz, et al. "Hamburger Connection Fuels Amazon Destruction'
[281] Chris Sudzina, "Final Methods and Effects of Tropical Rainforest
Deforestation," http://jrscience.wcp. muohio edu/FieldCourseOO/PapersCosta
[282] "A destructive megaproject for Tehuanepec Isthmus in Mexico,"
www.wrm.org.uv/bullentin/23/Mexico.html, May 1999
[283] Ibid
[284] Chris Sudzina, "Final Methods and Effects of Tropical Rainforest
Deforestation,"   http   //jrscience.wcp.muohio.edu/FieldCourseOO/PapersCosta
[285] "y flings y_{OU} can do to save the rainforest," www.ran.org/info_center/
factsheet s/01 c. html
[286] "Philippine Forest Fires Send Tribesmen Fleeing,"
http//forests org/archive/asia/phsendfl htm
[287] "Frequently Asked Questions About Forest Fires," http://fire.cfs.nrcan.gc ca/
faq_fire e php
[288] Ibid

289 Henry Chu, "Deforestation, burning turn Amazon rain forest into major pollution source, " www post-gazette.com/pg/05171/524318 stm, June 20, 2005

290 "Rainforests and Global Warming," www.ran org/info center/factsheets/04a html

291 http://home.alItel.net/bsundquistl df2.html#F

292 "Brazil launches ambitious plan to save rain forest," www.cnn com/EARTH/9804/29/amazon.rainforest/index.html. April 29, 1998

293 www. dhushara com/book/di versit/extra/deforest htm#anchor

294 "Brazil launches ambitious plan to save rain forest," www.cnn.com/EARTH/9804/29/amazon rainforest/index.html, April 29, 1998

295 www.dhushara.com/book/diversit/extra/deforest htm#anchor • (New Scientist, October 11, 1997)

296 Ibid (Scientific American, December 1997)

297 Henry Chu, "Deforestation, burning turn Amazon rain forest into major pollution source, " www.post-gazette.com/pg/05171/5243l8.stm. June 20. 2005

298 Ibid

299 http //home alltel.net/bsundquist 1 df2.html#F

300 "The Burning of Indonesia - an Ecological Catastrophe Unfolds," www.dhusharacom/book/diversit/extra/smoke.htm........

301 Ibid

302 "Fiddling while Siberia burns: 'lungs of Europe' under threat from forest fires,"www.fireuni-freiburgde/media/2005/news_2005060I ru.htm, 5/31/05

303 http //home alltcl net/bsundquist 1 ,dQ.html#F

304 Tim Radford, "Huge rise in Siberia forest fires puts planet at risk, scientists warn," www guardian co.uk/russia/articIe/0,2763,1495903,00 htm, 5/31/05

305 Ibid

306 "Fiddling while Siberia bums 'lungs of Europe' under threat from forest fires," www.fire.uni-freiburg.de/media/2005/news_20050601_ru.htm,5/31/05

307 Smoke form Agricultural and Forest Fires," http://aimow.gov/index.^{c}fm?acti^{oD}=sm^{o}ke_fi^{r}es main

308 "Smoke can signal health problems for those with lung and heart diseases." www.doh.wa.gov/Publicat/2003_News/03-123 htm, July 15, 2003

309 "Forest Fires and Respiratory Health Fact Sheet," www lungusa org/site/pp.asp?c=dvLUK900E&b=36064

310 "Smoke can signal health problems for those with lung and heart diseases," www.doh wa.gov/Publicat/2003_News/03-123 htm, July 15, 2003

311 "Forest Fires and Respiratory Health Fact Sheet," www.lungusa.org/site/pp.asp?c-dvLUK900E&b=36064

312 "Indonesia burning," www.cifor.cgiar.org/doc8/_ref7publications/newsonIine/33/in........

313 Shanta Christian Emmanuel, "Impact to lung health of haze from forest fires. The Singapore experience." www.blackwell-synergy com/doi/abs/10 1046/i. 1440-1843.20........June 2000

314 Ibid

315 "Money in the Rainforest," www.ran.org/info_center/factsheets/04f html

316 "Deepening crisis in Philippines over mining as it hosts the ASEAN Mining conference," www.minesandcommunities.org/Action/press759.htm, 10/15/05

317 www mongabay com/0808 htm

318 Jamaica Deforestation linked to mining, agriculture and tourism," www wrm org uy/bulletin/50/Jamaica.html, September 2001

319 Ibid

320 William B Depasupil, "Gov't, Church header for face-off over mining law," The Manila Times, December 8, 2004

321 Ibid

322 "Filipino $_{rc}$)>e|$ warn they will attack Canadian mining firms," www.asianpacificpost com/apnews/news/articlejsessionid, 2/10/05

323 Ibid

324 Ibid

325 "Deepening crisis in Philippines over mining as it hosts the ASEAN Mining conference," www,minesand<x>mmunities.org/Action/press759.htm, 10/15/05

326 "Filipino rebels warn they will attack Canadian mining firms," www asianpacificpost.com/apnews/news/articlejsessionid   2/10/05

327 "Deepening crisis in Philippines over mining as it hosts the ASEAN Mining conference," www.minesandcommunities.org/Action/press759.htm, 10/15/05

321 Ibid

329 www mongabay com/0808 htm

330 "Ghana: The World Bank in the gold scenario," www.wrm.org.uy/bullentin/80/Ghana.html

331 Ibid

332 Alyansa Laban sa Mina, "Case Brief The Mindoro Nickel Project," www. mangy an org/current/environment/casebrief-nickelproject

333 Ibid

334 Ibid

335 "Solon wants Palawan nickel mining stopped," www.ecologyasia com/ news-archives/2003/oct-03/manila-bulletin.......

336 Ibid

337 Ibid

338 "The case against a mining operation in Palawan, Philippines." www csiwisepract ices org/?read=467

339 Jefferson Mecham, "Causes and consequences of deforestation in Ecuador." www rainforestinfo org au/projects/jefferson htm, May 2001

340 Ibid

341 S Friedman, A.S Mehta and P L. Thigpen, "Wood-to-Oil Process," http://joumeyto forever org/bx> fue 11 i brary/wood-to-oi I. html

342 "Multinational mining in the Philippines," www.wrm.org.uy/bulletin/ 11 /Philippines html

343 "Central African republic: IMF, logging and mining," www.wrm org.uy/ bulletin/54/CAR html

344 Ibid

345 "IMF and deforestation in Indonesia," www.wrm org.uy/bulletin/95/ Indoneisa.html

346 Ibid

347 Ibid

348 Stine Lykkc Nielsen, "Improving Japanese Official Development Assistance Quality: Discussing Theories of Bureaucratic Rivalry "

349 Ibid

350 "Deforestation in Indonesia and the Orangutan Population," www American.edu/projects/mandala/TED/orang htm

351 Citigroup Leans on Logging Company to Clean up its Act," www.forestrycenter.org/News/news.cfm7News ID=858

352 Ibid

353 Ibid

354 "BB Adopts Equator Principles," Press release of Banco do Brazil Press Service, March 3, 2005

355 Ibid

356 Citigroup Leans on Logging Company to Clean up its Act," www forestrycenter.org/News/news cfm?News_ID=858

357 Mitesh Badiwala, "The Narmada Sagar and Sardar Sarova Dam projects," www.geocities.com/CollegePark/Library/9175/inquiry2.htm?

358 Shui Fu, "A Profile of Dams in China," www.im.org/programs/threeg/ shuifu.html

359 Mitesh Badiwala, "The Narmada Sagar and Sardar Sarova Dam projects," www.geocities.com/CollegePark/Library/9175/inquiry2.htm?........

360 Ibid

361 Jill Davis, "Alexander's Marvelous Machine," www nrdc org/onearth/ 05spr/gorlovl asp

362 Jill Davis, "Alexander's Marvelous Machine," www.nrdc org/onearth/ 05spr/gorlov2.asp

363 Jamais Cascio, "Gorlov's Helical Turbine," www worldchanging com/ archives/002383 .html

364 "The Causes of Rainforest Destruction," www rainforestinfo org.au/ background/causes, htm

365 "Deforestation in Asia by country," www tqnyc.org/NYC052139/Asia htm

366 Ibid

367 Ibid

368 Max Lane, "Off course golf in South-east Asia," www.greenleft .org.au/back/ 1993/lo3/103pl2 htm

369 Ibid

370 Ibid

371 http;//home alltel net/bsundquist 1 df2.html#F

372 Ibid

373 Ibid

374 Ibid

375 Ibid

376 Ibid

377 "Natural Forces," www mongabay com/0802 htm

378 Greenpeace," Partners in Ancient Forest Crimes," www.greenpeace.org,
April 2002

379 "Super Studs-A New Approach to Marketing Sturctural Lumber,"
www forestrycenter org/News/newscfm?News_ID=908

380 Divya Ramamurthi, "For design and <tecor," www.hinduonnet.com/
thehindu/thscrip/print/print.pl?file=200402........

381 G.S. Dhillon, "Novel wood substitutes, " wwwtribuneindia com/
2002/20020509/science htm

382 Michael P. Wolcott "Production Methods and Platforms for Wood Plastic
Composites."

383 Ibid

394 Alex Wilson, "Wood Substitutes," httpV/doityouseelf. com/info/
wouldbewood.htm

395 Ibid

396 Ibid

397 Ibid

398 lbid

399 Li Yi, "Promising Future for Wooden chopsticks,"
http //homepage, mac.com/mstrauch/greenchopsticks/read05bidne........

390 Philip P. Pan, "China's Chopsticks Crusade Drive Against Disposable Feeds
Environmental Movement," httphomepage mac mstrauch/greenchopsticks/
read01main.html, February 6, 2001

391 Ibid

392 Ibid

393 "Disposable Chopsticks 2003," www.ibpcosaka.or.jp/network/
e_trade j apanese market/house......

394 "Mitsubishi and Daisbowa's Involvement in Canadian Deforestation,"
www american.edu/TED/canchop.htm

395 Ibid

396 Ibid

397 Joshua Karliner, God's little chopsticks," http homepage mac mstrauch/
greenchopsticks/readO 1 main html

398 Li Yi, "Promising Future for Wooden chopsticks."
http//homepage mac com/mstrauch/greenchopsticks/read05bidne........

399 "World bamboo diversity falling to deforestation,"
www newfarm org/intrenatinal/news/060104/061404/bamboo........

[400] *Philippine Daily Inquirer*, August 18, 19%

[401] Robert Bryce, "Are We Running Out of Wood?' www austinchronicle.com/i ssues/spec/greenbui Id/timber/ht ml

[402] "Money in the Rainforest," www ran org/info center/factsheets/o4f html

[403] Ibid

[404] "Fast wood like fst food - not all good, not all bad," www.dfor.cgiar.org/docs/-p£ʳl/_rcf7publicationv'newsonline/........

[405] Greenpeace," Partners in Ancient Forest Crimes," www greenpeace org, Anri I 2002

[406] "Forests the earth's lungs," www.peopleandplanet net/doc php⁹id= 1480&section=l, December 16, 2004

[407] www ibiblio.org/pub/academic/environment/pesticide-education/general/tidbits

[408] www hoffmangraphics com/~efguides/ht ml/stationary, html

[409] Frank Grave, "Paper Chase," www forestrycenter org/Newa/news cfm ID=886, March 17, 2005

[410] Ibid

[411] Ibid

[412] Ibid

[413] Jane Brissett, Recycled paper demand booms," www forestrycenter.org/News/news. cfm?News_ID=916

[414] Howard Rheingold, "Digital Paper, Digital books and the Future of reading," www honco. net/archive/n-3. html

[415] www.globalhemp.com/News/2005/September/hemp-oil-canc......9/20/05

[416] Anne W. Wilke, "Rethinking hemp," www global hemp com/ Archives/Magazines/rethinkinghemp........

[417] Ibid

[418] Ibid

[419] Ibid

[420] www hoffmangraphics.com/-efguides/html/stationary html

[421] www.travellerspoint.com/foru m/cfm?thread= 15679

[422] Miguel Llanos, "Recycling's next frontier: Poop as paper," www forestrycenter org/News/news.cfm?News 1D=833

[423] Ibid

[424] "From Dung to God - The Ultimate in Recycled Paper," www hippy com/php/article-280 html

[425] "World Press Trends: Newspaper Circulation and Advertising Up Worldwide," www wan-press org/article7321.html

[426] Ibid

[427] Howard Rheingold, "Digital Paper, Digital books and the Future of reading," www honco . net/archive/n-3 html

[428] Ibid

[429] Liu Zhiming, "How Electronic Media can Reduce Paper Consumption," www.honco net/archive/n-3 html

[430] "Corrugated Cardboard Recycling," www.co.orange.nc.us/recyding/ corrugated asp

[431] http://home alltel net/bsundquist 1 df2 html#F

[432] Ibid

[433] "Forests: the earth's lungs," www peopleandplanet net/doc php?id^ 1480&section=l, December 16, 2004

[434] Ibid

[435] "EC and UNDP Address Forest Management in Viet Nam's Poor Mountainous Areas," www.undp org.vn/undp/unews/mr/2003/eng/0930e.htm

[436] Ibid

[437] "Species Extinction," www.ran org/info_center/fact$heeets/03b html

[438] "Java teak A livelihood hardwood," www.dfor.cgiar.org/docs/-pfi[l]/_ref7 publications/newsonline/........

[439] Ibid

[440] "Philippines: Graft blamed for reforestation failure," http://forests.org/ articles/print asp?linkid=36589

[441] Michael Bengwayan, "Illegal Logging Kills Philippines forests," http://forest.org/archived_site/today/recent/1999/phillog/htm

[442] Mark Clayton, "Now, bioengineered trees are taking root," wwwcsmonitorcom/2005/0310/pl4s02-sten.htm

[443] Ibid

[444] http //home.alltel.net/bsundquistl df2.html#F

[445] WRM Bulletin, Issue Number 85, August 2004, www wrm org uy/ bulletin/85/Asia, html

[446] Mark Clayton, "Now, bioengineered trees are taking root," www csmonitor.com/2005/0310/pl4s02-sten htm

[447] WRM Bulletin, Issue Number 85, August 2004, www.wrm.org.uy/ bul letin/8 5/Asia, html

[448] Supertrees, COj Eating Algae," www.globalwarming.org/ article. php?uid =*222

[449] www. dhushara com/book/genes/genaug/clonfbr htm#anchor........, 8/23/97

[450] Ibid

[451] "The Richard & Rboda Goldman Fund and The Goldman Environmental Prize Move into New Presidio Offices," www.goldmanprize.org/press/ pressReleaseltem cfm?prID=87

[452] Michelle Nijhuis, "Priest wins prize for defending forests," www msnbc.com/ id/7631990/print/1 /display mode/1098/

[453] Blanche Ss. Rivera, "Groups to restore 1M hectares of rainforests," The Philippine Inquirer, November 28, 2005

[454] Ibid

[455] Ibid

456 Florence A Samy & Kuldeep S. Jessy. "Rampant illegal felling of timber at Tasik Temenggor," http://thestar com my/services/printerfriehdly.ftsp?file
457 Ibid
458 "WWF Hails 'Giant Step' Forward in Amazon Conservation," ww.enn cora/aff PF.html?id=426, February 20,2005
459 Ibid
460 "Urban green belt," http://edugreen.teri res.in/explore/forestry/urban htm
461 "Debt for Nature Swap," www.bookrags com/sdences/biology/debt-for-nature-swap.en ...
462 Michela Wrong, "Environment Benefits from Madagascar's Foreign Debt," www safariweb/com/saferimate/benefrt htm
463 "Debt-for-Nature Agreements Will Help Conserve Jamaica's Forests, October 8, 2004," http://usunrome.usembassy.it/Forestry/docs/a4101403.htm
464 Ibid

READ * READ * READ

BOOKS ARE YOUR BEST FRIENDS

There is nothing more important in this life than preparing
for the next life. There are a lot of preachers who claim and preach
that they hold the key to the absolute truth when in fact they have
perverted the gospel of Christ. They have absolutely no right to
take others with them to hell with their distorted interpretation of
the Bible; let them be accursed. (Galatians 1:8) What better way
than knowing the truth behind one's faith and belief. Read and
judge for yourself the truth behind your faith.

The Dark Side of Catholicism
The Plain Truth About the Unorthodox Protestants

Read the book first and be forewarned before you buy or build
your first home. Beware of the many scams going on around you.
You may be in for some big surprises.

Tips and Traps When Buying or Building a Home
Greed & Scams, Inc.

You may think that Hitler's Germany annihilation of Jews
is the worst, but wait until you read the atrocities committed
by the Japanese Imperial Army in Asia during the WWII.

The Brutal Holocaust

We live in a world where even children are not safe
from the scums of this world. Know how to keep
your children safe by reading this book.

Child Abuse: A Growing Menace